3.00

P

Please return to

1977 o.p.

Polly Bloch
2532 Ransdell
Louisville, Ky.
40204

THE ARROW WAR

The Arrow War

An Anglo-Chinese Confusion

1856-1860

DOUGLAS HURD

The Macmillan Company

NEW YORK

Library of Congress Catalog Card Number: 68-20747

FIRST AMERICAN EDITION

Originally published in Great Britain in 1967 by Collins, London

The Macmillan Company, New York

Printed in Great Britain

To Tatiana

NOTE.   I have used the Wade Anglicisation of Chinese names except when another version is more familiar (e.g. Taiping).

Illustrations

Maps

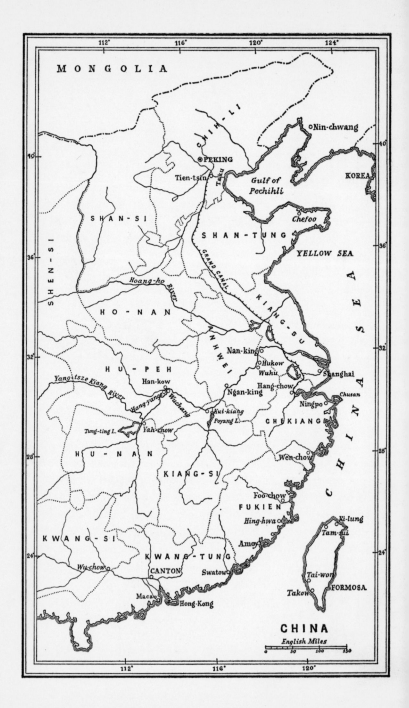

MONGOLIA

CHIH-LI

○Nin-chwang

◎PEKING

Tien-tsin

Taku

Gulf of
Pechihli

KOREA

SHAN-SI

SHEN-SI

Chefoo

SHAN-TUNG

YELLOW SEA

GRAND CANAL

KIANG-SU

Hoang-ho River

HO-NAN

ANHWEI

Nan-king

HU-PEH

Yang-tsze Kiang River

Han-kow

Hukow
Wuhu

Shanghai

Hang-yang
Wuchang

Ngan-king

Hang-chow

Chusan

Kui-kiang
Poyang L.

Ningpo

Tung-ting L.
Yak-chow

CHEKIANG

HU-NAN

KIANG-SI

Wen-chow

Foo-chow

FUKIEN

Hing-hwa

Ki-lung
Tam-sui

KWANG-SI

Amoy

KWANG-TUNG

Wu-chow

CANTON

Swatow

Tai-won

Takow

FORMOSA

Macao
Hong-Kong

CHINA SEA

CHINA

English Miles

0   50   100   150

I

AT EIGHT O'CLOCK on the morning of October 8th 1856 three young men were breakfasting together on the deck of a small British ship anchored in the river at Canton. Opposite them lay the prosperous line of buildings known as the factories which served as combined warehouses, offices and houses for the two hundred European and American merchants who lived at Canton. Between the factories and the river they could see the dismal strip of garden reserved for the use of the Europeans. Already perhaps some merchants were pacing up and down taking the only exercise which Canton could safely afford them. The river was already crowded with traffic, boats large and small, Western as well as Chinese. Canton was traditionally the only port in the Chinese Empire which Western traders were allowed to enter, and although for the last fourteen years four other Chinese ports had by treaty been opened to foreign trade, in practice Canton was still the centre of foreign enterprise in China. It was foreign enterprise which had brought the three young men to their breakfast together; each was the master of a small vessel of about 100 tons plying with merchandise and passengers up and down the Canton estuary between the city itself, the crumbling and picturesque Portuguese colony of Macao and the brash new British colony of Hong Kong. These vessels were called lorchas, were originally designed by the Portuguese and carried a crew of about fourteen. One of the breakfast guests was an American, the other was Thomas Kennedy, a young man of twenty-one from Belfast.

Kennedy had recently been engaged as master of the lorcha *Arrow* by her owner, a Chinese called Fong Ah-ming who had lived for ten years in Hong Kong and had been able to take out British papers for the *Arrow* by registering her under the colony's ordinances. The *Arrow* had arrived at Canton from Macao five days earlier with a cargo of rice, had deposited her papers in the usual way with the British Consul, and on the morning of the 8th was preparing to leave again for Hong Kong. She lay at anchor a little way downstream from the boat on which her master was break-fasting, so that he had a good view of his crew as they made ready to sail. The three young men noticed two boats pass, each with a Chinese mandarin and about thirty uniformed men on board; the morning was already hot, and the man-darins were protected by cotton umbrellas from the sun. A few minutes later the American remarked to Kennedy that the boats had stopped alongside the *Arrow*, but Kennedy merely supposed they were dropping off pas-sengers for her to take to Hong Kong. But the next thing they saw made them jump up from their breakfasts and row hurriedly upstream to the *Arrow* in a sampan. All three clearly saw one of the uniformed men from the boats pull down the British ensign from the stern of the *Arrow*, and immediately afterwards the Blue Peter (hoisted to show that the *Arrow* was about to sail) also disappeared. When Kennedy reached the *Arrow* he found that his whole crew had been arrested and were lying bound in the Chinese boats alongside. One old man had been tied with a thicker rope than the others and was being kept apart. Kennedy could make nothing of this, and did not know enough Chinese to ask questions. He managed to convey to the mandarins that he would be helpless if left without any crew, and persuaded them to leave behind two of their prisoners. The two Chinese boats then pulled away; Kennedy hoisted the ensign again, and hurried off to tell Parkes, the Acting British Consul, what had happened.

Harry Parkes was twenty-eight, and already a remarkable man of a type then relatively new but soon to become familiar to a generation of Victorian novel readers. He was strikingly good-looking with fair hair and blue eyes, and, though never physically strong, seemed impervious to fear. He was forthright in speech and deeply religious. In the uproar which followed the Government was often accused of leaving the important Consulate at Canton in the hands of a callow youth. This was unfair; quite apart from his exceptional quality, Parkes had fourteen years' experience of government service in China, which was as much as could then be said for any Englishman. In 1841 at the age of thirteen he had been shipped out as an orphan to Hong Kong to live with his aunt, who was married to the Prussian missionary, Gutzlaff. Gutzlaff belonged naturally to the chaotic freebooting 1820s and '30s after the monopoly of the East India Company in Chinese waters had been challenged, but before consuls had arrived at the ports and a Governor in Hong Kong to impose some restraint. He claimed almost every intellectual accomplishment and there were few to put him to the test. His straw hat, squat figure and old-fashioned German clothes were a familiar sight in many a market-place; his alternating bouts of bad temper and of generosity impressed both Chinese and Europeans. His zeal as a Christian was undoubted, and carried him far. He translated the New Testament into Chinese, and distributed his product from one side of the opium clippers while Jardine's or Dent's agents unloaded theirs on the other.

This enterprising man introduced his young nephew to Sir Henry Pottinger, who as British Plenipotentiary was in charge of all British interests in the closing stages of the first war against China. Sir Henry took young Parkes with him to Nanking in 1842 as a personal assistant, and the fourteen-year-old watched the signature there of the first Treaty between Britain and China. The Treaty of Nanking, by providing for British Consuls to be established at five treaty ports, made necessary a new British service.

Recruits who could speak Chinese were rare, and Parkes, whose Chinese was already excellent, was an obvious choice. He spent the next fourteen years in subordinate posts in the consulates at four of the five ports, Shanghai, Amoy, Foochow and Canton.

Today we think of the China Consulates as they were at the height of their power in the Edwardian era between the Boxer Rebellion and Sun Yat Sen's revolution. No one who has seen them, even now in their decay, can fail to be impressed by those enormous uncomfortable houses, always in the best site which the city could offer, the lawns stretching towards sea or river, the full-length royal portraits dominating ugly rooms, the bandstand for the birthday of Queen or King, the surrounding compound for the army of European and Chinese servants and for the Sikhs or Punjabis who guarded the gates under the massive coat-of-arms. In its heyday British influence in China was almost viceregal; but sixty years earlier when Parkes served his apprenticeship these palaces were not built and nothing could have been more lonely or uncomfortable than the life of a China Consul. He was hemmed in by hostility and difficulty of every kind. He represented a distant sovereign whose equality to the Emperor of China was recognised by the Chinese in the Treaty of Nanking. But this was an idea wholly alien to the local officials with whom he had to deal. To these mandarins the new consul was merely the local head of the British merchants, from whom they would receive respectfully worded petitions but with whom they would certainly not negotiate on equal terms. The consul usually had no force with which to assert his treaty rights. Occasionally a British warship might call at his port, and its commander might be persuaded (though he could not be ordered) to mount some demonstration to carry a point with the Chinese. But any commotion at a treaty port was likely to bring down upon a consul the rebuke of his immediate superior, the Superintendent of Trade, who combined that office with the Governorship of Hong Kong.

A consul could not usually ask for instructions in a crisis since it could take four or six weeks to get them from Hong Kong. (As we shall see, this did not apply so much to the Consul at Canton, who was much closer to his superior.) The Consul had to act as he thought best and hope that he would not be disowned. His difficulties were not confined to the Chinese. Before the Treaty of Nanking all foreign goods were supposed to pass through Canton, the only port at which the Chinese Government had traditionally allowed foreign trade. But in practice trading had taken place illegally at other ports and British merchants had become accustomed to come and go with little hindrance. Some sold opium, keeping the mandarins quiet with bribes. Others, who had smuggled goods in duty-free before the Treaty, expected to continue in the same way, even though the duties to be levied by the Chinese had now been agreed with their own British Government. It was not the job of the British Consul to collect Chinese duties or enforce Chinese laws against his own countrymen, and he had no legal power to do so. But he was held responsible for their behaviour by the local Chinese authorities, and in practice his position depended on the merchants' reasonable behaviour, at least while they were in the ports. (Partly for this reason most opium was sold not at the ports themselves but at receiving stations nearby, which both consuls and mandarins could pretend to ignore.) The British Consul also found himself made responsible for the behaviour of ships of other countries which had appointed no consuls. Over these he had of course no control, but only the most sophisticated Chinese distinguished successfully between one brand of big-nosed barbarian and another. He was not helped by his fellow-consuls of other nationalities who were almost always themselves merchants who had accepted an honorary office, and not servants of their government as he was. The task of a British Consul in the 'forties and 'fifties was indeed hard; it was carried out with the help of a staff of one or two, in an unhealthy climate, without congenial society, with inadequate pay and leave. This was the life which Parkes had led. He had watched different consuls react to it in different ways, and drawn from the results a theory from which he never wavered. He had served under poor Mr. Lay at Foochow who had been afraid to hoist a flag over his office, or find a decent house to live in, who had indeed for fear of making a commotion accepted the subordinate standing which the Chinese gave him, and done his best to forget the Treaty of Nanking. Later he served at Shanghai under Alcock, the most successful of the first generation of consuls. Alcock believed in the high style. He transacted business with the Chinese in full uniform with cocked hat and no less than six Spanish orders of chivalry acquired at a previous post. When a missionary was ill-treated in 1848 Alcock without asking for authority from Hong Kong stopped the Chinese grain junks in the Yangtze as a reprisal and eventually sent a warship up the river to Nanking, and there with Parkes' help negotiated a settlement. From his experiences Parkes became certain that the only way of avoiding trouble with the Chinese was to stand firm from the start on every part of one's rights, significant or insignificant. Once make a concession, and there would be no end to the demands which would follow. In dealing with Chinese officials, each detail of ceremony, each phrase in a document must be examined. There could be no greater mistake than to concede a point of form, however trivial it might appear, because Chinese officials had been trained to believe that details of form were a clue to the reality of power. Parkes held these ideas strongly and preached them so convincingly that when on home leave in 1850, a young man of twenty-two with no money or connections, he so impressed the Foreign Office that they arranged for him to see the Foreign Secretary. Lord Palmerston spoke kindly to this very Palmerstonian young man, and Parkes went back encouraged to a cramped and irksome tour of duty at Canton.

When Thomas Kennedy of the *Arrow* brought his story

16

to the Consulate on the morning of October 8th Parkes acted vigorously. The Chinese action seemed clearly illegal. Under the Supplementary Treaty of 1843 the Chinese authorities when they wished to arrest a Chinese serving on a British ship had to apply to the British Consul, who would examine the man and hand him over to the Chinese. This procedure had been ignored in the case of the *Arrow* and Parkes hurried to the spot to protest. He found the Chinese boat with the prisoners still on board and asked that they should be escorted to the Consulate for examination. The officer in charge explained that the old man who had been arrested had been recognised as the father of a notorious pirate; other members of the crew might also be involved, and all were needed to give evidence. He refused to do as Parkes asked and in the course of the argument one of the Chinese struck Parkes a blow. For the moment there was nothing more to be done and Parkes went back to his office. The same day he wrote to Yeh Mingchen, who was Viceroy of Kwangsi and Kwangtung, the province of which Canton is the capital, and Imperial Commissioner for relations with foreign powers. His tone was firm but not blustering: 'I hasten therefore to lay the case before Your Excellency, confident that your superior judgment will lead you at once to admit that an insult so publicly committed must be equally publicly atoned. I therefore request Your Excellency that the men who have been carried away from the *Arrow* be returned by the captain . . . to that vessel in my presence and if accused of any crime they may then be conveyed to the British Consulate, where in conjunction with proper officers deputed by Your Excellency for the purpose, I shall be prepared to investigate the case.' At no time did Parkes mention either to his superiors or to the Chinese that he had been struck during the argument on the Chinese boat.

As the case then stood Parkes' demand was reasonable, but he must have known that Yeh would not listen. Yeh was a fat sour intelligent man with a taste for astrology.

During seven years in Canton he had earned a high reputation as a conqueror of rebels and pacifier of the European and American barbarians. The two provinces of which he was Viceroy were notoriously turbulent, and had been the first base of the Taiping rebels who now dominated the centre of China. At one time it had seemed as if the rebels would drive Yeh from Canton, but he had rallied the imperial forces and by 1856 was again in control of most of his two provinces. His methods were recognised as exceptionally severe even by his colleagues. Rebels and their families were killed as soon as captured. The execution ground outside the walls of Canton was occasionally visited by adventurous Europeans, who reported that at times the output rose to two hundred heads a day. But it was as a pacifier of barbarians that Yeh was most highly esteemed. To the court at Peking the test of success for a Viceroy of Kwangtung and Kwangsi was whether or not the barbarians were quiet. It was the job of the Viceroy in his capacity as Imperial Commissioner to keep them quiet without making concessions of which the Emperor would have to take notice. The methods which he used were his business, and he rarely received guidance from Peking. By this standard Yeh had certainly been successful. When he first arrived as Governor of Kwangtung he had been responsible together with his superior the Viceroy Hsu for a major diplomatic success over the British on the question of entry into Canton. Since this success had much to do with what followed, something must be said of it. Until the Treaty of Nanking in 1842, as we have seen, Canton was the only city of the Empire at which Europeans were allowed to trade. They were not admitted into the city itself but built for themselves what were known as the factories between the city walls and the river. The factories were really warehouses, but also provided space for the merchants to live rather uncomfortably while they were doing their business. The Treaty of Nanking provided that Consuls and merchants should be allowed to live at five ports, one of which was Canton. In the

four newly opened ports although there were minor difficulties the Chinese allowed Europeans to live within the
walls; but at Canton they insisted that Europeans should
continue as before, confined to the narrow strip of factories
along the river bank, and excluded from the city itself. It
was just possible to interpret the Chinese, though not the
English, text of the Treaty of Nanking, as justifying this
restriction, but the Chinese did not base themselves mainly
on legal argument. They maintained that the people of
Canton were so hostile to foreigners that whatever the
Treaty said it would just not be possible to admit foreigners
into the city. There was some truth in this, but the mandarins whipped up local feeling to support their argument.
Whenever the British showed signs of pressing the point,
reports would come in of threatening placards appearing
in the city, of the militia arming in nearby villages, or of an
attack on some foreigner who had strayed outside the
factories. In 1847 Sir John Davis, the Superintendent of
Trade, extracted a promise that the city would be opened to
foreigners two years later. But when the time came his
successor Sir George Bonham was confronted with exactly
the same arguments. Palmerston had told him that entry
into Canton was not worth a war, and unable to threaten the
use of force, Bonham agreed not to press the question for the
time being. He wrote ambiguously to the Chinese: 'The
question at issue rests where it was, and must remain in
abeyance.' Hsu and Yeh at once announced that the British
had permanently abandoned their claim. Hsu was con-
gratulated by the Emperor and both were honoured in a
tablet of victory erected by the scholars and gentry of
Canton. British officials tried from time to time to reopen
the question, but without the backing of their own Government got nowhere. The foreign consuls and merchants
were still confined to their cramped quarters in the factories.
On fine evenings a crowd of Cantonese used to gather to
watch the barbarians exercising themselves in a little garden
nearby. The sight of grown men taking a walk for its own

sake provided an irresistible entertainment and a further proof of the invincible strangeness of the European.

This arrangement had one great advantage for Yeh. It meant that his own headquarters, or *Yamen*, was beyond the reach of the foreign consuls. He could and did hold himself aloof from them. He was slow to answer their letters and he met requests for an interview with a variety of excuses; he was busy dealing with the rebels, or he felt compelled to wait until he could find an auspicious day for the interview. The lot of a foreign representative trying to have businesslike dealings with Yeh was not happy, and most of them lost patience. 'His Excellency Yeh, in some respects,' reported the American Dr. Parker in the summer of 1856, 'stands alone and pre-eminent in his insane and insufferable conduct towards foreigners. . . . The same demeanour on the part of an officer of his rank of any other nation would be deemed an outrage justifying summary redress.' But there was no alternative to dealing with Yeh; attempts to correspond direct with Peking or to treat with high officials in other provinces were politely refused on the grounds that Yeh alone was charged with the handling of relations with foreign powers.

2

YEH WAS REASONABLY PROMPT in answering Parkes'
complaint about the arrest of the crew of the *Arrow*. On
October 10th he offered to send back nine of the twelve men
arrested with a letter in which he explained that the other
three were wanted on charges of piracy. One of them had
been recognised by his red turban and belt, and the fact that
some of his front teeth were missing, as the leader of an
attack made on a Chinese junk about a month earlier. The
man had admitted to another of the crew of the *Arrow* that
he had taken part in this attack shortly before he joined the
Arrow. According to the deposition of the crew the *Arrow*
had been built and was owned by a Chinese. She was not
therefore a foreign lorcha and there was no point in discussing the matter further. Yeh did not in this letter deny that
his officers had run down the British flag.

This reply together with the return of the nine men was
reasonably conciliatory by Yeh's standards, but was unac-
ceptable to Parkes, who now referred the case to his superior
in Hong Kong, Sir John Bowring. Parkes pointed out that
the British were not concerned with whether or not the
three men had been pirates before they joined the *Arrow*. If
Yeh believed that they had he should have asked Parkes to
detain them and hand them over as laid down in the Supplementary Treaty. The *Arrow* flew the British flag and had
British papers, as the Chinese authorities knew. If they
considered that she had no right to the flag and the papers,
then again they should have approached Parkes. Instead of
this Yeh had taken it upon himself to decide that the *Arrow*

was not a British vessel. If he was not checked there could be no safety for British commerce in the waters round Canton. Parkes recommended to Bowring that as a reprisal British naval forces should seize one of the official boats which had raided the *Arrow*. Meanwhile he refused to accept the nine men whom Yeh had offered to release.

Sir John Bowring, Governor of Hong Kong and Superintendent of Trade, was a passionate Victorian reformer whose learning and zeal throughout his life outran his discretion. He had started his career in a humble merchant's office in Exeter, where he snatched at whatever knowledge came his way. He early realised that he had a gift for languages, and was soon fluent in French, Italian, Spanish, Portuguese, German and Dutch; he also had by his own account a good knowledge of Danish, Swedish, Russian, Polish, Czech, Magyar, Arabic and Chinese. He published translations of Russian poetry, and wrote an excellent and famous hymn:

In the cross of Christ I glory,
Towering o'er the rocks of Time.

But to Bowring learning was merely a tool of reform. He became a disciple of Bentham and editor with him of the *Westminster Review*. After the master died in his arms, Bowring wrote his biography, and helped to carry on his work. He firmly shared the central Benthamite belief that the problems of any society could be solved if the clutter of tradition and prejudice were cleared away and its institutions reformed on logical utilitarian lines. He was learned, intelligent and sincere. His French colleague in Hong Kong declared that Sir John had one of the ugliest and most intelligent faces he had ever seen. He lacked charm, but that is a defect which need do no harm to a radical. His real failing in matters great and small was that he could not judge the time to act and the time to pause. His restless enthusiasm drove him onwards into the obstacles, and unfortunately the obstacles usually proved bigger than the man. In his twenties he had become involved in Orleanist intrigues in France against Charles X and spent six weeks in prison in Boulogne for unsuccessfully helping prisoners to escape. He returned from a visit to the Middle East with a bottle of Jordan water for Queen Victoria, an enthusiasm for Egyptian nationalism, and a conviction that the plague was not infectious. He explained that 'the Emperor of Russia sent many criminals to Egypt who were compelled to sleep in the beds of plague patients but not one of them caught the disorder.' In 1839 he turned his attention to Prussia and was so impressed by its tariff system that he told the Prime Minister on his return that the British Corn Laws would have to go. He was seven years early; Lord Melbourne 'exclaimed with an oath (not an unusual ornament of his conversation) that I was fit for Bedlam.' Bowring sat twice in Parliament as a radical and his votes were predictable. He was against the press gang and flogging in the army, in favour of decimal coinage and the ballot. He became a collaborator and friend of Cobden in the Anti-Corn Law League, and later in the Peace Society, of which he was for some time Secretary.

But parliamentary life did not suit Bowring. An old Cornishman came to him once on behalf of the Wesleyan Methodists to say that it was reported that Bowring did not believe in the Trinity, and therefore he must pay double for their votes. The winning of votes and in Parliament itself the unavoidable necessity of listening to other men's opinions did not come easily to Bowring. Besides money was short and an iron works in which he was interested came to grief. By 1849 he had had enough, and applied successfully to Lord Palmerston for the vacant Consulship at Canton. It was an odd request for a man of fifty-seven to make, and an odd appointment for Palmerston to agree to; probably he thought that this Government supporter would be less trouble in Canton than at Westminster.

Bowring arrived at Canton in time to watch his superior Sir George Bonham give Hsu and Yeh their success in keeping the barbarians out of the city. This British diplomatic defeat coloured the whole of Bowring's time in China.

The approaches to
CANTON

English Miles

113°

Samshui

West River

CANTO

Shiuhing

Fatshan

Shekw

23°

Shuntak

Koming

Kumchuk

Hokshan

Kongmoon

He

Sunning

22°

Chikkai

113°

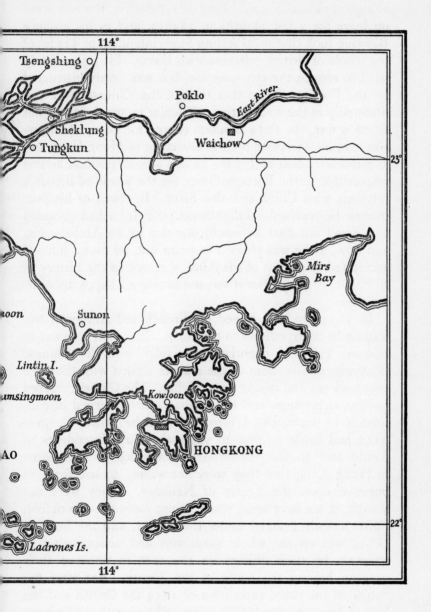

114°

Tsengshing

Poklo

East River

Sheklung

Waichow

Tungkun

23°

Mirs
Bay

Sunon

Lintin I.

umsingmoon

Kowloon

AO

HONGKONG

22°

Ladrones Is.

114°

It was the kind of concession to an effete tyranny with which as a good radical he could have no sympathy. Bonham went on leave for a few months in 1852-3, and in his absence Bowring took charge (as Acting Superintendent of Trade) of the whole of British relations with China. He immediately tried to reopen the city question, but was firmly instructed by the Foreign Office that though the Chinese were undoubtedly in the wrong, that particular treaty right was not worth a war. In 1854 Bonham retired for good, and Bowring was his successor both as Governor of Hong Kong and as Superintendent of Trade. In this second position he was responsible to the Foreign Office for the whole of Britain's relations with China and also Siam. In token of his promotion he received a knighthood. Sir John had dreamed as a small boy that he would one day be an Ambassador, and now, as he was pleased to point out, he found himself accredited to a third of mankind, a record in the history of British diplomacy. But it was not to prove a happy appointment.

In 1854 Sir John joined his French and American colleagues in an expedition to the north. Their purpose was to by-pass Yeh and negotiate peacefully with the Chinese Government a revision of the treaties signed with the three countries ten and twelve years earlier. The Chinese refused to discuss revision, and the Ambassadors returned disconsolately to the south. Up to this time the British Government had made it clear to successive Superintendents of Trade and to the vociferous community of merchants in Hong Kong that they were not willing to use force to improve upon the Treaty of Nanking. They were not always, as we have seen, ready to use force even to defend rights already granted under the Treaty, and the Foreign Office was on the whole suspicious and disapproving of attempts by their officers on the spot to improve their position beyond the terms of the Treaty. But after the failure of the peace expedition of 1854 the British and the French began to accept that a new collision with the Chinese was inevitable. The Treaty of Nanking and the similar treaties signed by the other powers had been an attempt by those powers to make the Chinese abandon their claim to superiority and enter the Western system of international law based on the idea of equal sovereign nations. In this central aim the Treaties had failed; the Chinese had with some exceptions carried out the practical provisions of the Treaties but they had not revised their conviction that China was a nation superior and indeed of a different quality to the peoples of the West. The British and French, and to a lesser extent the American Governments, came slowly to the conclusion that it was not enough to defend the letter of the existing Treaties; they must be prepared to use force to get themselves recognised, in practice as well as theory, as the equals of the Government in Peking. It was perhaps characteristic that the Americans, while less ready than the British and French to use force, wished to make even more sweeping demands of the Chinese. Bowring's American counterpart was Dr. Parker, an indefatigable former missionary, who believed that the Western powers should demand not only unlimited freedom of trade for themselves but also freedom of opinion and legal reform for the Chinese people. It was the kind of scheme which naturally appealed to Bowring's sanguine radical temperament, but even he had to advise the Foreign Office that there was no hope of its success. For two years the British and French were preoccupied with the Crimean War, but by the autumn of 1856 they were once more able to consider a forward move in China.

Most of those who thought about these matters on the Western side had concluded that the Chinese would never treat the Western powers as equals until the powers were represented by Ambassadors in Peking. So long as relations were handled by an Imperial Commissioner in Canton, the court at Peking could keep itself at one remove from foreign affairs. It would not concern itself with Western grievances, beyond entrusting the Commissioner with the traditional task of keeping the barbarians quiet. Bowring accepted this argument in principle but in practice he was far more interested in trying a fall with Yeh and the people of Canton. It was Yeh and the Cantonese who had in the eyes of all China humiliated the British by refusing them their acknowledged right of entry into Canton. The Chinese would never treat the British as equals until the right of entry had been successfully asserted and Yeh humbled. Bowring had been specifically told by his Government not to try to assert the right of entry. But what if Yeh played into his hands with some new infringement of the Treaty? Then surely he would be justified in using the naval force at his disposal not only to resist the new infringement but also to settle the outstanding question of entry into the city of Canton.

He did not have long to wait for his grievance. On October 9th he heard from Parkes of the seizure of the crew of the *Arrow* and the hauling down of the British flag. He promptly approved the line which Parkes had taken and authorised him to demand an apology, an assurance that the flag would be respected, and the return of the crew of twelve. If Yeh did not accept those conditions within forty-eight hours the British naval authorities were authorised to seize an imperial junk in reprisal. Yeh refused to budge, and on October 14th the small British gunboat *Coramandel* seized a Chinese junk without bloodshed and towed it down river to Whampoa. Unfortunately it turned out that the junk did not belong to the Chinese Government, and the reprisal had no immediate effect on Yeh. Bowring had by now reported to the Foreign Office about the *Arrow* but he knew that it would be three months before he could expect any comments or instructions. He was beginning to think that this was the opportunity he wanted to force a reckoning with Yeh. On the 16th he wrote to Parkes: 'Cannot we use the opportunity and carry the city question? If so I will come up with the whole fleet. I think we have now a stepping stone from which with good management we may move on to important sequences.' He hesitated for another week; even so enthusiastic a man must have seen that there were good grounds for hesitation. Already it appeared that on the *Arrow* Yeh had a better case than he knew. Bowring had noticed something which Parkes had missed: the *Arrow*'s Hong Kong register had expired on September 27th, eleven days before her crew had been seized. It was true that she had not put in to Hong Kong during those eleven days, and so had not had an opportunity to renew the register. It was also to be argued later by good lawyers that the failure to renew the register was a matter between the owner of the *Arrow* and the colonial authorities in Hong Kong; it did not affect the lorcha's status vis-à-vis the Chinese, or her right to fly the British flag. But at the time Bowring did not use these arguments. He wrote to Parkes bluntly on October 11th: 'It appears on examination that the *Arrow* had no right to hoist the British flag, the licence to do so expired on the 27th September, from which period she has not been entitled to protection.' Two days later in reply to a letter from Parkes which made the point about the *Arrow* having been at sea since September 27th, he repeated the same opinion: 'I will consider regranting the register of the *Arrow* if applied for: but there can be no doubt that after the expiry of the licence, protection could not be legally granted.' But to Bowring it did not follow that Yeh could be excused. Yeh did not know that the register had expired, but he did know that the *Arrow* claimed British nationality and flew the British flag. His offence was therefore as rank as if the register had been in order; he had still broken the Treaty. There was logic in this, but if Bowring had been more of a politician he would have seen that the insult to the *Arrow* was no longer a plausible pretext for reopening the old quarrel with Yeh.

While Bowring deliberated the diplomatic correspondence at Canton went on. On October 14th, the day the junk was seized, Yeh for the first time denied that the mandarins had hauled down the *Arrow*'s British flag. He said that according to their evidence no flag was flying. There is a direct conflict of evidence here which can never be finally resolved, but the weight of the evidence is against Yeh. His officers, who were clearly interested parties, denied that the flag was flying. On the other side the master, Thomas Kennedy, and his friend the British master of the *Dart*, who might also be said to be interested parties, deposed on the day itself that they had seen the Chinese haul down the flag. They were categorically supported by two witnesses who were not so clearly interested, a Chinese member of the crew, and an American called Charles Earl who made the third of the breakfast party on board the *Dart* and gave his deposition seven months later. It was not the custom to fly national flags when at anchor at Canton; but the *Arrow* was on the point of sailing, and had hoisted the Blue Peter to show this. If the flag was not hauled down by the Chinese it is odd that Yeh did not deny the allegation in his first letter of October 10th to Parkes.[1]

On October 21st, with Bowring's authority, Parkes gave Yeh twenty-four hours in which to comply with his demands, failing which 'Her Majesty's naval officers will have recourse to force to compel complete satisfaction.' The next day Yeh came very near surrender. He sent back all twelve of the crew of the *Arrow*, and he reaffirmed the procedure of the Supplementary Treaty: 'Hereafter if any lawless characters conceal themselves on board foreign lorchas you, the said Consul, shall of course be informed of the same by declaration in order that you may act with the Chinese authorities in the management of such affairs.' But he still maintained that the *Arrow* was not a foreign lorcha and that the Treaty did not apply to her; nor would he apologise or return the men in the public manner stipulated by the British. Parkes told Rear-Admiral Sir Michael Seymour,

[1] This conflict of evidence is dealt with by a Chinese scholar, Huang Yen-yu, in an appendix to an article in the Harvard Journal of Asiatic Studies (1941 vol. 6, p. 37). But he does not seem to be aware of Earl's detailed deposition of May 1857 (F.O.17.269) and appears to have slightly misunderstood the point about the Blue Peter.

who had moved up the river from Hong Kong, that the answer was unsatisfactory. On October 23rd Sir Michael captured and dismantled the four Barrier Forts which lay about five miles below Canton. Two of the forts resisted and four or five Chinese were killed, the first casualties of the war.

Sir Michael Seymour, who thus ordered the first shots in the *Arrow* war, was a navy man born and bred. He was the son of an admiral and joined his father's ship at the age of 11. He had bad luck in 1835 when H.M.S. *Challenge* which he was commanding was caught in an exceptionally strong current, swept on to the coast of Chile and wrecked. In the inescapable court martial which followed Seymour was acquitted and indeed commended for his behaviour. In 1854, when second-in-command in the Baltic, he suffered another mishap at the start of the Crimean War. While he was examining a Russian mine picked up off Kronstadt it exploded in his face, and he lost the sight of one eye. Seymour was now fifty-four, pompous, conscientious, and above all slow. He did not like Bowring but was no match for the latter's energy and ambition.

By the time the news of the naval action reached Hong Kong Sir John Bowring had made up his mind. In spite of the *Arrow*'s faulty register, in spite of the concession which Yeh had just made in sending back the crew, he told Parkes to use the dispute to reopen the question of entrance into the city of Canton. Admiral Seymour had doubted the wisdom of this, but now agreed; Parkes was wholly in favour. On October 25th Parkes wrote to Yeh that 'it will be necessary to guard against the recurrence of such difficulties by providing freer means of communication between Your Excellency and Her Majesty's officers.' Three days later he told a Chinese official that operations would be continued until all foreign representatives were allowed free personal access to all the authorities at Canton. This was less than the treaty right, acknowledged in principle by the Chinese in 1847, by which merchants and missionaries as well as officials would have been admitted to Canton; but it was a great deal more than Yeh could be expected to stomach. He rejected the demand in a letter to Admiral Seymour on October 31st.

The British had already resumed the use of force. Admiral Seymour had opened with one gun from H.M.S. *Encounter* on the 27th on the city wall of Canton and on Yeh's official residence within, firing one shell every five or ten minutes. Yeh played his part according to the expected tradition. He was found by his subordinates smiling over a book and only with reluctance allowed himself to be led away to safety. On the 29th the Admiral, having breached the wall, put himself at the head of a body of marines, entered the city and marched through Yeh's headquarters before withdrawing. The American Consul accompanied him in a high state of intoxication carrying the Stars and Stripes, an act of patriotism which was later disowned by the American Government.

Both sides now settled down to several months of desultory warfare. Each was hopeful that the other would give way, but neither in fact had the means to impose its will. Admiral Seymour quickly gained control of the river and estuary connecting Hong Kong, Macao and Canton. He dispersed hostile junks, demolished Chinese forts, and from time to time reopened fire on Canton itself. But his force of marines was not strong enough to take and hold the city, and Bowring could not spare him more than a handful of men from the 59th Regiment which provided the garrison of Hong Kong. Life in the European factories at Canton became less and less comfortable, shops closed, servants leaving, the Admiral's shells occasionally audible overhead, and the ladies of the Consulate already departed for Hong Kong. But Mrs. Parkes did not despond: 'Dear Harry, I am thankful to say, notwithstanding all his cares and responsibility, is wonderfully well and in good spirits, for he says with God's blessing he feels sure of a successful issue to this affair. . . . Sir John says he has done more than

The Anglo-French fleet in the river off Tientsin, 1858. From sketches in China and Japan, by F. le B. Bedwell

The Sikh camp at Kowloon, opposite Hong Kong, 1860

Commissioner Yeh, Viceroy of the two Kwangs, from a sketch by Colonel Crealock, 1858

The rear of the North Taku fort after its capture 1860, photograph by Signor Beato

admirably.' For his part Yeh could do nothing to counter the Admiral on the sea, but he made life extremely uncomfortable for the British on land. On October 30th he issued a proclamation offering thirty dollars for every English head. He refused to meet Bowring, and in writing lectured Seymour, in good Confucian terms, on the right of the people of Canton to refuse entry to the British if they wished: 'In the administration of all matters in China the rule adhered to is that which heaven shows is the right one to pursue; the chief consideration is the people. It is said in the Book of History, "Heaven sees as my people see; Heaven hears as my people hear." Is this not an additional reason why I should be unable to constrain the people? I must add that as it is the habit of Your Excellency's nation to adore the spirit of Heaven, it behoves you in my opinion so much the more to conform in your actions to the principle given us by heaven. Let Your Excellency maturely consider this.' This was sound doctrine to which on the whole the Manchu dynasty paid little heed, and Yeh's programme of mass executions showed that he was not averse in principle to 'constraining the people.' But he knew that he could rely on and exploit a genuine popular hostility towards Europeans in and around Canton. The Cantonese had no particular love of the dynasty and a few of the well-to-do stood to gain from European trade; but the ordinary people seemed ready to put up with and sometimes to help Manchu efforts to keep out the foreigners. This was not true of other parts of China, and it ceased to be true of Canton two years later; but in 1856 it was a fact in Yeh's favour.

Yeh was riding high through November and December. Bowring came up from Hong Kong to see him on November 17th but failed. 'I have exhausted all the means with which I could influence either the hopes or fears of this incarnation of ancient Chinese pride, ignorance and unteachableness,' he wrote to the Foreign Secretary, Lord Clarendon. On December 15th the foreign factories between the city wall of Canton and the river were burned to the ground. Parkes was in Hong Kong that day but Lane, one of the British Consulate staff, was killed in the fire. Yeh denied that he was responsible, but this was a matter of form; Chinese were seen running from house to house with lighted brands, and it seems likely that they acted on his orders or at least with his approval. The loss suffered by European firms was very great. Admiral Seymour continued for a few weeks after the fire to keep two ships, the *Niger* and the *Encounter*, anchored off the factories, but they were now in a dangerously exposed position and were soon withdrawn. So far from forcing their way into the city, the British had thus been expelled from their commercial and naval foothold outside the city walls.

Seymour continued to control most of the waterways between Canton and the open sea, but they were by no means safe for Europeans. On December 29th there was a mutiny on the small steamer *Thistle* on her way from Canton to Hong Kong. The eleven Europeans on board were beheaded by the mutineers, who wore the insignia of Yeh's militia.

An even greater calamity seemed possible in the opening weeks of 1857. The colony of Hong Kong had been in existence some fifteen years. It had a Governor, a Bishop, an Attorney General and most of the other ingredients of British colonial society. An American visiting the island at this time was reminded of one of the boom towns of the American West. He meant it as a compliment, being impressed by the commercial palaces of Dent and Jardine and the speed with which money was made and spent. But it was also true that, like the American West, the colony had grown too quickly for its own good. When the British took over the island, only a few fishing families lived on it; by 1857 it had attracted an astonishing multitude of Chinese, smugglers, opium merchants, Taiping rebels, members of secret societies as well as thousands of ordinary fishermen, shopkeepers and coolies who found life better than on the mainland. Sir John Bowring had long realised how vulnerable was the small British community, and how little either he or they knew of what was going on among the Chinese whom he ruled in the Queen's name. He wrote to Hammond, Permanent Under-Secretary at the Foreign Office, on November 25th: 'The colony is now quite tranquil. I feel no disquietude about our position though our numbers are so small, in the midst of a somewhat disorderly multitude. I imagine we have about 80,000 Chinese in the island, and plenty of mischief makers, both imperialists and rebels.' In the next weeks his fears rapidly grew. Mysterious fires broke out on the island. Servants suddenly abandoned their masters. Assaults upon Europeans became frequent. Yeh was known to be in close touch with the fishing villages on the Kowloon peninsula across the harbour from Hong Kong. The Europeans were convinced that he would try to seize the colony after a sudden massacre. As their pastor, the Bishop of Victoria, put it in a lecture at Manchester five months later, they felt 'exposed, not merely to the ordinary danger of a foreign residence, but to the cup of the poisoner, the knife of the assassin and the torch of the midnight incendiary.' Bowring recruited extra police and even had humbly to ask the French and American naval commanders for detachments to help keep order; both agreed. On January 15th the climax came. Bowring, his family and other leading members of the British community were taken suddenly ill. They were found to be suffering from arsenic poisoning, which was traced to the bread they had eaten that morning. The baker was found to have fled to Macao and it was universally supposed that he had been hired by Yeh. The poisoner had botched his job; there was so much arsenic in the bread that the victims vomited at once, and no one died. But Lady Bowring was seriously ill for some time, and Bowring himself much upset. The bag left that evening for London, and Bowring wrote a postscript to his despatches to Labouchere, the Colonial Secretary: 'I beg to apologise if anything should have been forgotten at this last moment. I am shaken by the effects of poison, every member of my family being at this moment suffering from this new attempt upon our lives.' The fugitive baker was later arrested, tried and acquitted for lack of evidence by a Hong Kong court. In fact while Yeh certainly encouraged acts of terrorism against the British, he had neither the imagination nor the means to subvert the colony successfully.

While the scare was at its height Bowring decided that he must ask for reinforcements. It had been obvious since the middle of November that unless the British could muster a sizeable military force the best they could hope for was stalemate. Parkes had written to his sister when he got to Hong Kong in mid-December: 'I am well and in the best of spirits. True, I am up to my neck in hot water, but I hope to use it in washing an immense amount of Canton filth that has been accumulating during years past. . . . We are just in this position that having taken everything but the city we cannot *take* it (though we can destroy it, though we do not wish to be compelled to do that) unless we have a land force both for the attack and subsequent occupation which the former renders necessary. Better not to attack at all than to take and then retreat from it.' A month later the French representative , de Courcy, reported to Paris that the situation in Hong Kong was 'thick with danger, doubts and threats.' Yeh was acting against the British with energy and perseverance, and there were rumours of a plot among the British in Hong Kong to overthrow Bowring and replace him with a Committee of Public Safety. Nevertheless, Bowring, backed up by Admiral Seymour, was most reluctant to ask for reinforcements. He always hoped that Yeh was about to give way; he knew that the British Government would be most unwilling to send troops for a Chinese expedition; and self-righteous though he was he must have realised that his action in tacking the city question on to the dispute about the *Arrow* would be controversial. But by the middle of January he could no longer hope that he and the Admiral could succeed with what they had, and on the 10th he wrote to Lord Canning, the Governor General of India, asking him to send five thousand men with artillery as soon as possible. By the same mail he justified himself to the Foreign Secretary in a letter which sums up his vehement stubborn character:

'My Lord, Our hopes continue to be disappointed of making any impression upon the Imperial Commissioner likely to lead to any satisfactory arrangement. Hostilities, open and covert, continue to be waged with a desperation and utter disregard of any of the Laws of Civilisation and claims of humanity which cannot but awaken the greatest solicitude for the results, not only as regards the local question at Canton, but the whole of our future relations with China.

'The gate of China is Canton, and unless we can subdue the resistance and force an entrance there, I believe the difficulties of obtaining any improved position in China will be almost invincible. But success at Canton will, I am assured, be followed by a general and satisfactory change in the state of our relations with the entire Empire.

'Everything that could be fairly hoped for from the prudence, enterprise and valour of H.M. naval forces has been accomplished, but they are not able to take the city of Canton, and I deem its capture absolutely necessary for our final triumph. I have had a conference with the Naval Commander-in-Chief and he deemed military aid to the extent of 5,000 men, with a small body of artillery, an absolutely necessary auxiliary.

'. . . I hope the Admiral will be able to maintain his position at Canton and its neighbourhood. The vessels are exposed to great danger from fire rafts, explosive machines and other incendiary appliances. Attempts have been made to close the channels of the river by sinking junks, and the service is become one demanding incessant watchfulness.

'In the colony I hope we shall be carried safely through our perils. A large premium is offered for our heads, enormous recompenses are promised to any Chinaman who shall fire the town, great part of our servants have left in consequence of the menaces of the Mandarins, and the severest punishments have been proclaimed in the neighbouring Districts on all who shall supply our markets. But behind the present darkness we see the promise of brighter days, in the full conviction that H.M. Government will come to our aid.'

Bowring's letter of January 10th reached Lord Clarendon on March 1st. By that time Sir John Bowring and the lorcha *Arrow* were the chief topic of political talk and disagreement in England.

3

Six years before these events Lord John Russell told Prince Albert that Lord Palmerston was too old to do much in the future, having passed his sixty-fifth year. Prince Albert in turn observed: 'The Queen could never reconcile it with her duty towards the country to allow Lord Palmerston to become its ruler.' Neither of them knew the man's strength. At the time of the seizure of the *Arrow* Lord Palmerston had been Prime Minister for eighteen months, and was to continue in office with one interruption for the remaining nine years of his life. His strength lay in his enormous popularity with the people; not particularly with the upper classes, and not exclusively with the electorate, which between 1832 and 1867 was solidly middle-class, but with the great mass of citizens, whether or not they had the vote.[1] Not that Lord Palmerston was a democrat. He had played a part in the great reforms of the second quarter of the century but he was a Whig[2] nobleman not a pro-

[1] As Mr. Southgate puts it in his *The Passing of the Whigs 1832-1866*, 'It was not from parties that Palmerston was to draw that support that would make him Chief Minister; it was from a public drawn from all classes; it was from John Bull.'

[2] The political labels of this time are confusing. The Whig and Tory parties were in slow process of changing to Liberal and Conservative, but there were many cross currents. I have used Liberal as the official name of Palmerston's party and Whig occasionally to distinguish the old-fashioned members of it (such as Palmerston himself). The Radicals were a group to the left of the Liberal Party but loosely connected with it. The Peelites were dead centre; the name explains itself. I have used Tory rather than Conservative because that seems the

fessional reformer and by 1856 had long been convinced that enough had been changed. He had often to work with younger, more zealous men calling themselves Liberals and not Whigs, but it was no secret that he skilfully blocked their proposals for further reform and that no Government of which he was the head was likely to extend the franchise to the working classes, to introduce the Ballot, or make further changes in established institutions. Disraeli called him 'a gay old Tory of the older school, disguising himself as a Liberal and hoaxing the Reform Club.' But his popularity had little to do with his opinions on home affairs. It was partly the result of personal character. Like Churchill, Palmerston stood out in small ways and in great as a man who had a style of his own which he was not prepared to trim to the fashion of the moment. The white top hat, the big parties at Cambridge House, the race-going and partridge shooting, the dyed whiskers, the upright figure jogging on horseback down Piccadilly, or across to Harrow for speech day, the stream of little witticisms at the expense of everything solemn, and the very fact that he was so old and had been in and out of ministries for so long, made him a well-loved figure, loved perhaps the more because most mid-Victorians lived so differently.

But it was above all his handling of foreign affairs which made him popular. To ordinary people Palmerston was the man who stood up to the foreigners for England. When Palmerston first took office as a young man the country was threatened with destruction by almost the whole continent of Europe in arms against her. Now in the 'fifties and 'sixties England was at the height of her power; never before or since has she possessed such material superiority over her neighbours and rivals. So great a change in so short a time went to the national head. The speeches, pamphlets and

---

most apt label for the party during the twenty years after the repeal of the Corn Laws. Peel had taught them to call themselves Conservatives, but they had revolted against Peel.

newspapers of the time are flavoured with a feeling of pride in British achievement, which is understandable, and of contempt for foreigners of all kinds, which is often disagreeable. This pride and this contempt were identified in the public mind with Lord Palmerston. In 1855 when Lord Aberdeen's high-minded and intelligent coalition seemed unable to cope with the Crimean War it was to Palmerston that the country turned. As a broadsheet of a few years earlier put it:

> Then Palmy he'll be at our head,
> And keep the tyrants all in dread,
> Austria and France will wish him dead
> And for a milksop in his stead,
> Haynau and the Russian Tsar
> Will curse him in their realms afar,
> And on their feelings it will jar,
>   To find old Palmy stronger.

'Keep the tyrants all in dread.' The point was that Palmerston not only stood up for English rights, but also encouraged liberal movements in Europe against the absolute rulers, following the example of Canning in Latin America. It was this which made him so unpopular with the courts of Europe and therefore so suspect to the Queen and Prince Albert. But we need not dwell on this side of his politics for the simple reason that it did not apply to China. Palmerston did not conceive that liberal thought or parliamentary institutions had any place in the Chinese any more than in the Ottoman Empire.[1] His policy towards

---

[1] In the era which reached its climax with President Wilson and ended perhaps with the U.N. Declaration of Human Rights, liberal doctrine held in general that all men were entitled to live in a democracy and enjoy constitutional rights. Now it is fashionable to assert that military dictatorships and one party states may often be the right answer for Asian and African countries whose history and political needs differ widely from our own. Palmerston would have agreed.

China was solely concerned with the defence of British interests.

It was the defence of British interests, not their forcible expansion, which interested Palmerston. The phrase 'Palmerstonian diplomacy' is often used loosely to mean 'imperialism.' This is inexact. Palmerston was quick to redress by force an infringement of British rights, and sometimes, as in the famous case of Don Pacifico, the force used was out of all proportion to the infringement. But he did not consciously follow a policy of expansion like Disraeli or Joseph Chamberlain. His policy towards China shows this. The British had in Palmerston's view a double right in China, first to be treated as equals by the Chinese in political matters, and second to enjoy reasonable trading opportunities. Both these rights were on paper secured by the Treaty of Nanking, and Palmerston and the Foreign Office were reluctant to accept the advice which they received from the spot that the Chinese had no more intention of treating the barbarians as equals after the Treaty than before it. During Palmerston's second period at the Foreign Office from 1846 to 1851, Britain was at peace and had forces to spare. It was clear that the Treaty was not working, and that in one important particular, that of entry into Canton, the Chinese were withholding what they acknowledged to be a Treaty right. But Palmerston refused to allow the use of force and was careful to obtain and follow legal advice on the interpretation of the Treaty. The official papers and letters of the time often express anxiety lest Britain should find herself forced to take over responsibility for China as she had for India, either to forestall Russia or else because the existing Chinese Empire fell apart in disorder. It was supposed that this would be a task beyond the resources of the country. The British Government had rather crossly accepted Hong Kong in 1841 after its cession had been arranged on the spot by the British representative acting without instructions; but for many years the island was regarded as a liability. There was talk from time to time of acquiring either in exchange or in addition the island of Chusan off the coast near Shanghai in order to forestall French ambitions, but the idea came to nothing. Successive Foreign Secretaries of both parties agreed that the British commitment in China should not be increased.

Palmerston's Foreign Secretary in 1856 was Lord Clarendon. He was not a national figure, but courteous, intelligent and hard-working, and an excellent Foreign Secretary. He shared Palmerston's ideas but not his instinct for making rough fun of everyone, particularly foreigners. He was a good master to his subordinates, and his skill at managing the Prime Minister soon reassured the Court and friendly foreign Governments, to whom Palmerston's return to office had not been welcome.

Bowring's despatch reporting the seizure of the *Arrow* and his first plan for counter measures reached Clarendon on December 1st. On December 10th Clarendon replied that he had consulted the Law Officers of the Crown and was of opinion that the Chinese had broken the Treaty, even though the *Arrow*'s register had expired. He approved Bowring's plan for seizing an imperial junk as a reprisal. Clarendon's letter reached Bowring on February 3rd, three and a half months after the measure which it authorised had been taken. Early in the New Year it became clear in London that whether or not he had acted wisely, Bowring had a war on his hands. The Government was immediately pressed to take this opportunity to insist on a new Treaty with China. In an editorial on January 2nd *The Times* urged the Government to demand entry to Canton as Bowring had done, and also the right to station a representative in Peking. It would be wrong to 'conclude a new peace till we have eliminated from it the conditions of a future war.' The cry for a new Treaty was taken up vociferously by the China merchants, who were by now a recognisable force in the political world, and could rely on the influence of a score or so of Members of Parliament of both

main parties.[1] Bowring had not hitherto been a favourite
with the merchants of Hong Kong or their connections in
England because he had on various occasions made it
difficult for merchants to avoid paying the agreed duties to
the Chinese authorities even when the Chinese were in no
position to collect. Probably Bowring's greatest accomplishment was his support for the scheme by which after
1853 the Chinese at Shanghai employed foreigners to
collect the duties, a scheme which later developed into the
famous China Customs Service under Sir Robert Hart.
Later generations of Chinese denounced the virtual running
of their Customs by foreigners as a surrender to imperialism,
but the immediate effect was to strengthen the Chinese
against tricky or fraudulent merchants. The British merchants had criticised the scheme and Bowring on the grounds
that it was not for the British to save the Chinese from their
own inadequacies. But their criticism was muted as soon as
it became clear that Bowring's rupture with Yeh might give
them the chance at last to break decisively into the Chinese
market which they believed to be so great but which had so
far proved so elusive. On January 6th Mr. Gregson, M.P.,
Chairman of the East India and China Association, wrote
to Clarendon with advice on what a new Treaty should con-
tain. It should of course secure entry into Canton, but it
should also provide for a revision of the tariff, the opening
of new ports to trade and access to rivers and the interior.

[1] In *Sybil* Disraeli describes a contest of the 1837 election:
'You had a formidable opponent, Lord Marney told me,' said Sir
Vavasour, 'who was he?'
'Oh! a dreadful man! A Scotchman, richer than Croesus, one
McDruggy, fresh from Canton, with a million of opium in each
pocket, denouncing corruption and bellowing free trade.'
'But they do not care much for free trade in the old borough?'
said Lord Marney.
'No, it was a mistake,' said Egremont, 'and the cry was changed
the moment my opponent was on the ground. Then all the town was
placarded with "Vote for McDruggy and our young Queen", as if he
had coalesced with Her Majesty!'

Similar letters came from Liverpool and Glasgow. Manchester suggested that Shanghai should be annexed but the Foreign Office, temperamentally suspicious of colonies and new commitments, promptly turned this down. Gregson wrote again on another point which caused much perplexity at this time: could not the Chinese be got to allow the emigration of females to Malaya, which already contained about 50,000 Chinese emigrants, almost all male? 'I forbear to enter,' observed Mr. Gregson primly, 'upon the immoral and unnatural state of things now existing at Singapore.'

Lord Clarendon made no promises, but by the middle of January the Government had decided to support Bowring not only in having taken up the case of the *Arrow* but in having tacked on to it the question of entry into Canton. They had also decided to press for a revision of the Treaty of Nanking. The British Government had been preparing to make a new move towards revision before they heard about the *Arrow*. The same force could now be used to humble Yeh and to press the Chinese into revision. On January 31st, before they received news of Bowring's request to India for troops, the Cabinet authorised Lord Canning, Governor General of India, to send a regiment with artillery to China. On February 9th Clarendon wrote to tell Bowring that Seymour was being authorised by the Admiralty to lead an expedition into the Yangtze river to cut the entrance to the Grand Canal by which it was supposed that junks carried tribute of rice to Peking without which the capital would starve. Bowring was to ask for a new treaty which would include British representation at Peking, new treaty ports, and freedom of access to the great rivers.

The Government had in fact decided to back Bowring without reservation. It is clear that some members of the Government had reservations about what he had done. Those Ministers, Palmerston and Clarendon included, who had known Bowring in his parliamentary days, seem to have had few illusions about his good judgment. But the argument which swayed them was that even if they repudiated Bowring they could not undo what he had done but they would expose him and their other servants in the Far East to ridicule and probably danger. Before the days of the long-range telegraph there was really no alternative to trusting the man on the spot when the spot was as far away as China. The Duke of Argyll recalled in his memoirs hearing the Attorney General explain the legal position in Cabinet: 'I did not care to ask whether the conduct of Sir John Bowring had or had not been somewhat more high-handed than was absolutely necessary. It was enough for me to see that the disavowal of our Commissioner, when such serious action had been taken, would inflict a severe blow on all our officers who might succeed him, and throw into confusion the whole system on which our commerce rested in that part of the world.' Canning, writing to Granville, the Lord President of the Council, from India, probably summed up the opinion of many: 'I think we (England) were wrong about the Lorcha and right about the entrance to Canton. But that Bowring's presumption in swelling the small case into the great one on his own hook was indefensible'—but nevertheless, Canning went on, had to be defended. Palmerston told the Queen that he had no doubt that it was right to approve what Bowring had done. The Prime Minister was not perturbed by close argument among lawyers. It was enough for him that the Chinese had offered a deliberate insult. His predominance was so great that his opinion would almost certainly have prevailed with his colleagues even if their doubts had been stronger than they were.

By supporting Bowring the Government put its life in jeopardy. Ministers must have known that they would run into trouble with the radical wing of their own party. In almost every British Parliament since the days of Fox there has sat a band of men, usually not very numerous or much loved, who have set themselves up as the guardians of the British conscience on foreign affairs, with a particular brief to check the tendency which they detect in every British Government of their own or another party towards wicked dealing. In 1857 this group was led by the Radicals Richard Cobden and John Bright. Bright, who had been stalwart beside Cobden in opposing the Crimean War, was now seriously ill and the task of denouncing Britain's latest sins fell squarely upon Cobden. There is no doubt that Cobden felt passionately about the subject and, more strangely, that he believed he would be supported by a surge of public opinion. He held the lowest opinion of Palmerston, the head of the party to which he was loosely attached, and had written about him to a Frenchman some months earlier: 'All men at the age of seventy-two, with unsatisfied ambition, are desperadoes.' Cobden must have regretted that his friend Bowring, with whom he had worked closely for several years in the Free Trade movement and in the Peace Society, should also, though only sixty-four, have turned desperado; but he did not allow an old friendship to interfere with the force of his denunciation. The Radical Bowring went abroad and discovered that only force would bring free trade to China; the Radical Cobden stayed at home and still believed that it could be done by persuasion and good example.[1] Cobden had a strong personal following in Manchester and other northern towns, but his opposition to the Crimean War had not been generally popular, and his new stand confirmed in many minds a suspicion which was crudely expressed by *Punch*:

> Richard Cobden has a knack,
>> Talk away, Yeh-o, boys!
> Of hauling down the Union Jack,
>> Assailed by any foe, boys.

[1] A shrewd critic has written: 'The self-confident idealism which formed so large a part of imperialism in its late-Victorian form was rooted in Liberal and Radical minds as well as in Conservative ones. The career of Joseph Chamberlain speaks for itself.' (Anthony Hartley, *A State of England*). In this sense Bowring was a precursor of Chamberlain, and Cobden of the pro-Boer Lloyd George.

Come Pope, come Czar, come savage, why
I know not, still his best he'll try
To make old England's colours lie,
In degradation low, boys.

The Radicals were joined by the bedraggled heirs of Sir
Robert Peel. The Peelites were the remnant of the brilliant
group who had followed Peel against the Corn Laws ten
years earlier. They were the men whom Peel had groomed
to be the leaders of the progressive Conservative Party
which he was fashioning out of the old Tory interest. But
in 1846 the mass of Tories had baulked at the repeal of the
Corn Laws; the party split and the leaders found themselves without followers. Gladstone, Sir James Graham and
Sidney Herbert were men of great parts who would shine
in any assembly. But for years after 1846 they led unhappy
political lives, oscillating between the Whigs and the Tories,
uneasily conscious of their own merits, anxious for office
yet unwilling to submerge themselves in either of the great
parties. Peel himself died, the Tories came in after six
years and failed to restore the Corn Laws; but though
Protection was dead there was no reconciliation between
Tory and Peelite. The small band of Peelites gladly entered
Lord Aberdeen's coalition, but could stomach only a few
weeks of his successor Palmerston and resigned in March
1855. Gladstone was the most energetic of the group, but
they all shared his contempt for what they held to be
Palmerston's blustering and frivolous handling of foreign
affairs.

To them was also joined the sad figure of Lord John
Russell. Lord John was a Whig temporarily adrift from
his party, but unlike the Peelites he had not broken away
on a great point of principle. His views on foreign affairs
did not differ much from Palmerston's and within three
years he was to be working happily as Palmerston's Foreign
Secretary. His trouble in the early 'fifties was personal; he
had been too succesful too soon. As a younger man he had
been enormously popular as mover in the House of Com-

Sir John Bowring, Governor of Hong Kong, photograph taken in 1868

Mr. Parkes negotiates the surrender of the Taku forts 1860, from a
lithograph by Colonel Crealock

mons of the Reform Bill of 1832 and all his life he hankered to repeat the success with a new and more liberal Bill. His reward had come after the breakdown of Peel's Government; the Whigs came in and Lord John Russell was Prime Minister for five years. At the end of 1851 he summoned up his courage with the Queen's vehement support to dismiss Palmerston from the Foreign Office. But Lord John was not strong enough to rule without his chief lieutenant; his Government was turned out and in the intricate manœuvres of the next few years he lost his influence over his own party. It is not easy for an ex-Prime Minister in his sixties to serve under other men without sulking, and by 1856 Lord John had not yet found the knack. He served in various positions under Aberdeen and then Palmerston in 1854 and 1855, but he was a crotchety colleague, quick to take offence and threaten resignation. He made a bad muddle of the negotiations with Russia with which he had been entrusted in the summer of 1855, and Palmerston was probably relieved when he finally resigned in the summer of that year. His reputation was at its lowest and his constant harking back to the great Whig triumphs of 1688 and 1832 did nothing to rescue it. 'Undoubtedly he did some considerable things in his day,' wrote *The Times*, 'but we don't want him to be always doing them. . . . Lord John is always landing at Torbay to deliver an ideal Englishman from some hypothetical bondage.'

The Radicals, the Peelites and Lord John added up to a formidable team of debaters who could make an uncomfortable evening for Palmerston's not very strong team in the House of Commons. But Ministers can cope with discomfort so long as they have the votes at the end of the day. Cobden, Gladstone, Lord John and their associates, whatever their eloquence, could hardly put seventy votes into the lobby. Only if they were joined by the bulk of the Tories under Lord Derby was there a chance of defeating the Government. The Tories quickly decided to take this chance. Their decision was essentially a simple one: they were in opposition, and here was a chance to oppose success-fully. In later years, whatever the tactical advantage, it would have been impossible to bring the Tory Party to condemn strong action by a British representative overseas to protect the honour of the British flag. But Disraeli had not yet led the party into the habit of almost instinctively supporting a strong overseas policy. Indeed the tradition of the party had up to then been mainly against overseas com-mitment and a bold foreign policy. In the eighteenth cen-tury what support the Tories had came largely from the objection of the smaller country gentlemen to paying taxes for the wars of Marlborough and the elder Pitt, which they thought benefited only the Whig merchants in the City of London and the royal interests in Hanover. Lord North was a Tory, but the War of American Independence was not the result of a deliberate forward foreign policy. The wars against the French Revolution and Napoleon were so obviously necessary to protect first of all property and the established order and later the very existence of the country that the Tories supported them enthusiastically. But after the war they reverted to their traditional reluctance to em-broil the country in foreign quarrels. The European policies of Canning and of Wellington, and later those of Palmerston and of Aberdeen show the contrast. This was partly because the Tories, with the Jacobins fresh in their minds, did not share the enthusiasm of Canning and Palmerston for encouraging foreign liberal movements against their own Governments. But it was also rooted in a general suspicion of entanglements and commitments over-seas. This applied to China as well as to Europe. The Tories opposed the Opium War of 1839 (the chief cam-paigner against the opium trade, Lord Shaftesbury, was a Tory) and brought it to an early end after their return to office in 1841. So that when in February 1857 the Tories found themselves with a magnificent opportunity for defeat-ing the Government on their China policy, they did not act dishonestly or inconsistently in seizing it. About their wisdom there were some doubts. Indeed it was noticed that Disraeli, Lord Derby's chief lieutenant and the leader of the party in the Commons, was by no means enthusiastic, probably because he saw further into the consequences than most of his colleagues. There were a number of Tories who could not be persuaded to oppose the Government. Some like the Marquess of Blandford simply disagreed with their leader on the merits of the case and could afford to say so. Others, such as Horsfall, the member for Liverpool, were part of the China merchants' lobby and so wholeheartedly behind Bowring. Another more influential group of ex-naval officers were quick to resist any suggestion that Admiral Seymour might have been wrong; but most of them were contented when Seymour's part was left in the shadows and the attack was concentrated on Bowring whom many of them remembered and disliked as a Radical windbag.

It became known in the middle of February that Derby was to move a resolution in the House of Lords condemning the Government for approving Bowring's actions, and that Cobden would do the same a few days later in the Commons. On the 16th Greville, the elderly diarist, called on Clarendon and found him 'low, worn and out of sorts, he said he wished to heaven he could be delivered from office. . . . I told him I thought the China case was a very bad one.' Members of both Houses began to compose their speeches. First-hand news from China was hard to find; but those who were interested could read a wide selection of Bowring's and Seymour's despatches and Yeh's correspondence with them, which the Government had already published. Members of Parliament today are rarely able to read what passes between the Government and its agents so soon after the event; they have to rely when writing their speeches about foreign affairs on what they read in the newspapers or can glean from their own sources. But a hundred years ago, when reliable news from unofficial sources was so scanty, it was a matter of course that the Government should almost at once agree to publish a great part of its own documents

51

on a matter of general interest. This was sometimes embarrassing to its agents, and inevitably these often wrote confidential semi-official letters to supplement the official despatches which they knew might be published. But the system did mean that those who spoke in Parliament, for instance in the *Arrow* debate, had a good knowledge of the basic facts, and that Parliament could exercise a knowledgeable control over the foreign policy of the Government.[1]

---

[1] In the case of the *Arrow* both Bowring's son Edgar, who worked in the Board of Trade, and Wade, Bowring's chief assistant in Hong Kong, criticised the selection of papers published on the grounds that they did not do full justice to his case.

4

In the ten years during which he had led the Tory Party Lord Derby had disappointed many of his followers, and if they had trusted Disraeli more or could have found someone else of equal ability he would probably have been supplanted. He had been a strong Whig in his early days. That might have been forgotten if he had shown more energy in his new role; but many suspected that his heart was elsewhere. During his years as an active racehorse owner he won £94,000 in stakes, and he was often heard to say that he was too busy with pheasants to attend to politics. The same pleasures did not prevent Palmerston from being behind the flippant exterior an extremely energetic and hard-working politician; but with Derby it was felt that the pleasures came first. There were several intricate ministerial crises during the early eighteen fifties which gave openings to the Tory leader, and many of his followers thought that if he had really wanted to be Prime Minister he could have gained more for them from these opportunities than ten unsatisfactory months of office in 1852. But however fitful his leadership there was no doubt that he was an excellent debater in the slashing style which the early Victorians admired. Bulwer Lytton's description is often quoted: 'frank, haughty, rash, the Rupert of Debate.' He had evidently decided that the case of the *Arrow* gave him the chance for an enjoyable cavalry charge. He spent unusual effort in assembling his forces, even threatening to retire from the leadership if he was not supported. By February 24th the forces were assembled and in the House of Lords Lord Derby led the attack. It was characteristic that having decided to attack he went the whole hog and unreservedly embraced the Chinese cause. 'I am an advocate for the feeble defencelessness of China against the overpowering might of Great Britain.' He went through the whole story, concentrating his attack upon Bowring, who had handled matters 'with the utmost arrogance and the most offensive assumptions of superiority.' The Government of Hong Kong had no right to licence the *Arrow* to fly the British flag, and even if it had, the licence had expired. There was no advantage in insisting on the right of entry into Canton, and certainly no justification for tacking it on to the case of the *Arrow*. But Bowring had a 'perfect monomania' about entry. 'I believe he thinks of it the first thing in the morning, the last thing at night, and in the middle of the night if he happens to be awake.' He accused Bowring and Parkes of rudely rejecting Yeh's offers because they were determined to force the question of entry. 'I must say that the language of the Chinese officials is throughout forbearing, courteous and gentlemanlike, while the language of the British officials is with hardly an exception menacing, disrespectful and arrogant.' By their barbarity the British Government had dislocated trade and finally alienated the people of Canton. Derby's peroration began with an appeal to the bishops as the keepers of the national conscience. 'I would appeal to them as the legitimate rebukers of oppression and tyranny; I would appeal to them as those whom their position peculiarly qualifies to impart and inculcate the adoption of those high and holy maxims by which we are commanded not to go beyond or defraud our neighbours in anything, and if it be possible so far as in us lies to live peaceably with all men. . . . To them I would emphatically appeal whether scenes such as those I have been describing, and enacted by a foreign on a heathen people, are calculated to advance the interests and diffuse the blessings of that holy religion of which they are the ministers and guardians? . . . but if, my lords, I should be disappointed in my hope as regards the right reverend bench,[1] then I turn with undiminished confidence to the hereditary peerage. I appeal to them by their vote this night to declare that they will not sanction the usurpation of that most awful prerogative of the Crown, the declaring of war; that they will not tolerate nor by their silence appear to approve, upon light and trivial grounds of quarrel, and upon cases of doubtful justice as far as regards the merits of our first demands, the capture of commercial vessels; that they will not tolerate the destruction of the forts of a friendly country; that they will not tolerate the bombardment and the shelling of a commercial and open city; and that they will not on any consideration give the sanction of their voice to the shedding of the blood of unwarlike and innocent people without warrant of law and without moral justification.' Lord Derby sat down amid loud cheers.

Hammond, the Permanent Under-Secretary at the Foreign Office, scribbled a note for Lord Clarendon on Derby's speech. Most of it dealt with small errors of fact and law: 'Lord Derby is wrong about the row at Canton affecting the trade in silk, for next to none comes from that port. . . .' Hammond went on to make a very practical suggestion for influencing the debate which today would come oddly from a civil servant and would certainly not find its way on to an official file: 'A report judiciously circulated of the declining health of the Archbishop of Canterbury would probably neutralise the effect of Lord Derby's wordy peroration as regards the Bench of Bishops; and a similar report to be contradicted on Friday as to the contemplated appropriation of vacant Garters might not be without its effect on others.' A man in a position such as Hammond's is apt to exaggerate the corruptness of politicians; but as Trollope's political novels illustrate, beneath the thunderous eloquence of the mid-Victorian Parliaments

[1] Lord Derby was evidently not sanguine. The appointment of bishops had been almost without interruption in Whig hands for ten years.

there remained a stratum of simple self-seeking of which the realist had to take account.

The Times thought poorly of Lord Derby's speech. 'Since the days of the French philosophers the Chinese have never received so many compliments as were crowded into Lord Derby's speech last night.' Three days later *The Times* thundered again; the editor's style is sneering and over-blown, but the point that the Tories and Peelites were more interested in office than in China had substance:

'Could we imagine the Emperor of China, or that amiable gentleman, Commissioner Yeh, present at our debates in Parliament, he would probably conceive the greatest hopes of a signal triumph over the Outer Barbarian. . . . On hearing these overpowering testimonies to the sim-plicity of his motives and the intrinsic justice of his cause, the silken savage would begin to flatter himself, not only that he was not the impostor, the charlatan, the tyrant that his conscience had formerly suggested, but that he might live to see the barbarian dogs compelled to lower their flag and do him that homage so dear to Eastern vanity in the eyes of his people. But, amiable Yeh, disciple of Confucius, teacher of virtue, interpreter of law, slaughterer of myriads, it is time to dispel the growing illusion. You are not the only impostor in the world, or even the greatest. The zeal which inspires all these powerful personages is an ambition, not to relieve you from the terrible consequences of your insolence and folly—not to avert the just vengeance gather-ing over your head—but to have the pleasure and honour of accomplishing it.'

The London correspondent of the New York *Daily Tribune*, a German named Karl Marx, was also interested in China at this time. Marx's weakness as an interpreter of current events was that he instinctively rejected the obvious explanation, and saw sinister motives and secret under-standings where there was often merely human stupidity. At this time he believed that Bowring had secret instruc-tions to pick a quarrel with the Chinese, a suggestion for which there is no evidence. But he saw better than *The Times* the irony of Lord Derby's speech: 'The Earl of Derby, the chief of the hereditary aristocracy of England, pleading against the late Doctor, now Sir John Bowring, the disciple of Bentham; pleading for humanity against the professional humanitarian; defending the real interests of nations against the systematic utilitarian insisting upon a punctilio of diplomatic etiquette; appealing to the "vox populi vox dei" against the greatest-benefit-of-the-greatest-number man; the descendant of the conquerors preaching peace where a member of the Peace Society preached red-hot shell. . . . The whole parliamentary history of England has perhaps never exhibited such an intellectual victory of the aristocrat over the parvenu.'

Derby was immediately followed in the Lords by Clarendon. The Foreign Secretary was clearly conscious that on the details he had a weak case. He asserted that the Hong Kong ordinance under which the *Arrow* was registered was legal, and that since the *Arrow* had been at sea before her seizure she had not had a chance to renew the register. He briefly defended Bowring and, more warmly, Parkes, who was 'a very intelligent, able and gentlemanlike man.' As Ministers in a bad posture are apt to do, he tried to draw a parallel between Bowring's action and a British show of force at Canton in 1846 under a Tory Government. But his main concern was to show in general terms that the Chinese had made no attempt to accept the Treaty of Nanking but had shown an habitual determination to humiliate the barbarians. If the British failed to insist that they should be treated as equals, further humiliations would follow. It was just not practicable for Bowring to wait for instructions before reacting. To condemn him now would put every British resident in China in a position of degradation and danger. These were fair points based on experience, but Clarendon did not make the best of them, and allowed himself to use a phrase which was a gift to his adversaries: 'I fear that we must come to the conclusion that in dealing with a nation like the Chinese, if we intend to preserve any amicable or useful relations with them, we must make them sensible of the law of force, and must appeal to them in the manner which alone they can appreciate.'

The debate continued in the Lords for another day and a half, and the Opposition had the best of it. They had persuaded into the field Lord Lyndhurst who had been Lord Chancellor under Peel and was now, at eighty-four, probably the most respected lawyer in England. The old man, already partly blind, had lost none of his capacity for tough legal argument. The *Arrow* could never be made a British ship because she was not owned by a British subject. The British Government could not bestow rights on a Chinese subject against the Chinese Government. Bowring was 'one of the most mischievous men I know' and his conduct was flagrant and abominable. It was extraordinary that he should have been allowed the power of declaring war. The Lord Chancellor, Lord Cranworth, never a strong performer,[1] was unable to cope with this onslaught and made a feeble speech unhappily protesting that we must resent outrages from semi-barbarous states. The Tories continued in a tone of high moral fervour. Lord Malmesbury, who had been Foreign Secretary in Lord Derby's short ministry of 1852, over-reached himself in attack upon Bowring, whose impolitic and immoral behaviour he contrasted with the wise caution shown by Admiral Seymour. This was a contrast which it was tactically clever to invent at Westminster where admirals were popular, but which had not much reality in fact. Malmesbury quoted a letter from a midshipman to show the one-sidedness of the fighting: 'Dear Mother, don't trouble yourself about me, for I am in no more danger than if I were practising against an old

---

[1] *The Times* had remarked on Lord Cranworth a fortnight earlier as 'a man whose legal reputation, never of very great proportions, has dwindled away ever since he sat on the Woolsack until the dignity of the office has become sadly impaired by the inefficient and impracticable nature of the man who fills it.'

tea-caddy.' Lord Malmesbury sat down declaring that he felt shame for his country. Lord Ellenborough, a former Governor General of India, continued the attack on Bowring, to which he tried to give edge by referring throughout to 'Doctor' instead of 'Sir John.' Bowring had disregarded the instructions of four successive Foreign Secretaries, had been 'the eternal obstacle to peace' and had now started a war against a vast empire with four hundred men. The best speech on the Government side came from Lord Granville, the Lord President of the Council. Granville was a natural courtier, a clever, polite, moderate man who thought little of Bowring and his works, but, as he admitted later, was provoked by the excesses of the Opposition into making a better speech than usual. He deplored the personal tone of the attacks. He showed that it was likely that the *Arrow* was flying the British flag when she was boarded. If Bowring had not reacted strongly, the Tories would have denounced him as a Manchester Radical careless of his country's honour. The Chinese attachment to form and ceremony made it essential to ask Yeh for an apology for what had been done. Bowring was not a monomaniac about entry into Canton; successive Governments of different parties had agreed that this was an important British right.

The Bishop of Oxford was the only speaker from his bench. Dr. Wilberforce, popularly known as 'Soapy Sam,' attacked Bowring as vigorously as any layman. His was the guilt of the strong man who exploited the weak. 'What,' interrupted the Duke of Argyll, 'thirty million against three hundred million?' Yes, replied the Bishop, Bowring was the wolf among the sheep. But neither he nor his country would escape judgment. 'Remember that He who made the sand so light and impalpable that the wind of the desert bears it away upon its wings, powerless as an element, has yet set it to be a sufficient barrier to the raging sea: that Power will if need be find in the weakness of China an element to chastise and rebuke the pride and strength of Britain.'

The debate had so clearly gone against the Government that it seemed possible that Lord Derby's resolutions of condemnation might pass. The vote on the evening of February 26th came as a relief to Ministers. The result was:

For Lord Derby's resolutions: 110 (including 57 proxies)
Against: 146 (including 75 proxies)
                                                   ———
Government majority   36

Only three Bishops, Oxford, Chichester and Salisbury, voted for the resolutions; thirteen voted against the resolutions and in favour of the Government.

5

ON THE LAST DAY of the debate in the Lords, Cobden opened a less polished but more powerful debate in the Commons. Cobden grappled at the outset with the difficulty of his own past friendship for Bowring. He admitted that he had known Bowring for twenty years and claimed that he could have no vindictive feeling against him. But his attack was not less savage than that of the Tories to whom Bowring had always been objectionable. The British Government followed one policy towards the strong and another towards the weak. If the *Arrow* had been at Charleston instead of Canton and the consul there had behaved as Parkes had done, he would have been disowned, not supported, by the British Ambassador. Cobden fastened on to the expiry of the *Arrow*'s register, and Bowring's letter in which he appeared to say that this need not be taken into account because Yeh did not know of it. Cobden described this letter as 'the most flagitious public document that I ever saw.' He discounted the evidence of Kennedy, the master of the *Arrow*, who was too young to be taken seriously. 'Any man with a round hat and a European coat on will do. . . . They have plenty of grog to drink, and have nothing else to do but drink it.' He drew a picture of Chinese policy which Yeh would hardly have recognised: 'The Chinese authorities in every part of the empire to which we have access, have manifested the most consistent and earnest desire to carry out the provisions of the Treaty.' He shrewdly criticised the campaign of the China merchants for a strong policy. War did not increase trade but diminished it. Admission to Canton would not be worth a farthing, and by pursuing it Bowring had brought trade to a standstill. Britain could not annex China, and must therefore disavow Bowring and settle her differences with China peacefully in concert with France and the U.S. Cobden ended with a disguised appeal for Tory support: 'Is not so venerable an empire as that deserving of some sympathy—at least of some justice—at the hands of conservative England?'

The two resolutions which Cobden moved were skilfully drawn to attract support. The first explicitly refused to express an opinion on whether Britain had cause for complaint against China, and simply held that the papers available to the House did not show satisfactory grounds for the violent action taken at Canton. The second moved for a Select Committee to enquire into the state of our commercial relations with China.

The debate in the Commons lasted for four evenings divided by a week-end. The Government was even weaker in debating power in the Commons than in the Lords. The Prime Minister alone was capable of standing up effectively to the broadsides of the critics, and it was tactically necessary for him to reserve himself for the last evening. The other side had enough talent to mount a major attack each day. At the end of the first day Lord John Russell intervened in a speech which was thought to be one of his best, but exceedingly bitter against those who had until a few months before been his colleagues. He concentrated tellingly on the argument that it was necessary to back up Bowring for the sake of prestige. 'Never will England stand higher in the world's estimation than when it can be said that though troublesome and meddlesome officials prostitute her arms and induce a brave admiral to commence hostilities which ought never to have been begun, yet the House of Commons, representing her people, have indignantly declared that they will be no parties to such injustice; and that neither for commercial advantages nor for political advantages, nor for any other immediate advantages to their country, will they consent to stain that honour which, after all, has been and must be the sure foundation of her greatness.'

On the second day the attack was led by Sir James Graham, who had been Peel's Home Secretary and was, after Gladstone, the leading Peelite. He spoke warmly of Admiral Seymour; but Bowring was 'more remarkable for his self-confidence than for the soundness of his judgment.' He was so intent on a triumph in Canton that he had been ready deliberately to deceive Yeh about the expiry of the *Arrow*'s register. Graham was followed by the Attorney General, Bethell, who confused the Government's supporters by producing a legal basis for Bowring's actions quite different from that advanced by the Lord Chancellor and other Government speakers in the Lords, and by Bowring himself. Up to now the Government had held that the *Arrow* was British by virtue of her registration by a resident of Hong Kong under the Hong Kong ordinance of 1855 and that her international status was not altered by the fact that through no fault of her master her register was a few days out of date. The Lord Advocate argued this case closely on the first day of the Commons debate. But Bethell virtually ignored the ordinance and argued instead from Article 17 of the Supplementary Treaty of 1843 which mentioned lorchas as one class of vessels to which British registers could be issued. The Opposition was not impressed and Roundell Palmer, later to be a Conservative Attorney General and Lord Chancellor, observed: 'If the right honourable and learned gentleman when in the schools of Oxford had proposed as an example of sound logic that because every British lorcha must have a British sailing letter or register, therefore every lorcha having a British sailing letter or register must be British, he could hardly have carried off the high honours which he won there.'

The back bench speeches in the first two days did not alter the balance of argument against the Government but they showed some of the cross currents at work. Bulwer Lytton, the novelist, declaimed in turgid style against 'wholesale massacre on our helpless customers at a remote corner of the globe,' and wound up with a quotation from Virgil and the sentiment that 'in dealing with nations less civilised than ourselves it is by lofty truth and forbearing humanity that the genius of commerce contrasts the ambition of conquerors.' The Government found a novelist to answer back. Mr. Warren, the member for Midhurst, had fifteen years earlier published a work entitled *Ten Thousand a Year* which had been quite as successful as Bulwer Lytton's *The Last Days of Pompeii*. His style was even more self-conscious: 'No, sir, wherever all over the terraqueous globe the sun shines on our blue jackets and red jackets, they only reflect lustre on their country.' Gregson, the Chairman of the East India and China Association, and Horsfall, the Tory member for Liverpool, spoke up for the China merchants and a tough policy. Lord Robert Cecil, who was forty years later to be Prime Minister in the heyday of imperialism, commented that he had been in a great many British colonies, and had never been in one where the residents did not want to go to war with the country next door. Several naval gentlemen robustly defended Seymour, notably vain pugnacious old Admiral Sir Charles Napier, under whom Seymour had served in the Baltic. He was quite clear that it was right to ask Yeh for an apology: 'Good God! there was nothing extraordinary in that. If a man knocked another's hat off and then knocked him down, surely an apology would be required.'

The Tories and their allies were scoring points in the Debate and it looked as if Derby had a triumph in his grasp. His difficulty lay with the stiffest of his own supporters, who objected not so much to the attack on Bowring as to the alliance with the Radicals and the Peelites.

Although the looseness of party allegiance made accurate calculation impossible, the alliance ought in theory to produce a majority of at least fifty against the Government. But if a sizeable minority of Tories voted with the Government that paper majority would be wiped out. Derby exerted himself to good effect. He held a meeting of his followers on the morning of February 27th. A hundred and sixty Members of Parliament were present. Derby hinted that he might give up the leadership if he were not loyally supported, and Disraeli made a speech in favour of the alliance with Cobden and Gladstone, concealing his doubts about the tactics of his leader. The meeting was impressed and Derby was assured of support. On the other side Palmerston was at work among the radical wing of his own party. He told the Queen on the 28th that some of them were swinging away from Cobden.

The third day of the debate, after the week-end, brought no surprises. The Home Secretary, Sir George Grey, plodded through the familiar Government defence. Sidney Herbert, perhaps the most attractive of the Peelites, mocked the way in which Palmerston had extended the rights of British citizenship since the famous Don Pacifico debate seven years earlier. The crew of the *Arrow* were 'Chinese, picked up from the very refuse and scum of the population along the Canton river, whom you put into this vessel with a register with no limit to it—a vessel therefore which might go into any port in the world, which might have come over to Hamburgh, to Constantinople or to Marseilles, and the crew might have got into a row in any of these places, and have gone with their Chinese faces and Chinese costumes up to the British Consul, when each one of them might have exclaimed to that astonished functionary, Civis Romanus Sum.'

On the fourth and final evening the chief gladiators at last appeared. Two well-known Radicals, Roebuck and Milner Gibson, were succeeded by Gladstone. Granville wrote to Canning: 'People think Gladstone mad which is of course false but he certainly is in an extraordinary state of excitement.' Lord Elgin wrote to his wife: 'The general notion is that Gladstone is going mad he is so excited—but his insanity runs all to talk, as mine does to silence.' In the evening of March 3rd Gladstone's talk was to good effect. He rose at half past nine and spoke for two hours. One of his audience wrote: 'Nobody denies that his speech was the finest delivered in the memory of man in the House of Commons.' It was characteristic of the man that he did not follow the Tories in their personal attack on Bowring. Bowring had been clumsy but it was the Government which was responsible. The Chinese had on the whole dealt justly with the British in China. In his long-winded way he poked more fun at the Attorney General: 'When the Lord Chancellor and others . . . his noble friends had with infinite labour constructed their little bulwarks and fortifications about them as they best could, from materials such as the Statute law and the colonial ordinance afforded, he swept them all away into the sea, as we are told in the story of the siege of Troy that Neptune swept away the bulwarks of the Greeks—he made completely clear decks, and began upon his own account, staking everything upon his own single argument and declaring that all that had been advanced before, drawn from the statute law and the ordinance, was either worthless or immaterial.' But Gladstone was really interested in the moral, not the legal foundations of policy. The lorchas which trafficked in the Canton river were mostly smugglers, and often smugglers of opium. This was the trade which British arms were now to protect. It must be judged 'on the higher ground of natural justice . . . that justice which binds man to man; which is older than Christianity, because it was in the world before Christianity; which is broader than Christianity, because it extends to the world beyond Christianity; and which underlies Christianity, for Christianity itself appeals to it.' He condemned the way in which fighting had begun: 'War taken at the best is a

66

frightful scourge to the human race, but because it is so the wisdom of ages has surrounded it with strict laws and usages.' The Government had dispensed with these. 'You have turned a consul into a diplomat, and that metamorphosed consul is forsooth to be at liberty to direct the whole might of England against the lives of a defenceless people.' The war had no purpose, for the *Arrow* question had already been settled by Yeh's concessions, and the right of entry into Canton would cause more mischief than good. It could not be argued that a vote for Cobden's resolutions would weaken British power, for this power could not be well founded on injustice. The Government and the House of Lords had failed to check the violation of right. But the House of Commons was the paramount power of the State. Let it show that 'the first, the most ancient and the noblest temple of freedom in the world is also the temple of that everlasting justice without which freedom itself would be only a name or only a curse to mankind.'

It was the Prime Minister's turn. The old man was ill with cold and gout, but even at his best he could not have matched Gladstone. Greville found him very dull in the first part and bow-wow in the second. The little witticisms fell flat and seemed to expose rather than mask the failure of the argument to reach the level of the debate. It was one of the several occasions when more serious men than Palmerston concluded to their peril that he was at last played out. Palmerston began by twitting Cobden on his friendship with Bowring. What injury had Sir John done to the honourable gentleman that he should forget the ties which formerly bound them? He recommended to Cobden the old saying on how friends should treat each other:

> Be to their faults a little blind,
> Be to their virtues very kind,
> And fix a padlock on the mind.

Bowring was essentially a man of the people, mild, amiable, a member of the Peace Society promoted not by influence but by his own talents. But in Cobden's eyes everything that was English was wrong and everything that was hostile to England was right. Palmerston dealt briefly with the *Arrow* itself, in a manner which showed his usual command of detail behind the appearance of frivolity. The legal arguments were interminable, but the essential question was whether Yeh believed the *Arrow* to have British papers, and there was no reasonable doubt that he did. He had intended an insult and deserved punishment. The Chinese story was inconsistent. At first they had said they wanted a member of the crew who was the father of a pirate, but later they said that the pirate himself had been recognised on board by his red turban and missing front tooth. 'A man who could distinguish in rapidly passing another vessel in a river whether one man of the crew had or had not lost a front tooth would be a valuable addition to one of our sharpshooting regiments.'

Then Palmerston turned to two themes which were calculated to appeal not to his immediate audience but to the country as a whole. He accused his opponents of forming a coalition and manufacturing this occasion to turn him out. He played on the traditional idea that opposition for its own sake was wrong, and that for groups holding different opinions to manœuvre to defeat the Queen's Ministers was factious and unpatriotic. He played also on the recent memory of Aberdeen's coalition whose incompetence had made the very name 'coalition' unloved in England, as Disraeli had already pointed out in his famous saying. But Palmerston's main theme was the savagery of the Chinese. To the personal attacks on Bowring he replied with an extraordinary attack on Yeh stimulated no doubt by the recent news of the murders on board the *Thistle* and the poisoning at Hong Kong. The man whom Cobden and Gladstone had praised was 'one of the most savage barbarians that ever disgraced a nation. He has been guilty of every crime which can degrade and debase human nature.' If Cobden's resolutions were passed Yeh would raise a song of triumph and adorn the palisades of Canton with English rather than Chinese heads. Cobden's policy amounted to abandoning the British communities to 'a set of kidnapping, murdering, poisoning barbarians.'

Disraeli was the last main speaker in the debate. He did not attempt to match Gladstone's thunder. He had a fling at the Prime Minister: 'Looking back upon the last half century during which he has professed almost every principle and connected himself with almost every party, the noble Lord has raised a warning voice against coalitions because he fears that a majority of the House of Commons . . . may not approve a policy with respect to China which has begun in outrage, and which if pursued will end in ruin.' But apart from a few such gibes of the kind expected of him, Disraeli spoke thoughtfully; indeed he was one of the few speakers to give the impression that he had been interested in China before Sir John Bowring's deeds had begun to reach the headlines. He did not join in the personal attack on Bowring, merely remarking that since his forthright views were well known before he was sent out, it was a pity that he had been chosen for the job. We had to develop a regular relationship with China. Only slow progress had been made towards this, and it was futile to suppose that force by itself would provide the answer, if only because other powers, and particularly the Americans, were on the scene. Disraeli did not develop this theme, but returned at the end of his speech to the scoring of party points. He foretold that Parliament would be dissolved if the vote went against the Government, and offered Palmerston an election cry: 'No Reform! New Taxes! Canton Blazing! Persia invaded!'

Cobden spoke a few dignified words in reply to Palmerston's accusation that it was hope of office which had led to the coming together of the Opposition groups on this occasion. Shortly before two o'clock on the morning of March 4th the House divided. The result was reported as follows by *Punch*:

For hauling down the British flag, apologising to
the Chinese and putting Derby, Dizzy and Glad-
stone in office   263
For maintaining the honour of England and
keeping Pam in place   247
                                                             ——
                    Chinese majority   16
                                                             ——

Forty-eight Liberals from the radical wing of the party
voted with Cobden in favour; twenty-five Tories voted
against. Gladstone wrote in his diary: 'March 3, 1857.
Spoke on Cobden's resolutions and voted in 263-247—a
division doing more honour to the House of Commons
than any I ever remember. Home with C. and read Lord
Ellesmere's Faust, being excited which is rare with
me.'
   The debate had indeed been impressive. It was one of
the set-pieces of Victorian eloquence; it was also a demonstration of the growing power of moral arguments in British
politics. There were, as there always are, party reasons
behind the casting of most of the votes; but it would be a
mistake, as it usually is, to assume that the denunciations of
the Government were born simply of a desire to have their
places. Greville believed that quite apart from the
manœuvres of parties 'there is in fact a strong feeling both
in Parliament and in the country against all that has been
done at Canton.' He was wrong about the country but right
about Parliament. Gladstone's speech was said to have
changed several votes. It was the kind of speech which,
though rare before his day, has been repeated *mutatis
mutandis* at intervals ever since; for he was one of the first
representatives of that distinguished and influential minority
whose main concern it has been to test and test again the
morality of their country's foreign policy.
   When one reads the documents and speeches about the
Arrow after a hundred years a number of impressions remain.

The first is that Parkes, Bowring and the Government had a good technical case. The critical legal point had nothing to do with whether the *Arrow*'s flag was flying or with the circumstances in which her register had expired. It was this: could the Government of Hong Kong confer the right to fly the British flag upon a vessel owned by a man who, though by birth a subject of the Emperor of China, was a resident of the colony? In 1857 precedents existed either way and the case was far from clear. But Palmerston went to the root of the matter when he argued that Yeh, knowing that the *Arrow* claimed British nationality, had no right unilaterally to treat her as a Chinese vessel. Parkes was justified in protesting at this, and in recommending a reprisal against a Chinese vessel. But the second impression which persists is that Bowring was entirely unjustified in tacking the question of entry into Canton on to the question of the *Arrow*, not because the British case on the *Arrow* was weak at the outset but because Yeh under the threat of force accepted all the British demands on the *Arrow* except the apology. The British had a good claim to the right of entry into Canton, which for equally good reasons they had decided to leave in abeyance. To revive it forcibly merely because an apology was not forthcoming for another injury which for all practical purposes had been repaired once Yeh had undertaken to release the crew of the *Arrow* was imprudent and hardly defensible. If the speakers against the Government had concentrated on this point they would read more convincingly today. But the final impression left by the debate is of the unreal idea of China in the minds of those who promoted it. Except for Disraeli all the main speakers against the Government stated or implied that the Chinese Government was ready to stand by the Treaty of Nanking and treat the British as equals, if only they were reasonably treated by the British representatives on the spot. This assumption, on which Derby, Cobden and Gladstone rested their speeches, was wholly without foundation. It showed a deep ignorance of the principles by which China

71

was governed. The hours spent over the blue books had given them a good knowledge of imports and exports and of the minutiae of the question of entry into Canton; but they were almost as ignorant of the ideas of Yeh and his superiors as he was of theirs.

The Chinese were assured that Peking was in all senses the centre of the world and that their Emperor, whether Chinese Mongol or Manchu by origin, was by virtue of being Emperor different in quality from other rulers of the world, a difference which they expressed by the system of tribute and the epithet of barbarians applied to all foreigners, which to them was not a term of abuse but a statement of fact. This assumption of superiority was the very basis of the Empire and could not be shaken by a few reverses. From time to time the barbarians established a physical superiority over the Chinese in some part of the Empire. This had happened at Canton in the 1830s and '40s. In such cases it was the job of the local Viceroy to keep the barbarians quiet by making as few concessions as possible. Such were the concessions embodied in the Treaty of Nanking and the other Treaties. The idea that these concessions made by a Viceroy as a result of several months of skirmishing hundreds of miles from Peking, could reduce the Emperor to a state of equality with barbarian chiefs such as Queen Victoria or the Emperor Napoleon III, and so upset the whole basis of the Chinese state was unthinkable to Yeh or to any other Chinese official.

The Foreign Office and Ministers were beginning to get close to the heart of the matter and see that neither Bowring nor Gladstone was right. Gladstone proclaimed that you should treat the Chinese as if they were Europeans within the framework of European-made international law. This ignored the basic facts about China. Bowring insisted that the British should go on hammering away against Canton to right their grievances. This ignored the fact that nothing done or agreed at Canton would alter the way in which the Emperor and Government regarded the barbarians. It was only at Peking, by the presence of a permanent Ambassador, that equality could be gained. This became more and more clearly the main issue of the next few years. The tragedy was that it was only by showing themselves superior in war that the Europeans could get themselves regarded as equals in peace.

6

PALMERSTON had been ill and exhausted on the last night
of the debate, but the morning after his defeat he was
decidedly brisk, though still plagued by gout. A defeat of
this kind could not be ignored. Palmerston could either
resign and advise the Queen to send for someone else to
form a new ministry, or else advise her to dissolve Parliament and hold an election. All the arguments pointed to a
dissolution. A new ministry would in the present confused
state of parties take a long time to form, and much of the
work of forming it would fall upon the Queen. But the
Queen was far from well, being at the age of thirty-eight
eight months pregnant, and Prince Albert was determined
to protect her from the wear and tear of a ministerial crisis.
He wrote to Palmerston on the last day of the debate asking
him to go down to Windsor the next day. The Queen, he
wrote, could not decide on a dissolution without seeing the
Prime Minister; she was unable to go through a ministerial
crisis, and would prefer any other alternative. The Queen
and Prince Albert were almost Palmerstonians now and the
Prince wrote again as soon as they heard of the vote:
'Though prepared for an unfavourable result, the Queen
is not the less grieved at the success of evil party motives,
spite and a total lack of patriotism.' The Cabinet met that
day, and decided to advise dissolution; only Sir Charles
Wood thought they should resign. The Cabinet was influenced by the news of the Queen's health, but there was
more to it than that. They thought they could win an election
on the Chinese issue and the personal popularity of the

74

Prime Minister. On the same evening Palmerston went down to Windsor and advised the Queen to dissolve Parliament. She was much relieved and they had a considerable talk, in which he was very bitter against Lord John Russell. The next day, March 5th, Palmerston announced the dissolution to the Commons. He was pressed hard to say what policy the Government would follow in China after the vote in the Commons. Cobden urged him to send out a man of the first rank to take over from Bowring. Palmerston replied robustly that there would be no change in Government policy. In fact he had already told the Queen that someone new would have to go out to China. It was impossible with an election pending to get rid of Bowring. Indeed Bowring's son was already complaining that no one in the Government had properly defended his father against the charge of deceit. He had supposed, he wrote to Granville, that the news of the poison in the bread at Hong Kong would have inspired at least a momentary decency among the Opposition. But now he heard at the Reform Club that his father's honour would be the main issue at the elections, and he proposed to stand himself solely in order to vindicate it. Granville replied politely that he hoped young Bowring would indeed stand one day but not alone for the reason he had given. The young man subsided and continued for a while to ply his pen at the Board of Trade. Clearly in the circumstances Bowring could not be recalled; neither, however, could he be allowed to run amok in the Canton river without restraint. Palmerston decided on one of those compromises which look politically neat but are the despair of the men who have to work them. Bowring was to stay and carry on his day-to-day duties as Governor of Hong Kong and Superintendent of Trade, but the political handling of the Chinese would be taken over by a special plenipotentiary. Several names were mentioned, the Duke of Newcastle was offered the job and declined, and eventually on March 13th the appointment was announced of James, 8th Earl of Elgin, with whom the rest of this book is mainly concerned.

By this time the election campaign was at its height. Palmerston concentrated on the Chinese issue and in particular on the iniquities of Yeh, whom he portrayed as a gross monster, half terrible and half ridiculous. As Kingsley Martin wrote of a slightly earlier period, Palmerston 'understood by instinct . . . that the English were not really interested in foreign politics but in individuals. While he was in charge European diplomacy took on the familiar appearance of a sporting arena. All was personal and vivid. Intricate questions of policy, which Prince Albert and Lord Aberdeen found subjects for anxious discussion and careful memoranda, were apparently regarded by Palmerston as challenges to a boxing match.'[1] His election address at Tiverton set the tone: 'An insolent barbarian wielding authority at Canton has violated the British flag, broken the engagements of treaties, offered rewards for the heads of British subjects in that part of China, and planned their destruction by murder, assassination and poisons.' At the Mansion House the Prime Minister said he was sure that the heart of the country was sound and would reverse the vote in the Commons. He asked whether the Opposition would follow the logic of their argument and rebuild the forts of Canton with cannon from Woolwich and pay for the arsenic in the bread of Hong Kong. His followers took the same line. One of the hottest contests was in the City of London, one of whose four members was Lord John Russell. The Liberals put up against him Raikes Currie, an orthodox Government man, who did his best to exploit the traditional radicalism of the City in good huckstering style: 'Was the name of Sir John Bowring that of a born aristocrat? No. Had he been the younger son of some great ducal family[2] or had he boasted great political connections they would have heard much less of this matter. But Sir John Bowring was a man of the people—he had sprung from the people— he had been sent to Parliament by the working men and

[1] Kingsley Martin, *The Triumph of Lord Palmerston*.
[2] i.e. like Lord John Russell.

there he had always advocated the principles of his master Bentham, the greatest happiness of the greatest number. (Cheers.) Would they then as Englishmen who loved fair play turn round upon the first possible occasion and crush such a man as that? (No! and Cheers).' The newspapers were full of letters from Hong Kong reporting tales of Chinese atrocities. A Dr. Gourley of Regents Park wrote to Lord Clarendon offering to persuade George Cruikshank to produce a series of sketches of atrocities practised by the Chinese on each other. The Foreign Office replied approvingly and on March 24th Dr. Gourley reported success: 'I have much satisfaction in informing you that our modern Hogarth Mr. George Cruikshank is now busily engaged in sketching some of the Chinese legal barbarities, chiefly taken from Chinese sketches I sent him, illustrating their punishments of Starving to death, Disjointing, Chopping to Pieces, Tearing the Body asunder by pullies, Skinning alive, etc. etc.'

The Opposition groups did what they could according to their different lights. At first Cobden thought that the China question was a good election cry. He wrote to Sir James Graham on March 16th that there was no safer battleground to choose, since a great principle was at stake, the responsibility of public servants to Parliament. Graham took this bad advice and set himself to rouse his constituents in Carlisle: 'The real object is to drug the people of China with opium and the effect of it here is to enhance the price of tea. . . . It is an additional tax upon the tea which is consumed by every old wife in the Kingdom and upon every lollipop which is sucked by innocent and unsuspecting children.' Cobden himself had sat for the West Riding of Yorkshire in the old Parliament, but was now standing with the absent Bright for the supposedly safer seat of Manchester. Here he was on his home ground, and defended his actions in a series of speeches which were probably the best of the campaign. But it was noticeable that as speech followed speech less and less was said about China.

Disraeli, who had been doubtful throughout about making an issue of the China question, tried in his election address at High Wycombe to exploit the appointment of Lord Elgin: 'Gentlemen, The House of Commons, having by a solemn vote in which the leading men of all parties concurred censured the cruel and double dealing policy pursued by the agents of the Government towards the Chinese, Parliament has been dissolved. Since the announcement of the dissolution the Minister has declared that his agents in China will be superseded, thus acknowledging the justness of the vote of the House of Commons. It is clear therefore that the plea for dissolution is a pretext. What then is the real object? To waste a year.' He then developed his favourite theme that Palmerston was 'the Tory chief of a Radical Cabinet,' who stirred up foreign affairs from time to time as a device for diverting attention away from the need for reform. There was probably truth in this, but it was sophisticated stuff and as Disraeli had not yet taught the Tories to think of themselves as reformers for many of them his argument pointed in favour of Palmerston. The Marquess of Blandford thought so, and told his constituents that he stood by his vote against his party and with the Government. Parliament had been reformed, but established interests were almost as strong as ever and the burghers of Woodstock would have elected a Marquess of Blandford whatever his views. But even park gates did not save from trouble some who had voted for Cobden against the Government; Sidney Herbert for example found himself fighting unexpectedly hard at Wilton. Several Tory and Peelite election addresses were distinctly apologetic about the attack on the Government's China policy. Sir Erskine Perry had made one of the fiercest speeches against the Government in the Commons, but back in Devonport among the Navy and threatened with opposition he swore complete confidence in Lord Palmerston's future handling of the matter. Lord Malmesbury, the Tory expert on foreign affairs, did his best to rally the party with an open letter to Palmerston which *The Times* published on March 26th. Malmesbury protested against the implication in Palmerston's election address that the outrages committed by the Chinese took place before the British did anything. In fact everything which Yeh had done, except the seizure of the *Arrow*, had been as reprisal for the actions of Bowring and Seymour. 'Sir John Bowring did obtain or secure important compensation for the first offence, and might then have stayed his hand until he received orders from home . . . the bloodshed and crimes that have followed are the consequences of other demands which you yourself in your wiser hours have officially pronounced to be dangerous and unprofitable. . . . The country having been committed, my humble vote will support a war which has now become necessary to English interests and honour but which at first might have been avoided without a sacrifice of either.'

Palmerston did not bother to make a reply of substance; he had no need. *The Times* thought he would win. So did another institution, perhaps better able by nature than *The Times* to understand the feelings of the British people. The Queen as usual kept King Leopold of Belgium fully informed. 'My dearest Uncle,' she wrote on March 24th, 'the Opposition have played their game most foolishly and the result is that *all* the old Tories say they certainly will *not* support them; they very truly say Lord Derby's party— that is those who want to get into office coûte que coûte— whether the country suffers for it or not, wanted to get in under *false colours*, and that they won't support or abide— which they are *quite* right in. There is reason to hope that a better class of men will be returned to support the Government, not a particular cry of this or that.'

Polling started on March 28th, and was spread as usual over several days, the boroughs generally polling before the counties. It soon became clear that Palmerston, *The Times* and the Queen had been right. The Government had been returned with an increased majority. Of the Government's opponents Lord John Russell succeeded in the City and

Gladstone was unopposed for the University of Oxford. But the Liberals made gains at the expense of the Tories in the counties. Their greatest triumphs were at the expense of the Radicals. Cobden, Bright and Milner Gibson were all defeated in their strongholds of the North and North West. Manchester rejected the Manchester School of politician, and showed that men who voted for radicalism at home were not necessarily in favour of a soft line abroad. John Morley, who inherited much of Cobden's outlook and wrote his life, commented on this election in his *Recollections*: 'To their surprise and vexation they soon discovered that in the arena of foreign policy the aristocracy had Demos on their side, and that the two together were their masters . . . Cobden . . . had fought his battle in reliance on a rational public opinion, and that proved a broken reed.'

It would be a mistake to suppose that the election was fought and decided solely on questions of foreign policy. Some of the Government's gains in the counties were the result of a predictable shift of Liberal country gentlemen and farmers back to a traditional allegiance. They had been frightened by the Repeal of the Corn Laws into voting for the Tories and Protection, but the Tories had shown that they could not revive Protection, and Repeal of the Corn Laws had not (yet) upset the prosperity of the countryside; so some of the farmers voted Liberal again and swung several county seats, particularly in the West and the Home Counties. But there is no doubt that in general the 1857 election was about Palmerston's foreign policy. Yeh and the *Arrow* were not in themselves particularly important, and Palmerston and his Ministers knew perfectly well that Bowring's judgment had been at fault, as the appointment of Elgin showed. But the Opposition had chosen this ground to challenge him, and Palmerston in accepting the challenge turned Yeh and the *Arrow* into the momentary symbol of his foreign policy. It was a campaign of great skill and determination. Palmerston was not content to show that on his record during the Crimean War and since he was better able to defend the interests of England than his opponents. He also contrived to make himself appear a warm-hearted amateur defending himself light-heartedly against a band of self-seeking professionals. The half flippant style which so exasperated Gladstone, the parties in Piccadilly and the race meetings were a genuine part of Palmerston's character; but he used them to create what is now called an image of himself which the mid-Victorian public liked and trusted. Of course only a fraction of the public then had the vote, but there is no evidence that those who had no vote thought differently about Palmerston from those who had. The non-voters jostled with the voters at election meetings and in 1857 set up those cries of 'What about China?' from the back of the hall which flustered Tory candidates trying to talk about something else. In the passage quoted above Morley does not attempt to argue that a larger electorate would have been more sympathetic to Cobden; later experience on the whole suggests that it would not.

So Palmerston won, and people quickly stopped talking about China and the *Arrow*. But nothing had yet been done to resolve the tangle into which Bowring had got himself, and there were to be dramatic twists of the road before peace with China was restored.

7

ON MARCH 12th, 1857, Lord Elgin wrote from London to his wife in Scotland: 'My Dearest, I have had a note from P. (almerston) followed by an interview. The proposal is to undertake a special mission of a few months' duration to settle the important and difficult question now embarrassing us in the East and concentrating the attention of all the world. On what grounds can I decline? Not on political grounds for however opposed I might be to the Govt. that would be a reason to prevent them from making the offer, but not me from accepting it. The very mission of a Plenipotentiary is an admission that there are errors of policy to be repaired.' Lady Elgin replied: 'Dearest, it was unexpected but if your conscience and feelings tell you to say yes I would not for the world dissuade you. God bless you my own darling. I promise you to do my best not to distress you. Forgive me if I can't write more today. Your own ever Mary.' Her letter crossed another from her husband: 'The deed is done. I have said Yes.'

At this time James Bruce, 8th Earl of Elgin, was 45 years of age, though his stoutness and early white hairs made him look older. He was the younger son of the 7th Earl, who rescued from the Parthenon the friezes which brought fame but not fortune to the family. James Bruce was too young to have any part in this transaction, but his life was to be deeply influenced by the fact that the Elgin marbles cost his father so much more than the British Government was ready to pay for them. He was educated at Eton, and at Christ

Church where he was a contemporary of Gladstone and Canning. He was elected to the House of Commons in 1841 as a supporter of Sir Robert Peel, but the next year succeeded to his father's earldom, his elder brother having died some years before. There thus passed into his hands the family house at Broomhall, which stands high above the southern coast of Fife, looking across the waters of the Forth to the great house of Hopetoun on the Lothian shore. The land round Broomhall is good, and the property included several coalmines which were profitable. But though his father had kept a handful of charming Athenian fragments to display beside the sword of Robert the Bruce in the entrance of Broomhall, he left the estate sadly encumbered as a result of his dealings in Greece and with the British Government. His son had not the means to sustain the life of a Scottish nobleman in Fife or of an unpaid politician in London. When he succeeded to the title he asked for a Government post, and in 1842, at the age of 31, became Governor of Jamaica. On the way out he and his wife were shipwrecked. She never fully recovered from the after effects and died in Jamaica the following year. His four years in Jamaica cannot have been happy, but he was certainly a successful Governor. The old planter society had been broken up by the freeing of the slaves nine years before Elgin arrived. Power lay increasingly in the erratic hands of Negro leaders and Baptist missionaries who whipped up feeling against the Established Church. It was a tricky period, and Elgin came through it well. In 1846 the Governor Generalship of Canada fell vacant, and though the Liberals were now in and Elgin was nominally a Conservative, he was appointed. He equipped himself for it admirably by marrying Mary Lambton, daughter of Lord Durham, whose famous report had shown Canada the way to self-government. It was a way thick with difficulties. When Elgin arrived he found that while as Governor General he was theoretically supposed to administer impartially a two-party system on the Westminster model, it was generally thought that his English Tory Ministers must continue indefinitely in office because the only alternative, a ministry dominated by French Canadians, would lead straight back to sedition and revolt. Elgin quickly decided to put this theory to the test, and in 1848 called into office a reforming Government which included a strong French Canadian element. The experiment was a success, and though the Tories stirred up riots against him, Elgin had proved that they had no monopoly of loyalty to the Crown. In the later part of his term he was concerned mainly to show the Americans that Canada was not a historical anachronism whose end must be annexation to the United States, but a useful trading partner whose independence and prosperity should be encouraged. The Treaty of 1854 with the United States was the climax of Elgin's career in Canada. The next year he returned to Britain and to private life, from which he was called by Lord Palmerston to deal with China and Sir John Bowring.

Elgin's good qualities, his faults, and his strong opinions will emerge with the story of his mission to China. All that need be said here is that he was respected but not popular among those who chose him for that mission. Politics in England were in the hands of a small number of men who knew each other very well. The circle was not closed and Elgin had the qualifications to enter it; but he had not done so. His time abroad had estranged him from the informal give-and-take of the politician's life. After thirteen years of writing and receiving despatches, he evidently found it hard to cope with a world where important decisions might be made by a muttered word between two Ministers in Cabinet or a note scribbled during a dull debate. Like many Government servants, he had come to distrust politicians through ignorance of their ways, and in private accused them of double dealing when they were really only guilty of the occasional laxness or flippancy which makes parliamentary life tolerable. In return they found him stiff and, because he belonged to no group or party, suspected him of trimming. When he tried to be pleasant, they thought him self-seeking. Two days before Elgin was offered the job in China, Granville wrote to Canning in India: 'Elgin like the stormy petrel has appeared for the first time in London, and is wonderfully courteous to me.' A few months later when it was suggested that Elgin might succeed Canning as Governor General of India, the latter's comment was 'he will sail with the wind.' Remarks about Elgin with this disagreeable flavour are not uncommon, though they are not to be compared with the spate of his own criticisms against those who employed him. Both were the result of misunderstanding, which sometimes threatened to become complete.

Elgin spent six busy weeks in England preparing for his expedition. He saw the Queen who 'was kind as usual.' He chose his personal staff and his tropical clothes. He argued with the Foreign Office about his instructions. These instructions eventually took the form of a despatch addressed to him by Lord Clarendon the day before his departure. The despatch shows how completely the Foreign Office disagreed with Sir John Bowring's analysis of the situation. Sir John, supported by almost every Englishman in Hong Kong, was certain that the essential thing was to humiliate Yeh and take Canton. The same cry had been heard on the hustings during the election. But the Foreign Office had now realised that Canton was essentially irrelevant, and that the Emperor's Government would only recognise the Queen's Government as an equal if the Queen had by right a diplomatic representative in the Emperor's capital. As Clarendon had written to Bowring on February 9th: 'Without such a guarantee for ready access to the Supreme Government, all other concessions will be more or less precarious.' Lord Clarendon's despatch made no mention of Yeh and instructed Elgin to go north from Hong Kong to the mouth of the Peiho river (the traditional gateway to Peking) and there open negotiations with a representative of the Emperor. He was to ask for reparation of losses and injuries suffered by British subjects and British-protected persons in the recent disturbances and for the complete observance of the Treaties in future, at Canton and elsewhere. These were the essential demands, refusal of which would entitle Elgin to use force. He was also to put forward two other proposals of a wider and more revolutionary nature. He was to ask 'the assent of the Chinese Government to the residence at Peking, or to the occasional visit to that capital, at the option of the British Government, of a Minister duly accredited by the Queen to the Emperor of China, and the recognition of the right of the British plenipotentiary and Chief Superintendent of Trade to communicate directly in writing with the high officers at the Chinese capital, and to send his communications by messengers of his own selection; such arrangements affording the best means of ensuring the due execution of the existing Treaties and of preventing future misunderstandings.' He was also to propose a revision of the Treaty to allow the opening of new cities to commerce. He was not empowered to use force solely to obtain these new demands; but if the essential demands for compensation and the thorough execution of the existing treaties were not met, he was entitled to use force, and was not to end hostilities until the Chinese had also agreed to his proposals for a British representative in Peking and for the opening of new ports to trade. If force became necessary the British were to confine themselves as far as possible to naval measures and Elgin was specifically warned against occupying Canton unless this proved absolutely necessary. The British Government were anxious that there should be no unnecessary destruction of life or property and that friendly relations should be maintained with the people of the treaty ports.

As the Peelite Sir John Graham commented ruefully to Sidney Herbert: 'If Elgin had been appointed with full powers to treat earlier, Cobden's motion would never have been made.' The Foreign Office underestimated the amount of pressure which would be needed to compel the Chinese to abandon their claim of superiority over other nations; but their emphasis on negotiations with Peking and on the minimum use of force was in healthy contrast with many of the bellicose speeches and newspaper articles which had appeared in the election campaign. It was clear nevertheless that however moderate his instructions, Elgin would need a sizeable military force at his disposal if he was to carry them out successfully. In January Sir John Bowring and Sir Michael Seymour had estimated that an additional military force of 5,000 men was needed to capture Canton. The Government now intended to by-pass Canton, and hoped thus to achieve its ends with a good deal less than 5,000 men. Elgin was promised 1,500 men who were to be sent from England to Singapore to await his instructions. In addition rather more than 1,000 men would be made available from the garrisons of Mauritius and Singapore. Admiral Seymour's naval force would be strengthened with several gunboats, and more troops would be sent later if necessary. Elgin does not seem to have asked for larger forces, but he was anxious that the forces which he had should be fully under his control, and that he should not be asked to carry out his instructions until the forces had reached Hong Kong. On this second point he was supported by the Foreign Secretary and by the Commander-in-Chief, the Duke of Cambridge, and got his way. On the first point he was defeated despite a threat to resign. Lieutenant-General Ashburnham was appointed to command the military force, and Elgin was told that while it was for him to decide when it was necessary to use force, it would be for Seymour and Ashburnham to decide upon and carry out the actual naval and military operations.

Elgin's road to China lay through Paris, where he had an important diplomatic task to perform. For several years it had been the custom of the British, French and American Governments to consult over Chinese matters. The British Government was far from wishing to win exclusive privileges in China. It strongly upheld the most-favoured nation principle, under which any advantage won by one nation was automatically conceded to the others, even though this meant in effect that concessions obtained from the Chinese with much effort by the British were enjoyed forthwith by the nationals of other countries who had done nothing to help gain them. Lenin's theory of imperialism, which describes the manufacturing powers as jealously carving out exclusive markets for themselves in Asia and Africa, is hard to reconcile with what happened in China in the 1850s and '60s. The British Government had no desire to shut out foreign competitors, and was frankly uneasy about the one exclusive privilege which it had obtained in 1841 through the zeal of its local representative, that is to say the cession of Hong Kong. It did not expect too much from the Americans. Their merchants made good use of the privileges obtained for them by British negotiators, and their local representatives tended to favour close co-operation with the British. They were also prompt to react to any provocation by the Chinese. On November 15, 1856, a month after the *Arrow* was seized, Chinese batteries fired on the American corvette *Portsmouth* on its way up to Canton although the Stars and Stripes were clearly displayed. Within a week the Americans had bombarded and captured the Barrier Forts from which the fire had come. Despite the robustness of its local representatives the Administration in Washington was traditionally suspicious of British and French motives and reluctant to join forces with the Europeans against the Chinese. Late in 1856 the Administration changed and the incoming President Buchanan in April 1857 appointed a new representative, Mr. Reed, with instructions to co-operate with the British and French, but to stop short of the use of force. Reed was of higher rank than his predecessors. His instructions explained hopefully why force was not necessary to transform the Chinese Empire into something more closely resembling the United States: 'Fortunately commerce itself is one of the most powerful means of civilisation and national improvement.

By coming into peaceful contact with men of other regions and other races, with different habits and greater knowledge, the jealous system of exclusion which has so long separated China from the rest of the world will gradually give way, and with increased intercourse will come those meliorations in the moral and physical conditions of its people which the Christian and the philanthropist have so long and so ardently desired.'

The British Government was more hopeful of co-operation with the French, and this remained a fixed point in its Chinese policy for several years. British public opinion did not understand why this was necessary. The British and French had been allies during the Crimean War which had ended only a few months before, but such enthusiasm as this short partnership had created was quick to cool, and the British public lapsed into their usual feelings of mixed contempt and fear for their closest neighbour. These feelings were not shared by Palmerston or Clarendon. They had no particular respect for Napoleon III, but they regarded him as a considerable improvement on his fellow-monarchs farther east. His liberal ideas were obscurely expressed, and vulnerable to the pressure of clerical and nationalist opinion in France, but he was the only substantial ruler on the Continent who in any way shared Palmerston's hopes for a liberal Europe. If Palmerston had been simply concerned with his own tenure of power he could have added to his popularity by snubbing or quarrelling with the Emperor of the French. As it was he showed himself anxious to co-operate with him wherever possible, and China seemed the obvious place to continue the partnership started in the Crimea.

There was another good reason for co-operating with the French; it was the best way of keeping a brake on their ambitions. The British were worried that the French, in addition to their pre-occupation with Indo-China, might try to match the annexation of Hong Kong with some Chinese prize of their own, perhaps the island of Chusan, off the mouth of the Yangtze. It happened that in 1856 the French already had a good reason of their own for quarrelling with the Chinese. The French, unlike the British and the Americans, were not at this time substantial traders with China. The main French interest, which they regarded as more idealistic than that of the Anglo-Saxons, was the protection of Catholic missionaries, and it was this interest which the Chinese strikingly offended at the beginning of 1856. On February 29th the Abbé Chapdelaine, a French missionary, was executed by order of the magistrates in a small town in the province of Kwangsi in the south of China, after living and peacefully preaching in the area for three years. It was said that his heart was cut from his body, cooked and eaten. The news of the murder, which did not reach Hong Kong until July, provoked an immediate protest from de Courcy, the acting French representative there, to Yeh in Canton. A fruitless correspondence followed. Yeh justly pointed out that the Abbé Chapdelaine had no right to have settled in the interior outside the five treaty ports. He also argued that Kwangsi was infested with Taiping rebels, whom Christian missionaries were known to support, and that this provided some justification for the magistrates' action. In fact only a handful of Protestant missionaries supported the Taiping rebellion and its semi-Christian trappings; it was strongly opposed by Catholics and in particular by the French. Apart from this, de Courcy was entitled to argue in reply that if Chapdelaine had been found to be trespassing, the Treaty provided that he should be sent to one of the Treaty ports, not put in a cage, decapitated and dismembered. The argument continued between de Courcy and Yeh while Bowring and Yeh were beginning the dispute about the *Arrow*. De Courcy did not however, feel drawn to make common cause with the British, and kept up a rather chilly neutrality. He refused to be associated with Parkes' demand for the right of entry into Canton and at the end of November the French withdrew from their factory outside the city. In January, when

90

it looked as if Hong Kong itself might come to grief, de Courcy and the French Admiral Guérin offered Bowring 50 men for the defence of the colony; but this was the extent of his co-operation, and in his reports to Paris he criticised Bowring's tactics as deplorably rash. But his Government was already committed to co-operate with the British. In the autumn of 1856 the two Governments, knowing about the fate of the Abbé Chapdelaine but not yet about the *Arrow*, agreed to make a joint approach to the Chinese at the mouth of the Yangtze to ask for reparation of injuries and revision of the Treaties. The French representative, M. de Bourboulon, returned to Hong Kong to resume charge from de Courcy at the beginning of March 1857. He was a formidable little man with a quick temper and reputedly left wing opinions. He was accompanied by his Scots wife, who became remarkable in Hong Kong society for her great height and boasts of royal ancestry. 'Quant à Madame De Bourboulon,' wrote a colleague, 'elle est aussi maigre que longue et point jolie du tout; mais elle sourit toujours.' De Bourboulon returned with instructions to co-operate with Bowring in an expedition to negotiate at the Yangtze; but by the time he arrived Bowring and everyone in Hong Kong were convinced that the first and essential step was to expel Yeh from Canton, for which de Bourboulon had no authority. It says much for the force of Bowring's character that he persuaded both his French and American colleagues that he was right in his passionately held conviction that, as he wrote to Clarendon on April 7th, 'any move towards the North would end in discomfiture and disappointment until the local question is settled at Canton.'

The British Government, as we have seen, disagreed, and the instructions given to Elgin in April 1857 were not very different from those agreed with the French six months earlier, before the troubles in Canton. Although there was no disagreement between the two Governments Clarendon thought it would be wise for Elgin to stop for a day or two in Paris on his way east. 'All Frenchmen,' he wrote, 'require a certain amount of cajolery, and to have confidence shown them, and to be made to think that they are not in the background playing second fiddle. I have no doubt that you will do this skilfully and that having got on so well with all Yankees [in Canada] you will have no trouble with the French Minister, who appears to be a *gentleman*, which is not a bad foundation.' Elgin saw Napoleon III on April 24th and found him very gracious but not knowledgeable about China. The Emperor was mainly worried as to whether he should appoint a special representative who would rank equal to Elgin or whether he should leave de Bourboulon in charge. He decided finally in favour of a special representative. The Prince de la Tour d'Auvergne, Minister in Florence, refused the post ('wise man' commented Elgin), which was then reluctantly accepted by Baron Gros. Elgin met Gros just before leaving Paris, and also had a talk with the Foreign Minister Walewski, who hoped that the Western powers would not have to push matters too hard against the Chinese. Walewski asked Elgin to take with him and deliver to de Bourboulon the official despatch announcing the appointment over his head of Baron Gros, a curious arrangement which as was perhaps foreseen caused the messenger some embarrassment.

During his short stay in Paris Elgin's native suspicion of politics and politicians burst out in an angry letter to Clarendon. *The Times* carried a leading article on April 21st implying that there would soon have to be fighting in China, and referring politely but not enthusiastically to Elgin's qualifications for his new position. The point of the article was that Elgin would need a first-class general at his side to command the British troops, and that General Ashburnham was not good enough. If Elgin had had a more detailed knowledge of British politics he would have realised that *The Times* of 1857, while on reasonable terms with the Government, was by no means its mouthpiece, and that its bellicosity towards China probably had more to do with the

China merchants than with Palmerston. Elgin thought that he had been tricked by the politicians; he deduced that they wanted a moderate figurehead in charge of their China policy in order to please Parliament and the electorate, but were quite ready to throw him over when public attention had shifted elsewhere. Elgin does not seem even to have read *The Times* article himself. 'I am told,' he wrote to Clarendon on April 29th, 'that the liberal Press, *The Times* en tête, is beginning to discover that a worse man for this China business than myself could not have been selected. It appears that I have not blood enough on my hand. This is ominous because it shows that disasters are expected and that to appease the national vanity victims must be dressed beforehand for the sacrifice. For my own part I am very little solicitous on the subject as I accepted the office with a full consciousness of what would follow when the elections were over.' Clarendon was an even-tempered man, but he could not pass over what was in effect an accusation against his own honour. He replied on May 11th: 'I received your last letter from Paris with some surprise and regret for it seemed to me as if you were seeking to make the Government in some way responsible for an article which appeared in *The Times*, and which does not, you must permit me to say, bear out your construction of it. . . . I cannot either understand your allusion to the elections or what you expected would follow when they were over, with a consciousness of which you accepted the office. You made no such intimation to me, and I won't suppose for a moment that you can think the Government are rogues and fools enough not to desire your complete success and not to take every possible means in their power for ensuring it. I attach very little importance to canards and reports, but they certainly were rife as soon as you left London that you were dissatisfied with the Government and with your instructions and that you would not be able to do anything in China. If you had any such feeling you must allow me to think that you ought to have frankly communicated it. . . . I can only hope that the spirit in which your last letter from Paris was written may long since have passed away.'

It was a magisterial and deserved rebuke, and Clarendon did not have to repeat it. Elgin kept his rooted distrust of his political masters of all parties, and in his private diary continued to attribute to them devious and sometimes improbable motives; but he did not challenge them openly again, and his correspondence with Clarendon in particular was to be correct and even friendly.

8

LORD ELGIN's journey eastward was swift by the standard
of his day. He had taken with him his younger brother
Frederick to act as Secretary to the mission, four attachés,
and Laurence Oliphant, his private secretary, who was to
write a stout volume describing the expedition. By May 9th
the party was in Egypt, and in Oliphant's words 'found ourselves rushing across the desert in the first train which had
ever carried passengers to the central station, enveloped in
clouds of dust, and indulging in the most sanguine antici-
pations of the future.' The next phase of the journey, by
P. and O. steamer to Singapore, was painfully hot, and
Elgin's letters home called forth a wifely cry of protest.
'I could not be surprised to hear of your suffering from heat
and discomforts,' wrote Lady Elgin, 'but it is hard that the
trial should have been unnecessarily aggravated by the
niggard and heartless First Lord. I wish I could give him a
taste of the heat and see how he would like to be left to his
fate without any of the things which at least lessen the personal misery of such a passage a little! The want of champagne makes me angry when it is the most effectual and
refreshing remedy.' Elgin was indeed in low spirits and
feeling his years. 'There is nothing congenial to me in my
present life,' he wrote home on May 24th. 'I have no elas-
ticity of spirits to keep up with the younger people around
me. It may be better when the work begins; but I cannot
be sanguine even as to that, for the more I read of the blue
books and papers with which I have been furnished, the

more embarrassing the questions with which I have to deal appear.'

On May 27th the ship touched at Galle in Ceylon and picked up General Ashburnham who had been serving in India until his recent appointment to command the land forces being sent to China. The General brought news of mutinies which had broken out in the Indian Army. He evidently had only a fragment of the story and Elgin's re-action was to press on to China so that he could complete his mission quickly and release the troops which had been put at his disposal for service in India if they were needed. On the next lap to Singapore, Elgin found the official documents on his mission to China gloomy shipboard reading: 'It is impossible to read the blue books,' he wrote in his diary, 'without feeling that we have often acted towards the Chinese in a manner which it is very difficult to justify; and yet their treachery and cruelty come out so strongly at times as to make almost anything appear justifiable.'

On June 3rd he reached Singapore. It had been arranged that he was to wait there until the frigate *Shannon*, which was to be his flagship in China, could pick him up. The *Shannon* of course had to round the Cape, and Elgin was in Singapore three weeks. The news which met him there was disastrous. The scattered mutinies which Ashburnham had reported had grown into a sudden great rebellion which threatened to destroy British rule in India. Canning, the Governor General, in his desperate need for reliable troops, inevitably thought of the transports converging on Singapore with the regiments for service in China. On May 19th he sent Elgin an urgent appeal. In an official letter he formally asked that the troops be diverted. In a private letter he pressed home the request: 'I wish I could give you more cheerful and acceptable greeting than you will find in the letter by which this is accompanied. As it is you will not bless me for it, but the case which I have before me is clear and strong. Our hold of Bengal and the Upper Provinces depends upon the turn of a word, a look. An indiscreet act

James 8th Earl of Elgin; a photograph taken in China, 1860

Major-General Sir James Hope Grant from a photograph taken in India 1858

Sir Frederick Bruce, from a portrait by James Swinton 1844

or irritating phrase from a foolish commanding officer at the head of a mutinous or disaffected company may whilst the present condition of things at Delhi lasts, lead to a general rising of the native troops in the Lower Provinces where we have no European strength—and where an army in rebellion would have everything its own way for weeks and months to come. We have seen within the last few days what that way would be. . . . If you send me troops they shall not be kept one hour more than is absolutely needed. If you come with them yourself you shall be most heartily welcome.'

Elgin was now in the classic position which his successors in the twentieth century are spared. He had precise instructions from the Government to carry out a mission in China for which certain military forces had been assigned to him. He had now received a request from a colleague that he should divert those forces elsewhere. He had no means of getting his instructions altered. The telegraph reached no farther than Alexandria. If he wrote asking for fresh instructions he would in effect be refusing Canning's appeal as no reply could be expected from London for about two months. Sitting sweltering in the Governor's house in Singapore he had no senior adviser except Ashburnham, who knew little of what was involved. The burden of decision lay on him alone.

Elgin does not seem to have hesitated. The 5th and 90th regiments, totalling about 1,700 men, had already reached Singapore and were despatched to Calcutta. Messages were sent to divert the further three regiments which were on the way from England. This last step proved unnecessary; in the event the Governor of the Cape Colony, Sir George Grey, diverted the troopships to India on his own responsibility. Elgin was left with nothing except the *Shannon* and her crew with which to strengthen the clearly inadequate forces with which Admiral Seymour and Sir John Bowring had been wrestling vainly against Yeh.

Elgin's decision was much praised; indeed he probably

received more credit for this single act than for any other of his career. Clarendon's biographer judged that Elgin probably saved the British Empire in India. The Governor of Ceylon writes: 'You have set a bright example at a moment of darkness and calamity.' There seems little doubt that the diverted troops gave decisive help in turning the scale in India. But some of the praise given to Elgin seems exaggerated. He would have been an abnormally selfish or stupid man if he had not realised that the stake in India was far greater than the stake in China, and that speed was essential to save the one, but not so necessary to safeguard the other. On the same day as he asked for the troops Canning wrote to his friend Granville in England that Elgin ought not to refuse. 'It cannot matter whether Yeh is coerced now or six months hence. Canton will keep: India will not.' It was a fair summary. Elgin could only reasonably have refused if he had distrusted Canning's judgment of events in India; but he had been at Christ Church with Canning, and though they were not close friends, knew him well enough to know that he was not a coward or an alarmist.

The only person in authority who seems seriously to have questioned Elgin's diversion of the troops was the Prime Minister. The Cabinet had argued about the wisdom of this step before they knew that Canning had written to Elgin, and Palmerston had objected. When Ministers heard of Canning's request, no one suggested that he should be over-ruled, but equally it was some time before they sanctioned what he had done. To the great indignation of Canning's friends, the First Lord of the Admiralty, Sir Charles Wood, merely announced to the House of Commons that Canning had made the request and that it was not yet known if Elgin had accepted it. Palmerston refused to agree that any contingent which had already reached Hong Kong should be turned back. He was showing an old man's reluctance to see his plans changed. He had personally interested himself in China and was probably the victim of some of his own lively propaganda about the vices of Yeh; now the settlement of accounts was to be postponed. Clarendon was sure that Canning and Elgin were right; but even he could not help writing wistfully to the latter on July 10th: 'It would certainly be a brilliant achievement if you could send away the troops and do all you want with the ships alone.' In any case it was too late to intervene. The Cabinet discussed the matter and Sir Charles Wood made his statement at the beginning of July, a month after Elgin had taken his decision. As the terrible summer wore on and the full dimension of the Indian danger became clear, there could be no doubt that Elgin's decision had been right. As Foreign Secretary, Clarendon had already learned that the politeness with which an overwhelmingly superior Power is generally received turns quickly to malice as soon as it receives a check. He wrote again to Elgin about the Indian Mutiny in the autumn: 'We have never before played for so great a stake, and the whole world is watching how we conduct the game upon which our national honour and our prestige and position among nations depend. I need not tell you that a large proportion of the spectators devoutly hope that we may lose this game, and that England may henceforward take rank as a second or third-rate power, and it is therefore all the more incumbent upon us to win it. I do not permit myself to doubt that we shall do so because we are determined upon it, but we can only expect to be successful by concentrating all our energies and resources upon India, and leaving other things—the national defences inclusive I grieve to say—to chance.'

The *Shannon* was helped by a south-west wind and brought Elgin and his party to Hong Kong on July 2nd. Their spirits were not high. Much about China was obscure, but it was quite clear to all that the Chinese were unlikely to negotiate a settlement with a High Commissioner who had no serious military force at his disposal. No one could tell how long Canning would need the diverted regiments or indeed if they would ever be sent to China.

99

The letters which Elgin had received during the voyage showed that the deadlock which had existed along the Canton river since January was unbroken. Admiral Seymour had managed to maintain small garrisons at a number of points along the river, the nearest to Canton being three miles away at Macao Fort. He had fought a number of successful engagements with Chinese Government junks. But their control of the main Canton river gave the British no hold over Yeh, who did not rely exclusively on it for the supply of the city. No doubt the Chinese merchants in Canton were hard hit by the disruption of trade, but to Yeh and probably to the greater number of those whom he ruled the important fact was that the barbarians had once again been shown that Canton was impregnable, and had indeed been chased out of their foothold in the factories outside its walls. Admiral Seymour wrote glowing accounts of the chasing and burning of war junks, but to most observers it seemed in July 1857 as in January that Yeh had slightly the upper hand.

The one person who entirely disagreed was Sir John Bowring. The news of Elgin's appointment must have been bitter to swallow. Bowring did not expostulate, he did not resign; in his immediate reply to Clarendon there was a genuine emotion beneath the fustian. He promised to support Elgin. 'A great success attends him, I doubt not—for out of the nettle of danger we will pluck the flower of safety. . . . We must trade from Corea to Cochin China on the coasts and visit the great marts on the navigable rivers. For this and more will I labour whoever shall reap the glory. I am getting old now, and there has been much trampling on my bald bare head, but I trust before I die to see the great purpose accomplished for which I wish to live, and for which I hope Providence may have spared me through many many troubles.' Clarendon had obviously expected worse and in a letter to Elgin gave Bowring what was for him probably the highest praise for showing 'a very gentlemanlike feeling as well as honest zeal for the public service.' Bowring's zeal had indeed never been in question, and after the shock of Elgin's appointment had worn off it began again to take an awkward form. He persuaded himself and set out to persuade others that there was little for Elgin to do. Yeh's position had already crumbled, and the smallest push was required to bring him down. 'I am happy to say,' he wrote to Elgin on May 13th, 'that you will find matters in an advanced state promising a satisfactory consummation. . . . Happily the Court of Peking is now much better informed than it was at first of the true state of matters and the Imperial Commissioner finds no support, but is left to get out of the difficulties of his position as best he may. In every port but Canton our relations are on the most amicable footing, and in Canton itself there is a strong party longing to come to terms. Yeh continues taciturn and obstinate. With him the machinery of resistance tumbles down and any hour may announce his overthrow and removal from the scene.' A fortnight later Bowring wrote again: 'Yeh is losing the little support he had and his garrulous pride is turned to morbid taciturnity.'

Few in Hong Kong of any nationality shared Bowring's optimism; but almost all agreed with him in the conviction which he had for months been vainly urging on the Foreign Office, and which he now urged on Elgin, that it would be useless and dangerous to make any move to negotiate with the Government in Peking until Canton had been taken and Yeh humiliated. In a later letter to Elgin he wrote: 'There is quite an explosion of public opinion as to the fatal mistake which would be committed by any movement upon Peking until the Cantonese question is settled. Many think such a movement might imperil the whole trade of China and encourage the imperial adoption of the Yeh system elsewhere —as it is no doubt believed to be triumphant. I do not share these views but I am quite of opinion that any action which refers the Canton question to the Emperor would be a most injurious and embarrassing step.' With Elgin's appointment Bowring had lost his right to decide or advise on the handling of Anglo-Chinese relations, and Elgin could have afforded to ignore his views even though they were supported by almost the entire British community in Hong Kong. The one man in Hong Kong whose judgment he was bound to respect was Admiral Seymour. Within half an hour of the *Shannon* dropping anchor the Admiral was alongside to pay his respects. Elgin was favourably impressed by Seymour, and therefore all the more dismayed to find that he too thought that the instructions which Elgin had brought with him from London were hopelessly wrong. Seymour was not a young man and he had spent eight exasperating months in the discomfort of the Canton river; but he put his case moderately. He said that he would of course escort Elgin to the mouth of the Peiho to start negotiations if that was what Elgin decided to do; but in his view the Canton dispute was a local matter which should be settled locally. The Cantonese had got it into their heads that their city was impregnable. That was why they felt able to deny the Western powers their treaty rights and continue their arrogant and exclusive system. If the British now shifted their activities to the north the Cantonese would be confirmed in their belief. Only if Canton were taken could the Chinese be brought to mend their ways. The Admiral also touched on the argument which appealed most strongly to the merchants. If Elgin went to the Peiho and, as seemed likely, his negotiations failed, the subsequent fighting could hardly be confined to Canton. There would be a general Anglo-Chinese war, as there had been in 1839-42, and so long as it lasted Anglo-Chinese trade would be interrupted. As things stood the merchants continued to trade profitably with the Chinese in the other treaty ports while pressing for the most vigorous action against Yeh in Canton. A quick sharp operation against Canton, leaving the other ports untouched, appealed to their pocket books as well as their indignant patriotism. Eighty-five merchants, headed by Jardine, sent Elgin a memorandum on July 9th urging this course. He had the same story over again when he first called on Bowring, who had been ill. 'It is clear,' he wrote in his diary, 'that there is here an idée fixe that nothing ought to be done till there has been a general massacre at Canton.' Bowring had been profuse in assurances of support, which Elgin received coolly. 'I thanked him and told him that if the matter ended well all who had been concerned would get credit, and vice versa.'

Elgin was shaken but not convinced by the universal criticism of his instructions. He pointed out that even if his instructions had allowed it he had not the means to mount an attack against Canton. He asked Seymour and Ashburnham how many soldiers would be needed for this operation in addition to the fleet. Seymour said 5,000, Ashburnham 4,000; there existed in Hong Kong 1,484, of whom 244 were sick. Even if the means had existed Elgin would not have been willing at this time to use them against Canton. He fully accepted the Foreign Office's argument that since Chinese policy was made in Peking, it was the men in Peking who must be persuaded to abandon their claims to superiority; however strong the passions aroused by what happened at Canton, no lasting settlement could be achieved there. Finally Elgin, now as throughout his mission, hated the thought of casualties, Chinese or British, and had a strong enough belief in his diplomatic skill to hope that he could get his way without serious fighting.

Elgin thus set himself against an attack on Canton, but he saw the force of the argument against at once starting negotiations in the north. The Chinese were copiously if somewhat inaccurately informed of what was happening in India. They would certainly know that Elgin had no force or immediate prospect of a force to support his requests. He would probably have to trail back to Hong Kong with no for an answer and without hope of early redress. It quickly became clear that there was another argument pointing in the same direction. Elgin's instructions said that he must act in concert with the French. He knew how strongly the

Prime Minister and Foreign Secretary had stressed this co-operation. But Baron Gros, the Emperor's special representative, had refused to take the new quick way to China which involved changing ships and scurrying by train across the Egyptian desert to Suez. The Baron was on his way round the Cape and was not expected till the autumn. This should not have been an insuperable obstacle. The French representative in China, M. de Bourboulon, had clear instructions to co-operate with the British, and a naval force with which to carry them out. But when Elgin sent him the despatch with which he had been entrusted in Paris, containing the news of Gros's appointment, de Bourboulon retired in a huff. He explained to Elgin that since he had been superseded by Baron Gros his previous powers and instructions must be considered to have lapsed, and he could not join in any initiative until Gros had arrived. Elgin pleaded with the French Admiral Rigault to intercede with de Bourboulon, but without success. He was advised that since Yeh had been claiming that the other barbarians did not support the British over the *Arrow* it would be an added sign of weakness if he moved north without the French.

Both possible lines of action in China were thus ruled out. Elgin could not attack Canton; there were overwhelming arguments against going north at once and trying to open negotiations. But the thought of staying inactive in Hong Kong until Gros or the regiments arrived appalled him. The *Shannon* at sea was a fine fast-moving ship; confined in the harbour of Hong Kong she was hot and smelly. But if he moved ashore he would have to stay at Government House, and that was the worst thought of all. Elgin had no respect for Bowring's judgment, but what really dismayed him was the old man's unending partisanship. Every conversation became an argument and every argument dragged on for hours. He wrote to his wife later: 'Among the consequences of remaining there [in Hong Kong] would have been, I believe firmly, that of never leaving it, for I do not think I could have lived through the summer cooped up in a ship in the harbour or as Bowring's guest. You may imagine, with all you have heard and know of Sir John Bowring, what it would have been to have occupied for months that position. He was civil enough to me, but everyone knows that he is a most dangerous person.'

On July 14th, twelve days after his arrival in Hong Kong, Elgin found a means of escape from his impossible situation. A ship arrived from Calcutta; the news of the Mutiny was even worse than before. There was clearly no chance of Canning releasing the China regiments for months to come. Elgin decided to go to Calcutta himself. He could bring Canning some support worth having, for three hundred marines had just arrived from England. Seymour agreed to release them for service in India, together with the corvette *Pearl*. These, with part of the crew of the *Shannon*, could form a Naval Brigade for use wherever Canning wanted them. Elgin's arrival might help the Government of India to steady the nerves of the British community. He could also keep an eye on his precious China regiments. General Ashburnham, with his recent knowledge of India, was enthusiastic for the scheme. Within forty-eight hours everything was arranged, and Elgin sailed from Hong Kong with a feeling of deep relief, having told Seymour and Bowring that he would be back in seven weeks and that they were to do nothing meanwhile except maintain the status quo. On his way south he noted his forty-sixth birthday: 'I feel sad when I look at this inhospitable sea and think of the smiling countenances with which I should have been surrounded at home, and the joyous laugh when papa with affected surprise detected the present wrapped up carefully in a paper parcel on the breakfast table.'

Elgin reached Singapore in time to hear news of the massacre of Cawnpore. The *Shannon* loaded 400 tons of coal in twenty-one hours, a considerable feat, and hurried on. During the onward journey to Calcutta the party heard a story that the city was about to be attacked by mutineers. On the 8th of August the *Pearl* and the *Shannon* entered the harbour of Calcutta and were enthusiastically received. Elgin's secretary, Oliphant, described the scene: 'First our stately ship suddenly burst upon the astonished gaze of two European gentlemen taking their evening walk, who seeing her crowded with the eager faces of men ready for the fray, took off their hats and cheered wildly; then the respectable skipper of a merchantman worked himself into a state of phrensy, and made us a long speech, which we could not hear, but the violence of his gesticulations left us in little doubt as to its import; then his crew took up the cheer, which was passed on at intervals until the thunder of our 68-pounders drowned any other sound, shattered the windows of sundry of the "palaces," attracted a crowd of spectators to the Maidan, and brought the contents of Fort William on to the glacis.'

The weeks which followed were an anti-climax for Elgin. He had made his second gallant gesture. A Naval Brigade was quickly organised from the marines and crew of the *Pearl* and the *Shannon* and sent to reinforce Sir Colin Campbell's army. Once they had gone there was nothing for Elgin to do, except go to parties. Calcutta was the seat of the Government of India and Elgin stayed at Canning's invitation in the Governor General's house. The European community was from time to time swept by rumours of mutiny within the city and disaster without, but its social life went on unchecked. Dining out had its hazards, particularly at Fort William, which according to Oliphant 'involved the risk of being bayoneted by a series of Irish sentries, who would not admit your pronunciation of the parole to be correct, and were haunted by the suspicion that you were the King of Oude in disguise escaping in a buggy.' Elgin found himself a society lion, and hated it. China weighed on his mind, and he longed for the return of his regiments, but no one in Calcutta took China seriously. He wrote later to his wife: 'Rather crude notions respecting the Chinese expedition prevail in India. The popular belief seems to be that by some lucky chance a large military force was despatched from England this spring to these Eastern Seas, and that the Indian Government have conferred a favour upon us by providing something for it to do. I tried when in Calcutta to persuade Canning that this was a mistake, and to convince him that a contest between English pretensions and Chinese prejudices and millions, with all the nations of the earth summoned as spectators or backers, was something more than a bad pleasantry. He used to listen to my declamations on this subject with admirable patience, but with something also of the benevolence which a kind-hearted man accords to a maniac.' It is difficult not to sympathise with Canning. The month of August 1857 which Elgin spent in Calcutta was perhaps the gloomiest of the Mutiny. The burden on Canning was fearsome, probably the greatest carried by a single servant of the Crown since Trafalgar. Elgin had given him valuable help, but it was hard for him in return to have to listen to tales of Yeh and Bowring when his mind was with the besieged at Agra and Lucknow. Lady Canning wrote to a friend: 'Lord Elgin himself looks more prosperous than ever, and in the most jolly old age; one cannot believe that he is but 45. He is entirely engrossed with China and everything Chinese, and I do not think it is merely that he has from a feeling of delicacy a wish not to meddle in Indian concerns, but that they really are not in his head just now.'

Elgin was depressed as well as bored by Calcutta. He thought he saw there on an immense scale the short-sighted English attitude towards Eastern races which he had already found in Singapore and in Hong Kong. Like almost every Englishman of his generation, Elgin did not doubt that Europeans were superior to Indians and Chinese in the sense that they had developed much further in the things that mattered. But he believed strongly that many Englishmen, and more particularly Englishwomen, were undermining their country's position by treating the Eastern races with a contempt and indifference which was almost as bad as the arrogance of the Chinese towards the barbarian.

He never expressed this fear more clearly than in a letter to his wife from Calcutta: 'It is a terrible business however this living among inferior races. I have seldom from man or woman since I came to the East heard a sentence which was reconcilable with the hypothesis that Christianity had ever come into the world. Detestation, contempt, ferocity, vengeance, whether Chinamen or Indians be the object. There are some 3 or 4 hundred servants in this House [Canning's]. When one first passes by them salaaming one feels a little awkward, but the feeling soon wears off, and one moves among them with perfect indifference, treating them not as dogs, because in that case one would whistle to them and pat them, but as machines with which one can have no communion or sympathy. . . . When the passions of fear and hatred are engrafted on this indifference, the result is frightful, an absolute callousness to the suffering of the objects of those passions which must be witnessed to be understood or believed.' To which one need only add that despite their party-giving the British in Calcutta in August 1857 were with reason a badly frightened community.

9

ELGIN HAD SAID that he would be back in Hong Kong by the end of September. The French admiral had thought that the leisurely Baron Gros would by then have arrived from France. There was no duty and certainly no pleasure to keep Elgin in Calcutta. The ships and men whom he had brought were doing valuable service, but he sat miserably among the gossip of Calcutta, unable either to advise on India or to interest anyone in China. Towards the end of August he heard that the Government was sending 1,500 marines to Hong Kong to replace the regiments diverted to India. It was not a large force with which to challenge the Chinese Empire, but at least it showed that Elgin was not entirely forgotten. The news from China itself was hardly encouraging. Bowring and Seymour had heard that Yeh was about to reopen Canton to trade for all except British merchants. Regarding this as an intolerable prospect, Seymour formally declared a blockade. This did not alter the existing situation, since no trade had been moving for months on the main river which Seymour controlled. The blockade merely gave warning to foreign shipping not to take up any offer which Yeh might make. Canton could continue to get sea-borne supplies by transhipping them into boats small enough to navigate the many back waterways up which the British gunboats could not move. The Admiral's blockade set the lawyers arguing unhappily; it was not easy to define the legal basis of a blockade imposed against a country with which one was formally at peace.

Bowring was fidgety, longing to take a hand himself, and irresponsibly suggesting in letters to London that military reinforcements were unnecessary because a naval force could do all that was required. Some of the British merchants were criticising Elgin for going to India and so giving Canning a second contingent of forces meant for China. Faced with these irritating reports Elgin decided that it was time to return and make a start in China.

He reached Hong Kong on September 20th in the P. and O. steamer *Ava*. Nothing seemed to have changed since he left two months before. No fresh troops had yet arrived from England. Baron Gros was still somewhere below the horizon. It was still insufferably hot; Bowring continued in full spate. Elgin's gloom and irritation deepened. He remained sure that it would be a mistake for him to go to the mouth of the Peiho and open communication with Peking without either the French or a military force to back up his requests. But the year was wearing on, and he was advised that in the winter he could not safely venture ships into the little known waters of North China. As he caustically wrote to Clarendon, Gros seemed to be delaying his arrival until the climate in Hong Kong became cool and healthy by which time it would be too late to go north until the spring. 'The practical effect of the nomination of a special Commissioner by the French Government has therefore been to deprive me for this year of the co-operation on which in the absence of such a nomination I might have counted.' Almost everyone he spoke to in Hong Kong was still in favour of an attack on Canton, for which he had as yet neither troops nor authority. He thought of sending his brother Frederick north to the mouth of the Peiho with a message for the Government at Peking, but the idea came to nothing.

Elgin was as determined as before not to expose himself to Bowring's hospitality and he and his party sweltered and suffered in the harbour on board the *Ava*. 'I have discovered the source of another smell by finding that Alexander (the steward) had ingeniously contrived to store his onions immediately below my cabin. Only conceive the abomination of such an arrangement.' September and October are typhoon months, and when the wind became too fierce the *Ava* sheltered under the promontory of Kowloon. The local British community was hospitable, but dinner ashore might mean two miles in an open boat in pouring rain. The gentlemen greatly outnumbered the ladies on such occasions, and to the untrained stomach the food was a hazard. You could walk along the shore to the left or to the right of the town; or at the risk of a fever you could scramble up the Peak; you could also play billiards at the Club. Despite these diversions the party's spirits were low and they suffered sadly from boils. Elgin momentarily succeeded in cheering them up by taking the *Ava* up the Canton river on a picnic. The day was fine and almost all the ladies of the colony were present. In the evening they danced on deck by the light of Chinese lanterns to music provided by the band of Admiral Seymour's flagship, the *Calcutta*. A little later Elgin visited the nearby Portuguese colony of Macao, and preferred its mellow charm to the parvenu brashness of Hong Kong. About this time he was much saddened by news of his sister's death. His family in Scotland were never far from his mind. He sent his wife tea and lichees and remembered the children's birthdays: 'Give Freddy a kiss and tell him that if I could get on the back of a flying fish I would fly over to see him.'

Elgin asked for exact information about the forces available in Hong Kong. Of some commodities he had more than enough; for part of the autumn, for instance, he had two military commanders. There had been a muddle over the intended transfer of General Ashburnham to India and his replacement by General van Straubenzee and for several weeks both generals were in Hong Kong, lacking only an army for either to command. There were plenty of supplies too, particularly for the military hospitals; fearful memories of the Crimea were too close for anyone to count the cost.

Elgin described 'oceans of porter, soda water, wine of all sorts and delicacies that I never even heard of for the hospitals,' 'a reaction after the economies practised in the Crimea and will be persevered in I suppose till Parliament gets tired of paying and then we shall have counter-action the other way.' But of troops he had only 1,150 of whom one-fifth were sick at the beginning of October. At least 350 men were needed to garrison Hong Kong, and Ashburnham calculated that at least an additional 1,500 Europeans, including a force of engineers, would be needed for an operation against Canton. As already mentioned, Elgin had heard unofficially before he left Calcutta that he was to be sent exactly that number of marines, but he was as usual sceptical of the promises of his masters. He wrote to Canning asking if there was any hope of troops from India, complaining that 'the Government at home have dropped us like a hot potato.' And to his wife the same week: 'The Government having sent me out with the intention that I should make war, and a war which would require a military force, are quietly giving the public to understand that I came here to make peace' and would need a naval force at most.

As the weeks went by it became clearer that the only action which could possibly be contrived before the end of 1857 was an operation against Canton. Gradually the various obstacles against this were removed. On October 14th Elgin received from the Foreign Office a despatch written some weeks before in which Clarendon authorised him, if he had not yet been able to go to the Peiho, to use force at Canton to bring the local government to terms. Two days later Baron Gros arrived on the *Audacieuse*, six months after his appointment as French High Commissioner. Elgin found him 'civil, cautious, diplomatic; does not commit himself.' Three years of difficult co-operation lay before them; and though the two men never became intimate Elgin learned to rely on Gros's calm judgment and to swallow occasional impatience at the Baron's slowness and resolute

Exterior angle of North Taku fort stormed by the French, August
1860, photograph by Signor Beato

Interior of North Taku fort

Tent of the 15th Punjabis at Pehtang 1860 from a sketch by C. Wirgman

The *Havoc* gunboat with Fane's Horse on board 1860 from a sketch by C. Wirgman

attention to his creature comforts. Gros's instructions favoured an approach to the Peiho, not an attack on Canton, but soon after his arrival he was given discretion on the point and was brought round by the weight of British opinion which since Clarendon's latest despatch was received had become unanimous in favour of giving Yeh a bloody nose. 'I stated to him some facts which I think moved him a little,' Elgin wrote to Clarendon, 'next day Bowring gave it to him for four hours, two on shore and two on board the *Audacieuse*. When I visited him in the evening I found him somewhat exhausted and ready to make almost any concession rather than entertain another assault of rhetoric.'

Two other Ambassadors arrived in Hong Kong in November, but rather to watch what was afoot than to take part. Reed, appointed American Minister by the incoming President Buchanan, flew his flag in the massive frigate *Minnesota*, whose size would have been more impressive if it had not prevented her from navigating the Canton river. Reed's instructions, which coincided with his personal views, were to be civil to the British, but stay neutral and look out for American interests. He found the British in poor shape: 'There is a great irritability among them all,' he wrote to his Secretary of State. 'They are fretful not only at their dependence on the French, without whom they could not take a step in advance, but by their inability to involve the U.S. in their unworthy quarrel. For such, as it now stands, I confess it seems to me. On the other hand the Chinese every hour are putting themselves in the wrong.' For Elgin the arrival of the Russian Count Poutiatine in a small paddle steamer was a more interesting event. Poutiatine had hung about the coast of North China for several weeks waiting for a reply to a letter he had delivered at the mouth of the Peiho asking to be received by the Emperor at Peking. When it came the reply said that he could not be received at present, and that in any case he would have to perform the ceremony of kowtow, or prostration before the Emperor. Poutiatine agreed with Elgin that whatever the merits of an attack on Canton the main issue could only be settled in the north, and he advised the British to take with them as many gunboats of light draught as they could muster so that they could if necessary sail up the Peiho river and bring effective pressure against Peking.

Planning now began for the operation against Canton, and proved a cumbersome business. Elgin moved ashore in mid-November into a house vacated by General Ashburnham who after many delays had finally left for India. 'Few people,' he wrote to his wife, 'have ever been in a position which required greater tact—four Ambassadors, two admirals, a general and Sir John Bowring, and notwithstanding this luxury of colleagues, no sufficient force.' And to Clarendon: 'It is necessary to pass a gentle hand over all these palpitating strings if we would produce from them none but accordant tones.' Despite his gentle hand discords were frequent, and he came finally to the classic conclusion of the exhausted diplomat: 'We are all more or less insane, but some are certainly more so than others.' It went without saying that nearest the line of insanity was Sir John Bowring, who vexed anyone he could find with passionate speeches of advice and self-justification. He continued to argue, to Elgin's particular irritation, that only a naval force was required against Canton and that the troops which had been asked for should be sent away. It also emerged that while Elgin had been in India Bowring, contrary to his explicit instructions, had let Yeh know that he was willing to hear from him. Elgin's patience, never his strongest point, wore out: 'I spoke to him pretty plainly and the way he dodged and insinuated revealed to me more than I had before seen of the man's character. . . . It is impossible to put the slightest trust in him.' Bowring was still Governor of Hong Kong and Superintendent of Trade with China, but since Elgin's appointment he had no responsibility for general British relations with the Empire, and it would have been possible to keep him at arm's length if he had not found an ally in Admiral Seymour. Bowring, wrote

Elgin, was on his knees to Seymour, 'only too glad that a man so respectable should take up his cause and work it out for him.' The two men had worked together smoothly in the troubles over the *Arrow* the previous autumn. They both knew that they had then failed to produce the right result, and that their professional reputations had suffered thereby. It was not surprising that they should form common front in favour of renewed toughness towards Canton. The first brush came at the end of November, when Seymour told Elgin that he proposed to re-establish a post on Honan Island, in the Canton river opposite the city of Canton, from which he had withdrawn nine months before. He argued that this would make his blockade more effective and would be a useful preliminary to an operation against Canton. Elgin disagreed, holding that before the allies made any change in the existing military situation they must give Yeh a chance to come to terms. Seymour argued, but in vain, and his proposal was dropped. As planning proceeded it became clear that to Seymour and Bowring the capture of Canton was an end in itself, and they did not particularly care how it was achieved or what happened afterwards. Seymour put forward a plan for landings and the scaling of the city walls which would almost certainly have meant heavy casualties on both sides and destruction of much property unless the Chinese immediately surrendered. To Elgin on the other hand the capture of Canton was only the first step to coming to satisfactory terms. If Yeh refused to make concessions the city must be taken with the least possible loss of life and property. It must then be held and conscientiously administered until the Government of Peking signed a new treaty.

In this opinion he was powerfully strengthened by Baron Gros. The Frenchman had many worries. As the shiploads of British marines began to appear in Hong Kong harbour he was worried that the French, with a useful naval force but no troops, would have too small a part in the forthcoming operation. He was probably aware of the general feeling in Hong Kong against co-operation with the French, illustrated in a letter from a Dr. Watson, formerly of Canton, to a friend in England which found its way into the archives of the Foreign Office. 'It is said the French are to have a hand in the pie, the more is the pity. Such a thing ought not to have been permitted and every man in China says the same thing. It will ruin us in the eyes of the Chinese. . . . They may do little but they will take all the honor and glory, mark my words.' Gros was also worried that despite the blockade Seymour had gathered little sure intelligence about the back waterways of Canton and the forces on which Yeh could rely. But above all he was afraid that Elgin would give in to the powerful British voices urging a swift and savage commando raid on Canton, undertaken without prior warning, and achieving almost certainly only adverse political results. After several talks with Elgin, Gros wrote a paper ably arguing the case for moderation. Gros and Elgin had the power to make their views prevail and despite much grumbling Gros's paper became the basis of allied action.

Canning had felt unable to let Elgin have any of his troops back from India, but by the beginning of December the three promised shiploads of marines had reached Hong Kong from England, and Elgin and Gros were advised that the allied force was now strong enough to attack Canton if need be. The two men began drafting their letters to Yeh. Elgin was uneasily conscious that the French had in the murder of Abbé Chapdelaine a better immediate cause for war than the British, and he said as little about the *Arrow* in his letter as he could contrive. 'My difficulties are of course much enhanced,' he wrote, 'by the wretchedness of the lorcha case on which our quarrel began and the utter want of judgment evinced by the whole party, Sir John Bowring, Seymour and Parkes in the proceedings last year.' Elgin's letter to Yeh of December 12th, 1857, reads well. He praised the benefits which both sides had received from the Treaty of 1842 in all the ports open to trade except

Canton: 'Commerce has presented itself with all its accustomed attendants, national wealth and international goodwill.' Unfortunately at Canton the treaty had not been observed, and Britain, France and America had all at different times been forced to seek satisfaction for repeated insults and wantonly inflicted wrongs. Finally Yeh had refused to grant reparation for or even to discuss an insult to the British flag, and a contest had thus begun which had been waged on the Chinese side with inhumanity and contempt for the rules of warfare. The season for mere remonstrance was now past. Elgin made only two demands: the complete execution at Canton of all Treaty engagements, including the free admission of British subjects to the city; and the compensation for British losses incurred in the late disturbances. If Yeh accepted these demands and those made by the French within ten days, the blockade would be raised, though the British and French would hold a number of forts on the river until a Treaty had been agreed 'for regulating these and all other questions pending' between the two Governments.

Elgin thought these requests were moderate. In particular he had forborne to ask for an apology for the seizure of the crew of the *Arrow*, on which Bowring had insisted in vain a year earlier. He wrote to General Charles Grey: 'I made mild proposals to Yeh with the conviction that if they had been accepted I should have been torn in pieces by all who were ravening for vengeance or loot. But Yeh was my fast friend . . . nothing would induce him to be saved.' There were certainly those in Hong Kong who distrusted Elgin for his moderation. They had found a spokesman in the newly arrived special correspondent of *The Times*, Wingrove Cooke. Wingrove Cooke wrote a book about the campaign, in which the prose style is as lavish as the criticisms of British policy. He was afraid that Elgin would ask for too little: 'The English people,' he wrote, 'should teach a starling to cry "Free transit through China" and should hang the bird in Lord Elgin's cabin. Nothing short of this will do; nothing short of this will prevent future wars.' In fact Elgin merely put to Yeh the two demands which arose directly from the local situation at Canton, reserving the right to make other requests when the time came to negotiate a new Treaty; but 'free transit through China' went far beyond what he could hope to secure.

IO

The British and French ultimatum can hardly have taken Yeh by surprise. He was excellently informed by his spies of what happened in Hong Kong and must have known of the arrival of British reinforcements and the drawing together of the British and French. Yet he took no particular precautions. He had other worries to fill his mind, for large parts of his two provinces were overrun by the Taiping rebels. But the Cantonese thought it strange that their Viceroy was so inactive and yet so confident, and some thought that he was in Elgin's pay. A lampoon appeared, in parody of the usual poem in praise of an outgoing governor:

> Neither fighting battle nor making peace,
> Giving no defence yet unwilling to die,
> Neither surrendering nor fleeing,
> In the stature of a Grand Secretary,
> In the aspirations of a Viceroy,
> The past has had none like him,
> They are at present rare.[1]

Yeh was fat, and it was still hot; he was superstitious, and his favourite oracle was optimistic. But the main reason for his sloth was probably that the tactic of sitting tight had worked before. Yeh had kept Bowring in check for a year not by any particular act of boldness, but simply by not allowing himself to be scared. It was known that the bar-

[1] The poem and other information comes from the memoirs of Hsieh Fu-ch'eng (1887). (*Harvard Journal of Asiatic Studies* 1941, vol. 6, p. 37.)

barians had ships which could defeat any junks which the Imperial Government could send against them. But they never ventured far from their ships, and their capacity for fighting on land was doubted. They had not taken Canton in the past and Yeh was confident that they would not take it now. Yeh was the successful expert on barbarian affairs and the doubts which others are known to have felt in Peking were not allowed to prevail over his judgment.

Yeh's reply to Elgin was brisk and negative. He argued that Sir George Bonham had eight years before finally abandoned the British claim to the right of entry to Canton. As a result the Queen had given him the Order of the Bath, and Elgin would do well to follow his example. In the case of the *Arrow*, Parkes, not the Chinese, had been at fault. As for a new Treaty, he argued ingeniously that the last Emperor had decreed that the Treaty of 1842 was to last for ten thousand years, and no Chinese official would dare to discuss its revision. He knew of Elgin's high reputation, and was sure that his letter had been the result of bad advice from those around him.

Yeh's reply to Gros was equally firm, and the attack on Canton became inevitable. On December 15th the British and French fleets moved up river and posts were established on Honan Island opposite Canton. To their surprise the allies found that nothing had been done to bar their way or to strengthen the fortifications of the city. The Canton river-front was still desolate from the fire which had destroyed the foreign factories a year earlier. The only sign of alarm was the melting away of the hundreds of junks and sampans which were normally moored along the bank and provided, then as now, homes for many thousands of Canton's inhabitants.

Elgin moved up river on the *Furious* on December 17th. Four days later he and Gros held a conference with the British and French Admirals and the British General, and formally entrusted to them the task of taking Canton. From then on he and Gros had no authority to interfere with the actual conduct of operations, but Elgin decided to stay at the scene of action in the hope of keeping down the loss of life and resuming control from the military at the first possible moment. To his diary, written for his wife's eye only, he entrusted his unhappiness at what was to come. He wrote bitterly of earning himself a place in the Litany after 'plague, pestilence and famine,' and of spending Christmas Day 'anchored within two miles of a great city doomed, I fear, to destruction from the folly of its own rulers and the vanity and levity of ours.'

Elgin in fact over-estimated the will of the Chinese to resist, and therefore the casualties and damage likely to be caused. The strength of Canton lay in its six-mile circumference of wall which enclosed the city (apart from suburbs) even on the river side and measured 25 foot high and 20 foot wide. The garrison numbered about 30,000 men of whom a proportion were Manchu troops likely to show particular loyalty to the Emperor's cause. The garrison had fortified several temples and other points in the cemeteries and small villages outside the city, in particular on a knoll called Magazine Hill about two miles from the river, not far from the north-east corner of the city wall. Two positions in this area, known to the British as Gough's Fort and Marines' Fort, contained more than twenty pieces of miscellaneous artillery.

Against these forces the allies could bring fewer than 6,000 men, made up as follows:

British and Indian troops	800
British marines	2,100
British naval brigade drawn from naval crews	1,829
French naval brigade	950
	5,679

At first sight the capture of a very large fortified city held by a garrison five times its own size would have seemed a hard task for the allied force. But the attackers had one overwhelming advantage; the city and the whole scene of operations lay under the guns of the British and French warships anchored in the Canton river and the allied batteries now established on Dutch Folly and other nearby islands. The range and power of those guns far outweighed the artillery mounted on the walls of Canton or drawn up on Magazine Hill, and left no doubt about the outcome. Yeh might have held Canton if he had concentrated on harassing the warships from the time they entered the river, with booms or fireships or intelligent fire from coastal forts. But he made no effort to prevent the fleet reaching its position opposite the city and throughout the engagement itself the Chinese artillery on the walls fired only two shots against the ships. His other hope would have been to incite the people of Canton and its suburbs against the attackers. A fleet cannot occupy a city, and 6,000 men are too few to hold down a million and a half hostile and determined civilians. In fact the allies found a patchy reception: some districts were hostile, some friendly, most unconcerned. The coolies recruited in Hong Kong to serve the allied force carried out their orders efficiently under the fire of their compatriots.

The original ultimatum to Yeh expired on December 22nd. On Christmas Eve he was given another forty-eight hours to hand over Canton. On the evening of the 27th reconnaissance parties were put ashore about a mile east of the city wall. In the early morning of the 28th the naval bombardment of the walls and nearby forts began, and at about the same time the main force of British and French landed. Their task on the 28th was to capture a position called Lin's Fort, which lay about a mile inland among the scattered graveyards to the east of the city, and held twelve small guns. This was achieved without difficulty and the allies fanned out towards the eastern wall of the city and towards Magazine Hill to the north and bivouacked for the night. They lay in open ground outside the walls and a determined attack that evening by overwhelming Chinese forces might have pushed them back to the river. The naval guns and mortars stopped any such attack from forming. *The Times* correspondent, Wingrove Cooke, waxed apocalyptic as he watched them at work towards daybreak: 'Some minutes elapse and the light strengthens. Then off goes one of the mortars upon Dutch Folly. It is fired upon Gough's Fort. The whistling shell speeds high over the city—just as I have often seen them and heard their plaintive whistle over the heights of Tchernaya or from the earthworks on the north of Sebastopol harbour. It does not reach its object. At its highest elevation—far far away—it puffs forth in a thin white cloud. I can now see the dark fragments falling, and in the cold cloudless morning sky that little cloudlet hangs

<blockquote>
As tho' an angel in his upward flight
Had left his mantle floating in mid air.
</blockquote>

Strange fancies seize us in these highly wrought moments —the angel of mercy has fled from the doomed city. Slow and continuous with a sombre monotony, like the firing of minute guns, the cannonade continues.'

The Chinese seem to have assumed that the allies would try to take Magazine Hill before they ventured against the wall of the city. But at dawn on the morning of December 29th the allied force which had landed the day before moved against the east wall. It had been arranged that the naval guns should stop firing at 9 a.m., but by a miscalculation the allied troops reached the wall half an hour earlier and were exposed for that time to the fire of their own guns. It was the only major hitch in what was otherwise a well executed operation. There was also heavy Chinese fire from the walls and from Magazine Hill; one ball killed Captain Bate of the *Actaeon* as he was looking for a lodging-place on the wall for the scaling ladders. The French were first up the wall shortly after 9 a.m. Little resistance was met on the wall; the Chinese had concentrated too high a proportion of the garrison outside the wall on Magazine Hill. By the end of the afternoon the whole wall and the forts on Magazine Hill had been taken, and resistance was petering out. From the wall the allied troops looked down from all four sides on the city of Canton, on which a great and apprehensive silence had fallen. The invincible city had been won.

British casualties were 8 killed and 71 wounded, French 2 killed and 30 wounded. The Chinese official list of casualties amounted to 450, in addition to which perhaps 200 civilians were killed by the naval bombardment.

During the next few days the allied troops established themselves in pouring rain along the wall but made no attempt to penetrate the city which they now dominated. The Chinese showed no further wish to fight. Yeh was said to be still in the city, but remained silent. His immediate subordinate, Pih-Kuei,[1] allowed it to be known that he and the leading gentry had been opposed to Yeh's policies. Elgin paid a visit ashore on New Year's Day 1858 and came back convinced that a further decision about the running of the city was urgent. Despite orders to the contrary the allied forces were beginning to loot. Oliphant noticed that the French were more skilful at this: 'While honest Jack was flourishing down the street with a broad grin of triumph on his face, a bowl of goldfish under one arm and a cage of canary-birds under the other, honest Jean, with a demure countenance and no external display was conveying his well-lined pockets to the waterside.' On a more serious scale were the outbreaks of pillaging by bands of Chinese. Within a few days the city might dissolve into anarchy. The first thing was to get hold of the three Chinese who had hitherto run Canton; on January 5th allied patrols entered the city and succeeded in capturing Yeh, Pih-Kwei and the Manchu commander-in-chief. Yeh's headquarters

---

[1] Yeh was Viceroy of the two Kwangs, i.e. the provinces of Kwangtung and Kwangsi. Under him Pih-Kuei was Governor of Kwangtung, the province of which Canton is the capital.

were hard to identify in the maze of drab one-storey streets. When they reached it the patrol found a confused bustle of officials trying to pack their luggage and escape. One of these selflessly gave himself up, claiming to be Yeh, but Parkes, who was with the patrol, judged that he was not fat enough, and the real Viceroy was soon discovered looking wistfully at a wall at the back of the compound. Yeh seemed assured and loud-voiced, but had nothing particular to say; he was kept in custody aboard the *Inflexible*.

The same day and the day following Elgin and Gros discussed the future of Canton with their commanders. All agreed that the city must be held until a new Treaty was signed. All agreed also that meanwhile the allies must rely on the existing Chinese authorities to run the city. They had with them only three men who spoke competent Chinese —Parkes, Wade and the French Captain Martineau. It was inconceivable that any kind of military administration could be set up on this foundation or maintained with the troops which could be spared from future operations. Pih-Kuei was the obvious man for the allies to rely on. The military commanders suggested that he should simply be told to get on with the job of governing the city, without any particular allied co-operation. Elgin, who was fast losing patience with his Admiral and General, argued that more was needed, and in the end he and Gros insisted on their solution. This was that Pih-Kuei should be formally installed by the allies as governor of the city, and that he should be helped at his headquarters by a tribunal of three allied officers. These should have power to try any cases in which a foreigner was involved, and to approve in advance all proclamations which Pih-Kuei might wish to issue. Pih-Kuei accepted this scheme and was installed at a ceremony on January 9th which was somewhat marred by the failure of the allied officer responsible to release the new governor in good time, so that through no fault of his own he kept Elgin and Gros waiting.

The members of the allied tribunal were Parkes, Colonel

Holloway of the Marines and Captain Martineau. Elgin cannot have been happy at appointing Parkes, whom he held partly responsible for the wrong handling of the *Arrow* question, and described in his diary at this time as 'clever but exceedingly overbearing in his manner to the Chinese.' For his part Parkes had resented Elgin's obvious distrust of the men on the spot, and wrote to a relative: 'Lord Elgin I do not consider a great man. He may be a man that suits the Government well, very cautious, having ever before him Parliament, the world, the public, etc. It is with him "What will these parties say to this or that?" not "What is best suited to the emergency?" ' Despite their poor opinion of each other, Parkes by his energy, courage and knowledge of China and Chinese was indispensable to Elgin as the main allied representative in Canton.

The new system worked well. The allied tribunal awarded severe floggings to a number of allied troops caught looting and so won a name for fairness among the Cantonese. Joint patrols of allied and Chinese police were set up. Pih-Kuei was elderly and polite and hoped for a quiet life. Only once in these early weeks did he resist and that was over the prisons. Gruesome stories were circulating about the state of Yeh's prisons and at the end of January Elgin made an inspection of two of them. He found a collection of beaten, broken convicts, the sick, dying and dead herded wretchedly together. *The Times* correspondent went with him and sent home a purple account. Mr. Gladstone had already made foreign prisons a favourite theme for British indignation. Elgin wrote a stiff letter to Pih-Kuei requesting him to bestir himself and telling him that he had given orders for the setting up of a prison hospital. The old gentleman was outraged at this interference in a domestic Chinese concern; he could hardly have heard of Mr. Gladstone. 'Would Your Excellency,' he wrote to Elgin, 'hold it correct or no, were I, for instance without giving you information, to desire anyone to remove by force British prisoners confined in a British jail? . . . I am not a man greedy of life, and sooner than be thus unreasonably oppressed, I would gladly give my life to the State.' His protest went for nothing and the prison hospital was established in his own compound.

Nevertheless Pih-Kuei's policy of co-operating with the allies quickly brought him two benefits. He asked for and on February 10th obtained the lifting of Admiral Seymour's blockade. The blockade had been illegal, since China was not at war with Britain, and ineffective since goods could travel to the city by the back waterways;[1] but its lifting was welcome in particular to the Chinese merchants of Canton. Pih-Kuei must behind his philosophical calm have wondered how the Emperor would react to the news of his co-operation with the allies. In its oblique way the Government at Peking quickly came to terms with the obvious. A decree was issued at the end of January dismissing Yeh from his position for undefined inefficiency, appointing Huang Ts'un-han in his place, and announcing that until he arrived Pih-Kuei was to take charge.

Although Elgin's arrangements for Canton were a success locally, he soon understood that they were being criticised in Hong Kong and London as too lenient towards the Chinese officials. As usual opinion in Hong Kong was the most virulent. 'I learn from Loch,' Elgin wrote in his diary on January 24th, 'who has just returned from Hong Kong that the thirst for blood is not yet slaked among the meek Christians of that locality.' One of his predecessors, Sir John Davis, wrote advising him to make Canton a heap of blazing ruins. Elgin was firm that 'No human power shall induce me to accept the office of oppressor of the feeble.' *The Times* on February 27th wrote of a 'strange and overweening modesty on the part of the plenipotentiaries' and criticised Elgin for the civilities exchanged with Pih-Kuei at the ceremony of January 9th. Parkes wrote to Hammond at the Foreign Office that the Chinese were misin-

[1] Elgin also heard and believed a story that some British officers took bribes to let ships through. This added to his distrust of Seymour.

terpreting Elgin's leniency. Clarendon came to the same judgment and even delivered a mild rebuke; he was inclined to think, he wrote to Elgin on March 9th, 'that rather too much respect had been paid to that barbarian Yeh and to Pickwick (as he is called here).' As usual Elgin felt bitter at these criticisms and his distrust of his employers deepened. In fact his critics were falling into the common error of willing the end without willing the means. Elgin was not instructed or equipped to conquer China, but to treat with her. Treating with China meant on the way being civil to Chinese, and eventually when they were ready to treat meeting them on the terms of equality which they denied to others. If Elgin had had an army five times the size and a corps of interpreters he could have annexed Canton and would not have had to be polite to 'Pickwick'; but no result could have been further from Lord Clarendon's wishes.

The allies did not know what to do with Yeh. He spent six weeks in the Canton river aboard the *Inflexible*, apparently little moved by his fall or worried by his prospects. But Parkes was told, perhaps by Pih-Kuei, that Yeh's presence in the river unsettled the Cantonese who evidently thought that he might one day return to govern them and that it would be better to hedge their bets. Elgin and Gros decided to move him and arranged to send him to Calcutta. He left China on February 20th, still on the *Inflexible*. Wingrove Cooke had had enough of China, scented a scoop and sailed with him. His despatches to *The Times* on his voyage to India with Yeh make one feel slightly sick. With lavish bad taste he described Yeh as an uncouth and savage criminal, and so filled in for the British middle class the portrait of a monster which Palmerston had sketched so vigorously on the hustings a year before. A few extracts show the authentic tone: 'I have been shut up for many days with the great Chinaman of the present day. Yeh must be hereafter one of the men of Chinese history. . . . A face of dull heavy stolid impassive cruelty.' Yeh did not brush his teeth, wash, or use a handkerchief; he was very seasick. He was quite willing to talk and claimed to have executed 100,000 rebels. The Bishop of Victoria sent him a Bible; Yeh replied that he had already read it and thought it a good book. 'No one can look upon that face without feeling that he is in the presence of an extraordinary man. There is a ferocity about that restless roving eye which almost makes you shrink from it. It is the expression of a fierce and angry but not courageous animal—while the long nails of his dirty fingers are trembling against the table, and his eyes are ranging into every part of the room in search of every face, his pose of dignity is too palpably simulated to inspire respect even if you could forget his deeds. But no one can look upon him with contempt.' Despite all the adjectives, nothing which Wingrove Cooke wrote destroys the impression that Yeh was really rather an unremarkable man.

Yeh was decently received and housed in Calcutta. The Lieutenant-Governor invited him to a ball but he declined firmly on the grounds that he understood that on such occasions the gentlemen spent their time in embracing each other's wives and standing first on one leg and then on another. Despite such occasional flashes of spirit Yeh remained on the whole apathetic and listless. His health gave way and he died after little more than a year of exile. He wrote a poem in Calcutta:[1]

> While my heart is disturbed by
> leaping tigers and the insistent bugles' blast,
> I watch the white-throat blackbirds
> until they disappear with the sunset;
> Only the spring returns as of old,
> Everywhere are cotton flowers red against the wall.

---

[1] *Harvard Journal of Asiatic Studies* 1941, vol. 6, p. 37.

II

THE ALLIES had captured Canton, dethroned Yeh, and salved the wounded pride of the Hong Kong merchants; but they were not much nearer a lasting settlement with the Chinese Government. The four Ambassadors now agreed on a leisurely diplomatic approach to Peking; they would write to the Chinese Government suggesting that negotiations on outstanding matters should begin at the end of March at Shanghai, the most northerly of the five ports at which Europeans were allowed to trade by the Treaties of 1842-4, roughly halfway between Canton and Peking. In a letter of February 11th to the Senior Secretary of State in Peking, Elgin gave his version of the events at Canton, suggested that the Chinese Government should send a negotiator with full powers to Shanghai, and touched briefly on the points which a new Treaty should cover. He reserved the right to take further measures if no negotiator had appeared at Shanghai by the end of March. While waiting for a reply to this message Elgin moved slowly northward, visiting various South China ports on the way, and reached Shanghai in the middle of March. There he stayed for nearly a month.

It was now a year since Palmerston had asked Elgin to go to China. For a year his reading and thinking had been almost entirely of China and of the British in China. This year's experience had deepened his knowledge but had not altered the opinion which he had instinctively formed at the time of the *Arrow* debate. Then he had disapproved of

Sir John Bowring and his works; a year later he was still rejecting the premises from which most of the British in China started, whether they were traders or missionaries. His stay in Shanghai gave him the chance to put his thoughts into public words.

The premise from which most British traders started was that an almost unlimited market for British goods existed in China if only the Chinese Government were persuaded or forced to remove the obstacles which it imposed. The Treaty of Nanking of 1842 had opened four ports to trade as well as Canton and organised a uniform tariff. When these changes failed to lead to a marked increase in British exports the traders were quick to ask for more. Other ports should be opened, perhaps one in every province as suggested to Clarendon by Gregson, their chief spokesman in the House of Commons, in May 1857. Merchants should be free to travel in the interior. Internal taxes levied by the Chinese after the external treaty tariff had been paid should be abolished. Some of the wiser traders such as Dent and Matheson doubted whether all this could be achieved at once. Dent wrote on Gregson's suggestions: 'The Chinese are not at present ripe for most of the stipulations proposed; indeed to enforce them it would be necessary to conquer and take possession of the entire country.' But to most of his colleagues it seemed that what was needed was a simple act of will by the British Government, a short military campaign, a strong new treaty; the Chinese would then remove the obstacles in the way of Western trade, and that huge market would at last begin to yield the fruits of which it was capable. Their stock quotation was from Sir Henry Pottinger, who had signed the Treaty of Nanking and in a euphoric moment of export promotion a little later had said of China 'that all the mills of Lancashire could not make stocking stuff sufficient for one of its provinces.' That was the vision; the reality was that in 1851 British exports to China consisted of £1.5 million only of manufactured goods (one-half of the exports to Holland the same year),

£6 million of opium, and £1.5 million of Indian goods. But the vision did not fade before these facts; the traders waited, impatient for the hour when the British Government would muster the courage to make a thorough job of forcing free trade on China.[1]

It is easy to dismiss the principles of the China traders as simply a cloak for their greed, and the fact that many of them made more money out of opium than from legal trade makes it more difficult to take their protestations seriously. But we must not forget that the genuine idealism of free trade still ran strongly in the 1840s, '50s and '60s. Jardine, Matheson, Dent and the others had a keen nose for profit, but most of them believed that the opening of China to Western trade would benefit above all the Chinese. They saw themselves as doing in China what their immediate predecessors had done in Britain, sweeping away the hampering traditions of the centuries, the ancient restrictive rubbish which prevented the people from achieving prosperity and freedom. It may seem paradoxical, for example, that Bowring who in his early life was identified with almost every orthodox 'left-wing' cause in Britain should in China have followed a strong forward line of the kind now associated with 'right-wing' colonial governors. But the associations of 'left' and 'right' have changed, and Bowring could argue that he **was** continuing his old efforts in another sphere; the disciple of Bentham was true to himself in denouncing the prisons of Canton, the enemy of the Corn Laws in fighting high Chinese tariffs, the critic of the Duke of Wellington in turning his lance against the Viceroy of the two Kwangs.[2]

[1] The vision of a vast Chinese market still convinces some Western traders; but the political restraints of which they now complain are imposed not by the Chinese but by the West.

[2] In his book *The Boxer Uprising* the late Dr. Purcell, describing the situation forty years later, supposes in a polemical moment that the Old China Hands learnt their ideas at their public schools. This would be wide of the mark as a comment on the 'fifties. There was no smack of

By the end of his first year in Chinese affairs Elgin was convinced that the vision of the merchants was unreal. He was much impressed by a five-year-old paper which he found buried in the archives of Hong Kong. In 1852 a Government servant named Mitchell wrote a report on the prospects for trade with China for the then Superintendent of Trade, Sir George Bonham. The report in plain robust language argued that the growth of British exports to China would be slow and difficult, not because of any political restrictions, but simply because British textiles could not effectively compete with native industry. In China 'the loom is to be found in every well-conditioned homestead.' By luck or good management the economy of the north of China was complementary to the economy of the south, so that together they supplied the main wants of the country without need for any quantity of imports. The Chinese would continue to take some British goods because they wanted to sell us tea. Sir Henry Pottinger's rosy prophecy had been contradicted by the failure of British exports to rise significantly after the Treaty which he signed had opened four new ports. 'We have nothing whatever to complain of if we will only view the thing soberly and forget for ever the monster blunder of our first expectations.' This was strong stuff for a civil servant and Sir George Bonham had suppressed the paper. Elgin now unearthed it and sent it to the Foreign Office with an approving despatch. At the end of March 1858 he had a chance to make his views known. The British merchants of Shanghai presented him with an address of welcome, and he replied with a stately speech of warning:

'The expectations held out to British manufacturers at the close of the last war between Great Britain and China,

---

the public school about Bowring or Parkes; it was Elgin, their liberal opponent, who went to Eton. The public schools trained their pupils to govern and defend the British Empire once it existed, but it was largely acquired by men of quite a different stamp.

when they were told that a new world was opened to their trade so vast that all the mills in Lancashire could not make stocking stuff sufficient for one of its provinces, have not been realised; and I am of the opinion that when force and diplomacy have done all that they can legitimately effect, the work which has to be accomplished in China will be but at its commencement. When the barriers which prevent free access to the interior of the country shall have been removed, the Christian civilisation of the West will find itself face to face, not with barbarism, but with an ancient civilisation in many respects effete and imperfect but in others not without claims on our sympathy and respect. In the rivalry which will then ensue Christian civilisation will have its way among a sceptical and ingenious people by making it manifest that a faith which reaches to Heaven furnishes better guarantees for public and private morality than one which does not rise above the earth.

'At the same time the machina-facturing West will be in the presence of a population the most universally and laboriously manufacturing of any on the earth. It can achieve victories in the contest in which it will have to engage only by proving that physical knowledge and mechanical skill, applied to the arts of production, are more than a match for the most persevering efforts of unscientific industry.

'This is the task which is before you and towards the achievement of which, within the sphere of my duty, I shall rejoice to co-operate.'

The phrases were decorous and well-rounded, as became a reply to an address of welcome; but the merchants long remembered, and some resented, his warning that once he had got them a treaty and sailed away they were at the beginning not the end of their task.

His word for the missionaries was much the same. They like the merchants had already in practice overstepped the boundaries set by the Treaties of 1842-4. There were a considerable number of English Protestant missionaries working in the interior of China where the Treaties gave them no protection. It was inevitable that the Chinese authorities should look on them with deep suspicion, not because of their religious beliefs towards which most officials would have been tolerant, but because of their possible connection with the network of rebellious sects and secret societies which lay just below the surface of Chinese life. Suspicion was particularly natural in that the Taiping rebels professed a form of Protestant Christianity. As Consul Alcock wrote at the time of the Abbé Chapdelaine's murder, 'It must be a matter of surprise that a single missionary of the many hundreds in the interior has been left alive, not that one should have been sacrificed.'

The missionaries were asking for a clause in the new treaty giving them freedom to travel in the interior, and guaranteeing toleration for themselves and their converts. The British Government seemed more conscious than the missionaries of the danger that if the converts were given special privileges or protection they would multiply for reasons which had nothing to do with religious faith. Elgin had already found signs of inadequate theological grounding among them; indeed one may feel sorry for the clergyman at Ningpo whom 'I cross-examined about his converts. When pressed he could only name one who seemed conscious of the want which we believe to be supplied by the Atonement.' The Bishop of Victoria (Hong Kong) ran into worse trouble later in the year when he admitted to Elgin that he knew that missionaries had travelled illegally in the interior but begged that the fact that he knew should not be revealed. 'I told him that I had all my life been constantly in the habit of saying disagreeable things to people when it was my duty to do so, and that I could have no sympathy with the anxiety which he expressed on that head.' Elgin showed himself ready to challenge the missionaries as well as the merchants when he replied to their address at Shanghai: 'It is most right and fitting that

Chinamen espousing Christianity should not be persecuted. It is most wrong and most prejudicial to the real interests of the faith that they should be tempted to put on a hypocritical profession in order to secure thereby the advantages of abnormal protection.'

I 2

THE PACE OF EVENTS had slowed since the capture of
Canton at the end of December 1857, and in the following
three months Elgin had time as we have seen to visit the
treaty ports and indulge in stately dispute with merchants
and missionaries. The Chinese reply to his Note of February 10th reached Shanghai at the end of March, and stirred
him again to a rush of activity. The Governor General
and Governor of Kiangsu, the province in which Shanghai
lies, conveyed the bland reply from the Senior Secretary
of State in Peking: 'There being a particular sphere of duty
allotted to every official on the establishment of the Celestial
Empire, and the principle that between them and the foreigner there is no intercourse being one ever religiously
adhered to by servants of our Government of China, it
would not be proper for me to reply in person.' The right
person for Elgin to address was Huang, Yeh's successor
as Viceroy at Canton, and his right course was therefore
to return to Canton and make his representations there.

This reply was in direct breach of the Treaty of Nanking
which gave the British representative in China the right to
correspond with (though not to visit) Chinese officials at
Peking. The Chinese were harking back to the traditional
arrangement by which all diplomatic intercourse with the
barbarians was confined to distant Canton, an arrangement
too convenient to them to be lightly abandoned. Elgin refused to receive the Chinese reply, and prepared urgently
to leave Shanghai for the north.

Elgin was now venturing outside the range of his country's practical experience. Although British missions had reached Peking British troops had never fought in North China and British ships were not familiar with its seas. But the main geographical facts were well known. The imperial capital, Peking, stood well inland, connected by canal and river with the port of Tientsin, which in turn lay 60 miles from the Gulf of Pechihli to which it was joined by the river Peiho. Where the Peiho flowed into the sea, near the little town of Taku, the Chinese had built a number of forts. These Taku forts were protected by a bar some five miles out to sea, over which only boats of shallow draught could pass. The waterway from Taku to Tientsin by river and then from Tientsin to the neighbourhood of Peking by canal was much used in the spring by junks carrying rice as tribute from the south to the capital, the traditional route by the inland Grand Canal having been cut by the Taiping rebellion.

Knowing these elementary facts Elgin planned to bring pressure on the capital by concentrating the Anglo-French naval force in the Gulf of Pechihli, stopping the onward passage of the junks bearing the tribute rice, and if necessary moving swiftly up the river to Tientsin. In making his plans he relied greatly on the practical advice of the Russian envoy Count Poutiatine, who knew North China well. Poutiatine had stressed two points, one exaggerated, the other well founded. He said that it would be impossible to continue useful operations in North China after the end of May because of the great heat. This was wrong, as anyone who has lived in Peking or Tientsin can testify, and as the events of 1860 clearly showed; but Elgin was convinced, and much of his anger and anxiety in this spring of 1858 sprang from the belief that nothing could be done in the summer. Poutiatine's second point was that the allies could only bring effective pressure to bear on Peking if they could muster gunboats of a draught shallow enough to cross the bar, enter the Peiho and pass up the river to Tientsin. 'Gunboat diplomacy' is now a cliché but it happens to describe aptly the kind of operation in which Elgin was engaged; only gunboats could carry him to the point (Tientsin) where diplomacy could bring the Chinese Empire to recognise the Western nations as equals, in practice and theory.

Having listened to Poutiatine, Elgin did his best to make sure that gunboats would be in the north when wanted. At the beginning of March he asked Seymour to collect at Shanghai 'towards the end of March, or as soon after as may be convenient, as large a fleet, more especially of gunboats drawing little water, as can be spared from service elsewhere.' Seymour replied at once, saying that he had already planned to meet this need, and adding that he himself proposed to sail to Shanghai from Hong Kong on his flagship *Calcutta* on or about March 16th. The Admiral implied that Elgin should not fuss; and yet by the time specified, the end of March, there was no Admiral and (what was worse) only one gunboat, the *Slaney*, at Shanghai. There followed for Elgin six weeks of intense frustration during which his mood deepened from disappointment to fury at the failure of the Admiral to support him. His official feelings were expressed in a series of despatches to the Foreign Office; privately he poured out his anger in his diary. Taken by themselves the entries in his diary suggest that for a time his bad temper upset his judgment and pushed him near to breaking point; but the diary was probably a safety valve and in public he seems to have remained calm and magisterial.

Elgin decided not to wait at Shanghai for Seymour or the gunboats. He ordered the senior naval commander Captain Sir F. Nicolson to sail with him to the Gulf of Pechihli with the three ships on the station. He left Shanghai on April 10th, and the French, Russian and American Ambassadors went with him. The next day he wrote in his diary: 'I requested *officially* and he promised *officially* to send up here all the gunboats drawing little water (so I phrased it) which he could spare. He sends only one or two and instead of sailing on the 16th from Hong Kong as he also promised to do, puts off his departure without giving any reason for it, to the 25th. The truth is that being a man of but small intellect he is very unmanageable when he gets an idea into his head, and apt to fall into the hands of people about him.'

Worse, much worse, was to come. By April 14th the *Furious* with Elgin on board was anchored in the Gulf of Pechihli, outside the bar which protected the forts and the mouth of the river at Taku. On a clear day they could just see the forts, but the days were rarely clear. 'Nothing could be more dreary than the scene,' wrote Oliphant. 'It was dreadful to contemplate the prospect of remaining at anchor in so forlorn a spot. Not a sign of land broke the monotony of the dim hazy horizon. The turbid waters were lashed into foam by gales which spun round to every point on the compass with incredible velocity, and kept the gulf in the condition of a caldron of boiling soup.' Not far away the Secretary of the American Ambassador, Wells Williams, was equally depressed on board the steamer *Mississippi*. 'Wind blows incontinently from all quarters, lulling and swelling to gusts in the most capricious manner . . . in many respects we have come to a lawless outlandish part of the globe. . . . This shallow water is a better defence to Peking than all the forts and troops in the country.'[1]

Elgin might just as well have waited in Shanghai. He had only one boat, the *Slaney*, which could cross the bar (on which there was 11 foot of water at a high spring tide) and so could neither put pressure on the forts nor intercept the junks full of tribute rice which sailed light-heartedly within full view of his tiny force. Seymour arrived on April 24th on his flagship the *Calcutta*. This hardly improved matters, for the *Calcutta* drew 25 foot of water and Seymour brought with him only one ship capable of crossing the bar. In despatches to Clarendon of the 23rd and 29th April Elgin rehearsed his grievance. If he had had ten or twelve gunboats with him by mid-April as he had expected, he might

[1] *Journal of N. China Branch of Royal Asiatic Society*, vol. XLII, 1911.

well have been able to move swiftly and without fighting up the river to Tientsin to negotiate, thus cutting off the tribute junks. Seymour had never warned him that the promised gunboats would be late, and even now produced no reason for the delay. 'It is therefore with a degree of surprise which I have difficulty in describing that I learn from the information which he has now for the first time furnished to me that his arrangements are so made that the very inadequate force which he is about to supply will not arrive here until the approach of the season when the climate is more unfavourable to the European constitution.' Elgin wrote in the heavy measured prose of his generation, but behind the formality appears the angry man, tossing for weeks uselessly and uncomfortably on a godforsaken sea.

In his diary the words are shorter and the phrases sharper. 'Nothing to do except meditate on the folly of this charming colleague my admiral. . . . He must be in his dotage. It is a stupidity beyond anything I have ever met with in my public career. . . . He does not seem even to read what is written to him.' And on April 29th: 'My letter goes today and carries many loves to you and the children. It leaves me in the most humiliating position in which I have ever found myself during my public career. The Flag of France is at the moment represented by two gunboats within the bar of the Peiho river, that of England by two despatch boats aground on top of it. I have a perfect driveller for an admiral, a general not much better, a sot for a commodore, and an old woman for the second in command up here (Sir F. Nicolson). Gros has a very small force but he has a man with a head to command it and he will beat us all. . . . I cannot write; I am like a person in a bad dream.'

Elgin thought that his chances of making a settlement were slipping away with the spring, and that he would have to go home with the job undone or spend another year in China. Either prospect was intolerable, and in his anger he came to believe that Seymour, egged on by Bowring, was deliberately frustrating his plans. The truth was simpler:

the Admiral thought and acted slowly. The gunboats for which Elgin was impatient were not lying inactive at Hong Kong. They were bustling up and down the Canton river, keeping open the line of communication with the garrison in the city, and also with the minor treaty ports between Hong Kong and Shanghai. They had to be detached from these duties and some of them overhauled before they were fit for service in the north. They then had to beat up the coast against the winds of the monsoon; Seymour wrote five months later: 'It is utterly impossible to move a force of gunboats up a stormy coast with the precision of a railway train; and though his Lordship makes so light of the monsoon and suggests towing the gunboats up the coast by paddle steamers . . . my arrangements for getting the gunboats up to the north were made with the view to see them arrive in an efficient state, and not torn to pieces by being towed against a head sea, an object which I fully accomplished by causing them to coast the shores and anchor in bad weather.' Gradually in late April and early May one by one the precious boats appeared through the murky sandstorms of the Gulf of Pechihli and were pushed forward over the bar. But it was too late to prevent the breach between High Commissioner and Admiral; the two men sat in their ships, separated by a mile or so of water, rarely meeting or corresponding, active only in the penning of stately remonstrances to their departments in distant Whitehall.

Elgin's worries at this time were increased by the news that Palmerston's Government had fallen two months earlier. A man named Orsini had thrown a bomb at Napoleon III. The French Government asked the British to control the activities of alien refugees in Britain. The Government introduced a Bill in the House of Commons; the Conservatives accused the Prime Minister of truckling to the Emperor, and mustered enough support to defeat the Bill; the Government resigned and Lord Derby took office. The Conservatives had strongly attacked the China War; they were now saddled with the handling of it, and no one knew what they would do. Clarendon, rid of office at last, wrote a cheerful letter to Elgin which can hardly have raised his spirits:

'I have not the remotest idea how our successors mean to deal with the China question upon which they have committed themselves so violently and with so little foresight and sense of national dignity, but now that they have got Yeh on board the *Inflexible* they will be able to apologise to him more conveniently for our rudeness, and they might send him one of the vacant Garters with a letter explanatory of it not being necessary for him to hang himself with it. . . . Goodbye my dear Elgin. I hope it will not be long before you return home in triumph and in health.' Elgin had never felt any enthusiasm for the outgoing Government, and believed that they had foisted the Chinese mission on him for electoral reasons and had then failed to support him fully in Parliament and the Press. He was bitter now about the criticisms at home of his leniency towards Canton which were beginning to reach his ears. But it was hard to be faced at this the toughest moment of his mission with the news of a change of Government and the strong chance that a despatch radically altering his instructions might already be on its way to him from the new Foreign Secretary, Lord Malmesbury.

13

ALL FOUR representatives had by now made contact with the shore. The British and French were in a different category from the Russians and Americans because they had a more serious dispute with China and the military means to settle it. The Americans and Russians were in effect there as interested observers, ready to lend their good offices in negotiations and to profit from any concessions which the Chinese might make to the two Ambassadors who had the gunboats. Elgin did not hope for any concessions at Taku, mainly because the gunboats were lacking; there was no reason why the Chinese should agree to negotiate seriously at Taku when they had refused at Shanghai a month earlier. Since however he and Gros were for the time being prevented from moving up the river to Tientsin, where hopes for a negotiation would be much better, they decided to use the time by another test of the Chinese attitude. On April 24th Elgin sent a letter ashore offering to negotiate with any 'Minister duly authorised by the Emperor of China' who might appear at Taku within six days. Within four he had a reply from T'au, the Governor General of the province of Chihli saying that he was authorised to negotiate. Someone noticed that in this letter and the corresponding one to Gros the character representing the Emperor of China was in accordance with Chinese tradition raised above the characters representing the Queen of England and the Emperor of the French. This was the kind of scholastic point which bedevilled China's relations with the West. The Chinese had recognised by the Treaties of 1842-4 the sovereign equality of the nations of the West, but in their day-to-day business the old assumptions of superiority persisted. T'au had to rewrite his letters, but a greater difficulty then appeared in them. T'au wrote that he was authorised to receive the ambassadors, to report to the Throne, and to request instructions as to the steps to be taken. He had thus no powers to conclude a Treaty. After careful thought Elgin and Gros decided that this would not do. Bowring and the American McLane had tried to do business at Taku in 1854 with Commissioners with similar powers and had been sent empty away. Unless the Chinese negotiator was known in advance to have authority to conclude, he would spin out negotiations indefinitely by referring every point to Peking.

It was now the end of April. According to the advice of the Russians, only a month remained before the onset of summer made it impossible for Europeans to operate in North China. The allied fleets had been considerably reinforced in the last week. Elgin and Gros decided not to be drawn into further correspondence with T'au at Taku. Elgin invited Gros and the British and French Admirals to a conference on the *Furious* on May 1st. The allied fleet expected immediate orders to attack the forts. 'Excited midshipmen, staggering under blankets, canteens and haversacks, rushed frantically about the deck; the landing parties had their rations served out and were told off; the paddle-box boats were lowered, and the guns put in them; and all were on the tiptoe of expectation until the afternoon, when it began to be whispered that a change had taken place in the views of the naval commander-in-chief, and that an attack on the forts was indefinitely postponed.' The Ambassadors were as baffled as the midshipmen; the two admirals, Rigault de Genouilly and Seymour had told them flatly that they had insufficient ships to attack the forts, that they had not had time to reconnoitre, and that they must wait for more gunboats whose date of arrival was uncertain. Another bad-tempered fortnight passed. Elgin and Seymour had a confused correspondence about what could be done, Elgin insisting that he must be able to negotiate from Tientsin, Seymour pleading that even if he could take the Taku forts he could not guarantee to take Tientsin, and proposing as an alternative means of pressure a blockade of the Yangtze-Kiang. At weekly intervals Elgin despatched salvoes to Lord Malmesbury detailing the Admiral's defects and omissions. They would find a place in any anthology of inter-departmental strife. Of Seymour's refusal to go up to Tientsin, 'I feel it my duty to state to your Lordship in the most distinct and emphatic terms that in my belief this decision, coupled with Admiral Seymour's omission to send up the Gun Boats at the time originally agreed on between us, has deprived the Allied Powers of an opportunity for placing the Western Nations and China upon an improved footing, which may very probably never again present itself under conditions equally promising.' Seymour did not know of these savage complaints until the Admiralty enquired politely after the facts in a letter which he received four months later.

As the admirals refused to act Elgin and Gros felt bound to keep up some semblance of activity by continuing their correspondence with T'au. They wrote reminding him that in 1842 the Emperor had given Ch'i Ying full powers to conclude a Treaty; why could he not do the same for T'au? This was a bad argument, for it soon appeared that Ch'i Ying had misled the British about his powers in 1842 and that he had had no more authority than T'au now possessed. The Russians and Americans accepted T'au's powers and tried to mediate between him and the British and French. The Russian Count Poutiatine, who seems to have impressed favourably almost all who met him, was at one time hopeful of success. T'au was inclined to agree to a declaration of toleration for Christians, to the opening of new treaty ports, and to the payment of compensation for the foreign fac-

146

tories destroyed at Canton in December 1856. Gros was tempted by these terms; but the rub was the allied demand that Western diplomats should be allowed to live at Peking. T'au referred this to the Emperor, and the Emperor refused. This was and remained the most difficult point for the Chinese; to grant it meant a revolution of thought, a visible recognition of the equality of other powers. According to a story which the French reported to the Quai d'Orsay, Poutiatine urged the Chinese to give in and so save innocent lives; the Chinese official smiled and said: 'They are only Chinese lives.'

Diplomacy was exhausted, and the Admirals were finally satisfied of their power. By the third week of May sixteen British and ten French warships were gathered in the Gulf of Pechihli, a large part of them gunboats able to cross the bar and sail up the river. On May 19th the Admirals agreed to attack the Taku forts. So ended five weeks of inactive frustration. The American Ambassador and his secretary had not wasted their time. 'During the evening I had a conversation with Mr. Reed respecting the principles of Romish and Protestant Missions and the impossibility of the former ever elevating a heathen people as long as they refused to give them the Scriptures and teach them to live by faith and not by good works.' The British were less profitably employed: 'We had been hot and hopeful, cold and despondent, shrouded in fogs, beset with doubts, choked with sand and disgust, tempest and passion-tossed, becalmed and torpid. We became wonderfully expert at games with rope quoits, and profoundly indifferent to sublunary affairs generally. News of the change of ministry at home, which arrived about this time, did not create nearly so much sensation as a present of fresh fish, for we were reduced to living on potted meats.'

During their five weeks of impotence outside the bar of the Peiho the allies had watched the Chinese fortify and reinforce the forts at the mouth of the river. Earthworks, sandbag batteries and parapets had been erected on both sides along a mile of the banks. Eighty-seven guns were visible and the whole shore had been piled to oppose a landing. Fifty more guns had been installed farther up the river, and several entrenched camps were to be seen in the rear, full of troops arriving from Peking. These defences looked formidable, but they collapsed even more suddenly than the defences of Canton. At 10 a.m. on May 20th, the Chinese not having replied to a request to hand over their positions, six gunboats (four French and two British) were detailed to silence the forts on either side of the entrance by engaging them at close range. Led by the *Cormorant*, which smashed through a barrier of bamboo, the gunboats entered the river. Heavy fire was exchanged for an hour and a quarter. The Chinese held to their guns well, but these were neither accurate nor powerful enough, and most of their shot passed through the rigging of the gunboats. The range was about 400 yards. When the Chinese fire slackened the main allied force, led by the two admirals, passed up the channel and put ashore landing parties above the forts. There was little further fighting; the Chinese artillerymen were not prepared for attack from the rear and the troops who should have protected them immediately retreated. By the end of the day the whole position and the village of Taku were in allied hands. The only riposte made by the Chinese was to send down river a string of junks filled with burning straw, which grounded before they reached the allied ships. The British casualties were 5 killed and 17 wounded. The French were heavier, six killed and 61 wounded, largely because of the unlucky explosion of a Chinese magazine in one of the forts which they occupied.

The ease with which the Peiho was forced surprised the allies. In his despatches Admiral Seymour argued speciously that the previous delay had given an added advantage to the allies, since they had now soundly defeated a substantial Chinese force whereas if they had attacked a month earlier the victory would have been easy and negligible. There was a corresponding disadvantage; the walk-over on May 20th 1858 bred over-confidence among the allies and led to disaster a year later.

Three days later the two admirals started up the river to Tientsin with a force of eight gunboats. The Ambassadors took their advice and stayed at Taku until the way forward was clear. In fact there was no further opposition. The lower reaches of the river were crowded with hundreds of junks which had been penned in by the presence of the allied fleet outside the river, and the traffic jam thus created reminded Oliphant of Temple Bar on a wet day. The Peiho is a formidably winding river which had never before been navigated, let alone charted, by European ships. The channel was so tortuous that the larger gunboats sometimes ran aground and had to be towed off. The danger from fire-boats was great, and the sailors burnt the stacks of straw which they found along the banks of the river in case it should be used for this purpose. In spite of this they had a cheerful reception from the mud villages along the river, most of whose inhabitants believed that a new foreign dynasty was being established and the Manchus chased out. On the 26th the gunboats reached Tientsin and the Admirals were greeted by a deputation of gentry and merchants anxious to trade and believing that the gunboats must be full of cottons and woollens, if not opium. Of the Chinese authorities there was no sign. Four days later Elgin came up from Taku, and was moved in his diary to a slightly stilted eloquence.

'Through the night watches, when no Chinaman moves, when the junks cast anchor, we laboured on, cutting ruthlessly and recklessly through that glancing and startled river which, until the last few weeks, no stranger keel had ever furrowed. Whose work are we engaged in, when we burst thus with hideous violence and brutal energy into these darkest and most mysterious recesses of the traditions of the past? I wish I could answer that question in a manner satisfactory to myself. At the same time there is certainly not much to regret in the old civilisation which we are thus scattering to the winds. A dense population, timorous and pauperised, such would seem to be its chief product.'

14

ON THE BANK of the river at Tientsin stood a temple to which the Emperor Ch'ien Lung had given the name of Supreme Felicity. The authorities of the city handed it over to Elgin, de Gros and their followers and in it they lodged for four weeks, within hailing distance of the line of gunboats anchored beyond their windows. The heat was intense during the day and the British and French covered the courtyard with matting. On weekdays it served as a skittle alley, and on Sundays as a place of worship. The rooms of the temple were likewise temporarily transformed; altars were turned into washstands, and looking-glasses propped against little gods. It was a considerable improvement on the mouth of the Peiho. Ice, meat, and fresh fruit were easy to find, the last indeed too easy for the health of the sailors. Apart from occasional surfeits of this kind the health of the expedition remained good, and the proportion of sick far lower than it had been in the Canton river.

On May 29th an imperial decree named two very senior officials to negotiate with the four Ambassadors who had thus unceremoniously thrust themselves within striking distance of Peking. Kuei Liang was seventy-four, a senior grand secretary, captain-general of the plain white banner of the Manchu contingents and comptroller general of the Board of Punishments; a courteous, experienced and apparently peaceable man. Hua Shana was fifty-three, president of the Board of Civil Office and captain-general of the bordered blue banner of the Chinese contingents; a Mongol who to one observer seemed dissipated, to another strikingly like Oliver Cromwell. It was clear from the choice of these men and the speed with which they travelled to Tientsin that the Chinese Government was reconciled to serious negotiations. The Temple of Oceanic Influences, outside the city to the south-west, was chosen as the meeting-place. On June 4th Elgin travelled there in state for his first meeting with the Commissioners, escorted by one hundred and fifty marines in scarlet and the band of H.M.S. *Calcutta*. The crowds about them, wrote Oliphant, were as thick as on Epsom Downs on Derby Day. At the temple the proceedings were entirely formal. The two sides exchanged their documents of authority, and this time no fault could be found with the powers delegated to the Chinese Commissioners. They lacked however a particular seal of authority; Elgin used this as a pretext for a display of annoyance and left the temple without tasting the food spread on trestle tables for his refreshment, brushing aside the dismayed protests of the Commissioners.

Elgin was not naturally a rude man and this calculated show of bad manners gave him no pleasure. But he had by now been persuaded by those about him that brutal tactics would bring the quickest results. He did not himself meet the Commissioners again until the day the Treaty was signed. Negotiations were in the hands of his brother, Frederick Bruce, and of two brilliant younger men, Wade and Lay. Of the three Lay had the strongest character and it was he who, at the age of 27, was responsible more than anyone else for achieving the Treaty of Tientsin. His tactics were simply those of the bully; when the Chinese stuck at a point or asked for delay or a British concession, Lay shouted and threatened, until the Commissioners saw in their imagination the allied forces marching upon Peking and perhaps this terrible young man lecturing the Emperor as he lectured them. Lay's ferocity was the more remarkable as he was technically in the employ not of the British Government but of the Chinese Customs; it was in fact to his own superiors in the Chinese hierarchy that his threats were addressed.

A pathetic incident showed the lengths to which Lay, with Elgin's support, was prepared to go. On June 9th the British party was astonished to receive an official notification that the aged Chinese statesman Ch'i Ying had arrived in Tientsin and wished to see Elgin. Ch'i Ying had negotiated the Treaty of Nanking with the British in 1842. He had gone out of his way to be friendly to the barbarians and indeed for a short time been the lion of Hong Kong society. He had drunk and eaten and laughed at English tables, and his fame had spread into the London Press. Then he had been recalled, disgraced and by the Western world forgotten. Now he appeared in Tientsin, over seventy, blind and halting, but still in a parody of himself producing the social patter and the little jokes which had once made his name among the ladies of Hong Kong. No one knew whether he had himself proposed this mission or whether his enemies in Peking had forced it on him as a means of compassing his final downfall. Lay was sent to see him; the old man mistook him for his father, wept at the mistake, and in 'a perfect clatter of compliments and moral sentiments' urged that the British withdraw from Tientsin so that the atmosphere for negotiations would be improved. Lay of course gave no ground. The British quickly learned that Ch'i Ying had been officially added to the number of Commissioners, but that he was at odds with his two colleagues. They were told that Ch'i Ying was trying to redress his reputation for appeasement by urging Kuei Liang and Hua Sha-na to take a strong line. They decided that his presence was an unwanted complication and that they must be rid of him. The material was at hand, and Lay was authorised to use it. He called on Kuei Liang and Hua Sha-na, unexpectedly found Ch'i Ying there, and produced his bombshell. Among the papers captured in Yeh's headquarters in Canton six months earlier had been one written by Ch'i Ying in 1850 defending his policy towards the barbarians. In it Ch'i Ying argued that the only way of keeping the British, French and Americans quiet was to humour them in small matters and concede to them the appearance of equality. As an example Ch'i Ying recalled that he had eaten and drunk with the barbarians despite the embarrassment which he suffered from some of their social habits: 'It is the wont of the barbarians to make much of their women . . . when your slave has gone to the barbarian residences on business, their foreign women have suddenly appeared and saluted him. Your slave was confounded and ill at ease, while they on the contrary were greatly delighted at the honour done them. The truth is, as this shows, that it is not possible to regulate the customs of the Western States by the ceremonial of China; and to break out in rebuke, while it would do nothing to remove their stupidity, might give rise to suspicion and ill feeling.' Similarly Ch'i Ying wrote that he had not insisted on giving the Emperor of China the formal prescribed style of superiority in various documents which he had negotiated with the barbarians; nor had he refused to accept small gifts from them. Ch'i Ying's paper was a defence of appeasement and flexibility in small matters. It probably seemed strange at first to Kuei Liang and Hua Sha-na that the British were bringing forward a document so favourable to the barbarians as proof of its author's treachery. To the British of course the document read quite differently. It showed that Ch'i Ying had been insincere, that his professions of friendship and admissions of equality had not marked as they had hoped a real change in China's policy to the outside world, but were simply stratagems, and what was worse successful stratagems, to lull them into quietness and so preserve for a little longer the myth of Chinese superiority which was as axiomatic for Ch'i Ying as for any other Chinese official. The truth is that the British and the rest had been naive in supposing that one campaign and a batch of treaties in the 1840s had been enough to turn the Chinese world upside down. It would have been remarkable indeed if Ch'i Ying with his education and background had really thought Sir Henry Pottinger worthy to sit down at dinner with him, or Queen Victoria entitled to the same honorific titles as his Emperor. His deceptions had been those of a diplomat, small and venial, but they had now caught up with him. Lay handed the incriminating paper to Kuei Liang and Hua Sha-na, and insisted that they prove that they unlike Ch'i Ying were sincere by accepting in writing Elgin's terms for a treaty. Ch'i Ying asked to see the paper and read it by a window apart. That evening he had a meeting with his colleagues and two days later he left for Peking. Before he reached the city he received an order to return to his post at Tientsin. He knew that there was nothing for him at Tientsin but humiliation, and he pressed on to Peking claiming that he had an urgent proposal to make to the Emperor. It was generally supposed that this proposal was war. It found no favour, and Ch'i Ying was thrown into prison and condemned to death for disobeying his orders; 'he treated our commands as a thing to be dispensed with.' Because of his age and past services he was spared a public execution. An imperial decree ordered two officials to go to his prison and 'having desired Ch'i Ying to read this our autograph decree to inform him that it is our will that he put an end to himself, that our extreme desire to be at once just and gracious be made manifest. Respect this!' According to one account Ch'i Ying drank poison; according to another he strangled himself with the silken bow-string provided by the Emperor for such occasions.

The Chinese negotiators now tried to outflank Lay by complaining to the Russian and American Ambassadors of his bullying and intransigence. The American Reed passed the complaint direct to Elgin, and was snubbed for his pains. Poutiatine, who was an excellent diplomat, instead asked Gros, whose personal relations with Elgin were good, if he could put in a tactful word. Gros decided that he could not, although he too disliked what he had heard of Lay's behaviour. As he explained to Paris: 'Ces faits qui m'ont été rapportés confidentiellement par Lord Elgin me semblent regrettables, mon silence le lui a dit assez, mais enfin puisque de si singuliers procédés paraissent réussir auprès des autorités chinoises, j'en viens presque à ne pas oser m'en plaindre.' That indeed was the point; at the same time as the Chinese were complaining about Lay's conduct behind his back, they presented him with a horse saddled and bridled as a mark of their esteem.

As the thermometer climbed steadily each day into the nineties Elgin sat inactive in his temple by the river. Intellectually he had been persuaded, like most men who did business with the Chinese at this time, that tough tactics were necessary and justified. He knew that Lay and Wade under Frederick's supervision were using very tough tactics indeed, and he was determined not to interfere. His demands were not those of a conqueror, he was merely asking that China should treat his country as sovereign states in the Western world were accustomed to treat each other. This was to him a just demand, and it was in the real interests of China as well as Britain that the Chinese Government should be forced as quickly as possible to accept it. So Elgin argued to himself and others. But he was uneasy at what was happening and his uneasiness characteristically took the form of savage private irritation against almost everyone with whom he dealt. Not even during the frustrating weeks afloat off the mouth of the Peiho were the entries in his diary as ferocious as now when the treaty was in his grasp. He was hot against the Russians and Americans for their complaints about Lay: 'These sneaking scoundrels do what they can to thwart me and then while affecting to support the Chinese act as their worst enemies.' Admiral Seymour was not yet forgiven: 'The one piece of strategy to which my admiral is competent is making arrangements for the despatch of letters. To this everything is sacrificed.' His denunciations of the British in Hong Kong were the fiercer because he had now accepted part of their traditional doctrine on the management of the Chinese:

'I did not know what brutes, lying, sanguinary, cheating, oppressive to the weak and crouching before the strong— I did not know I say what they are those smooth-faced countrymen of ours who look at home as if butter would not melt in their mouths.' He was still furious with the late Government of Palmerston for failing to defend his decisions in public: 'Anything more blackguard than the conduct to me of the last Government considering the circumstances under which I consented to come here it would be difficult to imagine.' But he was if anything more angry with their successors. Clarendon at least had known something of China and his letters had always been civil. Lord Malmesbury, the new Tory Foreign Secretary, was only interested in bringing to an end as soon as was possible without disgrace an undertaking which he and his party had opposed, and which tied up at the other end of the world resources which were needed nearer home. How this could be done Lord Malmesbury had no idea, and his letter of April 9th which Elgin received about this time was the type of instruction well known to servants of the Crown in which they are enjoined in general terms to secure the best of all possible worlds:

'A Cabinet has been held today and it is our anxious wish to see this Chinese business settled if it can be done without loss of honour and commercial interests as at present enjoyed. Our reputation is sufficiently vindicated at Canton and we do not look at the chance of a war with the Chinese Empire without much apprehension. I trust therefore that you will not engage us in a contest of this sort if you can possibly avoid it.' The Tories were clearly of one mind with John Bright, who in the House of Commons on June 4th urged 'that they will not, because this legacy is bequeathed them at the Foreign Office, think that they are to array themselves in all the wretched and verminous rags they find there.'

Each of the four Ambassadors at Tientsin was by now negotiating separately with the Chinese, while keeping his

colleagues partly informed of how he was faring. The first
to sign a treaty, on June 13th, was Count Poutiatine of
Russia. His task had indeed been the easiest, as the frontier
problems between China and Russia had been settled in a
separate treaty signed a fortnight earlier on the boundary
by the Governor General of Eastern Siberia and the local
Chinese official. Poutiatine's Treaty was a simple affair.
A Russian envoy might be sent to Peking on special
occasions (but not live there); Christianity was to be
tolerated; the Russians were free to trade at the five existing
Treaty ports and at a port on Formosa and another on
Hainan. The American treaty was signed with toasts of
champagne on June 18th, Reed having for some reason
insisted that the anniversary of Waterloo was the appro-
priate date for the occasion. It was similar to the Russian,
but contained a wider toleration clause. The two neutral
Ambassadors, having secured their countries' minimum re-
quirements as a result of the military pressure of the British
and French, now had greater leisure to besiege the latter
with sage advice. The moderation which they had shown in
their own demands was more apparent than real, for both
the Russian and American treaties included a most favoured
nation clause by which they were to enjoy on an equal
footing any further concessions which China might later
grant to other powers. This meant in effect that Reed and
Poutiatine were free to disapprove of Lay's bullying tactics,
secure in the knowledge that any advantages which Lay
could force from the Chinese would be automatically extended to themselves. To do them justice, both Reed and
Poutiatine realised the shaky moral base on which they
stood. Nevertheless they felt that they should pose what
now seemed the real problem: how far could the British and
French press the Emperor to accept their demands without
fatally undermining his authority over his own subjects?
This was the central problem of China's relations with the
West during the next ten years. It was clearly put forward
in the letter to Elgin and Gros with which Poutiatine sent

them copies of his treaty: 'C'est à votre Excellence de décider maintenant du sort futur du Gouvernement actuel, et il dépendra d'elle de mettre le frein indispensable au flot qui pourrait autrement inonder la Chine nouvellement ouverte et causer bien des désordres. Des concessions trop grandes qu'on exigerait d'un Gouvernement si fortement ébranlé ne ferait que précipiter sa chute, laquelle n'aménerait que de nouvelles et bien plus graves difficultés. C'est le repos qui est nécessaire à la Chine.' The same thought was more clumsily expressed in the diary of Reed's secretary: 'It is a difficult point to attain by foreign envoys not to destroy the prestige of the Emperor's supremacy, when it is almost all the real influence he has over his own subjects and dependencies, and at the same time teach him to say no more about it towards foreign nations.'

The French treaty was the next to be negotiated. The only important point which Gros gained by comparison with the Russians and Americans was that the exchange of ratifications of his treaty should take place in Peking. He did not insist on the right to station a French Ambassador permanently in the capital, nor on the freedom of French merchants to travel in China outside the treaty ports, both proposals having run into strong Chinese opposition. His treaty was ready on June 23rd, but he found himself much embarrassed by his obligations towards Lord Elgin. Unlike the Russians and Americans the French were in this China affair the allies of the British. Gros was throughout a loyal colleague and was not willing to sign his Treaty before Elgin too had reached an agreement. But the British were asking for more than the French, and Gros had no sympathy for Lay's tactics. On June 18th he had reported to the Quai d'Orsay that Elgin was pushing too hard, and asked himself whether if positions were reversed the British would support him as loyally as he was supporting them. Five days later Gros was ready to sign but the British were still bogged down. Gros decided to give Elgin four more days. He announced that he proposed to sign his treaty on the 27th and warned

Elgin that he could not decently delay signature beyond that date. The implication was that the French gunboats and Gros himself would have no business to detain them in Tientsin after the French treaty was signed and that if the British were unreasonable they would have to shift for themselves.

The British negotiations seemed to have succeeded on the 24th when agreement was reached on a text, but the next day all was in the melting pot again. The Chinese negotiators said they could not after all agree to two difficult articles not included in the three other treaties; the first gave the right of residence in Peking (which of course once granted to the British could be claimed by all other nations under the most favoured nation principle), the second the right of traders to travel freely outside the treaty ports. The same day the Chinese showed Reed and Poutiatine what purported to be an imperial decree forbidding them on pain of death to yield these two points, and appealed also to Gros to persuade Elgin not to press them. Elgin must have felt tempted to yield, doubtful as he was of his own Government's backing and of the support which he could expect from the French if he persevered. But he could not get rid of his conviction, with which it is hard to quarrel, that the right to keep an Ambassador in Peking lay at the heart of the whole matter. So long as the Chinese Government could send subordinate officials to treat with the barbarians in some provincial city so long would they regard these same barbarians as inferior. Only when a British Ambassador had access in Peking to the highest authorities of the Empire could political equality be achieved. So strongly did Elgin hold this view that he authorised Bruce on the morning of June 26th to refuse to make the Chinese negotiators any concessions on the two points which they had asked should be re-examined. It was a delicate moment. The only threat at Elgin's command was to break off negotiations and march on Peking. It was an empty threat as he had not nearly enough force to carry it out; unlike the towns which he had already taken, Peking does not lie on a navigable river. If he tried to advance he would probably be deserted by the French as well as by the two neutral Ambassadors; he might very probably be disowned by his own Government. Nevertheless with Admiral Seymour's backing he made the threat and it worked. The Chinese Commissioners withdrew their objections to the text already agreed, and on the evening of June 26th Lord Elgin paid his second and last visit to the Temple of the Oceanic Influences to sign the Treaty of Tientsin, escorted by a naval band and four hundred men. The treaty was signed without incident and the party was entertained by the Chinese with tea and savoury dishes. They returned late to their headquarters and as they reached the river the band on the French flagship greeted them in the dark with 'God Save The Queen.'

The next day the French signed their Treaty. After all his anxieties and embarrassments de Gros could not resist a flourish of satisfaction when announcing the news to Paris: 'Je suis heureux de pouvoir annoncer aujourd'hui à Votre Excellence que la Chine s'ouvre enfin au Christianisme, source réelle de toute civilisation, et au commerce et à l'industrie des nations occidentales.' The British were equally relieved and satisfied. As Oliphant wrote: 'Hostilities with the Empire of China had terminated with a loss to the British arms of about twenty men killed in action . . . and a treaty had been signed far more intensive in its scope, and more subversive of imperial prejudices than that concluded fifteen years before, after a bloody and expensive war, which had been protracted over a period of two years.' Oliphant and most of his contemporaries had no qualms about the tactics which had been used to achieve this result. In Elgin's letters and diary however we find a different strain of thought added to the natural satisfaction. He and his brother Frederick Bruce knew well the kind of private comments being made by the French, Russians and Americans about Lay's bullying and the final British intransigence on June 26th. They were men of a type to feel such criticism; and in this case they resented it bitterly as unfair.

They genuinely believed that what was being asked of China was in the interests of China as well as of the West. It was maddening that the Chinese Government did not see where its own advantage lay, and so forced the British into bullying them into an agreement which would in fact suit both sides well. As Elgin wrote to Malmesbury on July 6th: 'Bruce felt very sensibly the painfulness of the position of a negotiator who has to treat with persons who yield nothing to reason and everything to fear, and who are moreover profoundly ignorant both of the subjects under discussion and of their own real interests.' During the negotiations Elgin wrote in his diary: 'I have an instinct in me which loves righteousness and hates iniquity and all this keeps me in a perpetual boil.' After the treaty was signed he wrote: 'Though I have been forced to act almost brutally I am China's friend in almost all this and I suspect I have put a spoke in the wheels of Russia.'

Elgin had hoped to visit Peking after signing the Treaty to deliver to the Emperor in person a letter of greeting which he carried from Queen Victoria. Regretfully he decided that he could not now go. It would be rash to make the journey after the British and French forces had evacuated Tientsin, and messages now arriving from Canton urged that these forces be released as soon as possible for service in the south. General van Straubenzee had got himself into a mess. The military government of Canton established in January continued to function smoothly but the villages round about had turned hostile and there were more and more attacks on small British and French detachments. Van Straubenzee had obeyed Elgin's order to send the 59th Regiment to Taku in case land operations were needed against Peking; but with it he sent a plaintive appeal for reinforcements and fresh instructions. Elgin had no patience with van Straubenzee for allowing himself to be harassed by handfuls of village braves, but he felt obliged to bring his stay in the north to an end. He and Gros had decided to stay in Tientsin until they heard officially that the Emperor had approved the British and French Treaties. The usual diplomatic game was renewed. The Commissioners produced with smiles of pleasure an imperial decree announcing that the Emperor had *noted* the contents of the Treaties. Elgin and Gros produced in return a copy of the decree by which the last Emperor had actually approved the Treaty of Nanking, and insisted that a similar act of approval was needed for the new Treaties. At the same time Elgin ordered the 59th Regiment up from Taku, and applied to the Chinese for barrack accommodation in Tientsin. Promptly an imperial decree arrived approving the Treaties. On July 6th Elgin and Gros left Tientsin, speeded on their way with handsome gifts from the Commissioners, Elgin receiving nine enormous earthenware jars of wine.

The Treaties provided that the new tariff arrangements and various other minor commercial matters should be left for later discussion by experts, and it was tacitly agreed on the Western side that these discussions should be conducted by the British, who had the greatest interest in the result. As it turned out, neither Elgin nor Kuei Liang and Hua Sha-na were content to leave these trade negotiations to their subordinates. The Chinese Commissioners had as we shall see their own reasons for seeking another round with Elgin. Elgin was afraid that if he left for England the tariff negotiations would be mismanaged by Bowring. It was thus agreed that the two sides should meet at Shanghai in September.

Elgin meanwhile set out on a peaceful and highly successful expedition to Japan, which lies outside the scope of this book. Before he left he promised Seymour and van Straubenzee that when he met the Commissioners in September he would speak to them severely about the turbulent state of affairs at Canton; but he added pointedly that he would have a greater chance of success if the Admiral and General had meanwhile contrived some vigorous and decisive action of their own against the braves. Indeed everyone was criticising van Straubenzee for his sluggishness in allowing his army of 3,000 men to be pinned down in Canton by ir-regular troops, and Parkes, who was still the leading light of the city's administration, was so disgusted that he thought of resigning and going to sheep-farm in New Zealand. But the fault belonged partly to Admiral Seymour, who had given his naval commanders at Canton no discretion to move their gunboats while he was in the north.

Elgin and his party returned to Shanghai at the beginning of September, refreshed by their visit to Japan, which they thought a much more attractive and welcoming country than China. There was no sign of the Chinese Commis-sioners, the news from Canton was still bad, and the party settled down to wait. Shanghai was the most agreeable of the Chinese cities which Elgin had so far visited, but it did not have much to offer in the way of entertainment, par-ticularly in the hot damp month of September. The country around was flat and uninteresting and smelt strongly of night soil, game was rare, and it was more pleasant to ride round the new race-course than to pick one's way across the canals and ditches. Racquets, American bowls, billiards and walks along the Bund were popular, and there was an occasional ball at which the gentlemen outnumbered the ladies by ten to one. Elgin read *Vanity Fair*: 'It is certainly very clever, though one would hardly have liked to have written it.' He also read the Hong Kong Press, which was beginning to criticise the Treaty of Tientsin and the method of negotiating it as too mild. Elgin now believed that many Hong Kong merchants did not want the peaceful and orderly opening of China to Western trade; they seemed to prefer the restricted competition, occasional smuggling and high profits which the old disorderly system gave them, and also were strongly in favour of using the Chinese with violence so long as their trade was not thereby endangered. 'Anyone could have obtained the Treaty of Tientsin,' he wrote in his diary. 'What was really meritorious was that it should have been obtained at so small a cost of human suffering. . . . But this discredits it for many: the announcement was received with a yell of derision by connoisseurs and baffled speculators in tea.' He believed that Sir John Bowring had inspired the criticisms, but now that he had won his Treaty he could afford a little pity. 'Of Sir John Bowring I say nothing,' he wrote to Malmesbury on September 20th. 'All allowance should be made for a man in a position so false. If his first aim since I have been here had not been to prove that the supercession of himself by a special British plenipotentiary was a blunder he would have been more than human.'

As the Commissioners still failed to appear for the tariff negotiations Elgin wrote to them to suggest that he should return to Tientsin, to spare them the trouble and fatigue of the long journey to Shanghai. This threat produced the Commissioners without delay, and negotiations began at the beginning of October. The British negotiating team consisted of Wade and Oliphant, with Lay advising on customs matters in the background; the Chinese of two local officials. Elgin, Kuei Liang and Hua Sha-na exchanged hospitality and the atmosphere was much more jovial than at Tientsin four months earlier. Elgin complained of the conduct of Huang (Yeh's successor as Governor General of Kwangsi and Kwangtung) in stirring up trouble around Canton, and asked that he and the local militia commanders should be removed. The Chinese Commissioners agreed to recommend this to Peking. It took a month to work out the tariff and other arrangements. The most revolutionary change agreed in Shanghai was the legalisation and taxing of the trade in opium, which will be discussed with the Treaties as a whole in the next chapter.

On October 22nd Kuei Liang and Hua Sha-na explained why they, two of the most senior officials of the Empire, had come to Shanghai to discuss the lowly subject of tariffs. They wrote to Elgin asking the British not to exercise the right which they had obtained in Article III of the Treaty of Tientsin to send a British representative to live in Peking. The Commissioners explained that this concession had been wrung from them by force, pointed out that the Article gave the British Government the option merely to send an occasional representative to visit the capital, and urged that this should be the British choice. They at first argued that the people of Peking were not used to foreigners, and might provoke incidents; but the real reason emerged in a second letter of October 28th: 'The permanent residence of foreign ministers at the capital would . . . be an injury to China in many more ways than we can find words to express. In the present critical and troubled state of our country this incident would generate, we fear, a loss of respect for their government in the eyes of her people.' The letters of the Commissioners were couched in friendly, almost humble, terms and after much thought Elgin decided to agree. He wrote to the Commissioners on October 30th promising to report to the British Government 'and humbly to submit it as his opinion that if Her Majesty's Ambassador be properly received at Peking when the ratifications are exchanged next year, and full effect given in all other particulars to the treaty negotiated at Tientsin, it would certainly be expedient that Her Majesty's representative in China should be instructed to choose a place of residence elsewhere than at Peking, and to make his visits to the capital either periodical or only as frequent as the exigencies of the public service may require. Her Majesty's treaty-right will of course in any case remain intact.'

There were strong arguments in favour of this momentous decision. It was difficult to see how British or Western Ministers living in Peking could be protected against a change of policy by the Chinese. The fearful prospect of the Ministers in Peking being besieged in their Legations, far from the safety of the sea, became a reality forty years later at the time of the Boxers; it was already present in the minds of practical men. Gros was against residence in Peking and so was Malmesbury, who wrote to Elgin on August 9th: 'Peking would be a rat trap for the envoy if the Chinese meant mischief.' Indeed, although Elgin did not know it, the Cabinet had agreed in July that it would be acceptable for the diplomats to live in Shanghai.[1]   In exchange for his concession Elgin gained the agreement of the Commissioners to a project on which he had set his heart, a voyage down the Yangtze to Hankow, further than any European ship had yet penetrated.   But his main reason for recommending the concession was simply that he did not want to press the Chinese too hard.   Kuei Liang and Hua Sha-na had consistently told him that residence at Peking was the bitterest concession for which he could ask, and that the consequences of insisting on it would be dire for themselves and for the Chinese Empire.   It was in the interests of Britain that the Empire should hold its authority over its subjects, and that this authority should be exercised by moderate men such as the Commissioners.   Elgin wanted to leave to his successors a reasonable chance of building a relationship with China based on something better than the periodic use of force.   He had felt compelled to act the bully in Tientsin;   he judged that in Shanghai he could be his liberal self.   His judgment was unhesitatingly endorsed by the British Government.

These were all sensible motives, but the decision was surely wrong.   As Elgin and the Foreign Office had hitherto consistently held, the presence of a British representative living permanently in Peking would be the clearest possible sign that the Chinese Empire had agreed to treat the British as equals.   In June Elgin had formally obtained the right of residence, and at Shanghai merely recommended that it should not be exercised;   in theory the right remained undiminished.   But it was the exercise of the right, not its survival on paper, which counted.   Elgin should have remembered the story of Canton.   There too a right had been secured in a treaty, the right of entry into the city.

[1] This decision was never followed up because the Colonial Secretary had not been listening to the discussion in Cabinet, and as there were no Cabinet minutes in the nineteenth century his department did not agree that a decision had been taken.

There too a liberal-minded British plenipotentiary had agreed that the right should not be exercised, while insisting that legally it still existed. It had not been long before the Chinese claimed that he had abandoned the right for ever. Elgin should have had enough experience of the way in which Chinese affairs were conducted to know that his concession would be presented to the Emperor as a brilliant example of pacifying the barbarians by showing them the error of their ways, and as a sign that all could continue as before. The arguments put forward by the Commissioners made this clear. They argued that the authority of the Empire would be gravely shaken by the presence of Western Ambassadors in Peking. One can understand a negotiator arguing at any time that the presence of an occupying army in his capital would shake the authority of his Government. But an Ambassador is not the same as an occupying army, and the Commissioners' argument could only mean that if the authorities of Peking were seen to treat the representatives of Western powers as equals their power would crumble. The Imperial power thus was said to depend on the survival of the myth of Chinese superiority, and this was the claim which Elgin was implicitly supporting when he recommended that the right of residence at Peking should not be exercised. As often happens with such vacant gestures of good will the consequences for both sides were grievous, probably more damaging than if a less liberal man than Elgin had insisted from the outset that a British representative must live in Peking.

Elgin spent four months in China after the end of the negotiations in Shanghai. The first two of these were largely passed on the Yangtze river. His journey to Hankow and back was picturesque and successful; it is fully described in the pages of Oliphant. Elgin came for the first time into contact with the semi-Christian Taiping rebels, who still held Nanking and several other riverside cities by which he passed. The rebels indeed fired on his flotilla, believing him to be in league with the Imperial forces, and there was an artillery duel before the misunderstanding was cleared up. His conclusion from what he heard and saw was that the rebels were even more unpopular in the Yangtze than the Imperial forces because of the destruction which they inflicted.[1] Before finally leaving Shanghai in January he fired a splendid parting salvo at the businessmen of the city who had presented him with an address of congratulation: 'Uninvited, and by methods not always of the gentlest, we have broken down the barriers behind which these ancient nations sought to conceal from the world without the mysteries, perhaps also in the case of the Chinese at least, the rags and rottenness of their waning civilisations. Neither our own consciences nor the judgment of mankind will acquit us if when we are asked to what use we have turned our opportunities we can only say that we have filled our pockets from among the ruins which we have found or made.'

Elgin spent January and February 1859 in Hong Kong and Canton. He had been successful in getting Yeh's successor removed and the situation round Canton, though not easy, was quieter than it had been. The British were entitled under the Treaty of Tientsin to stay in Canton until the Chinese had paid the agreed indemnity.

Finally on March 4th Elgin left China, as he hoped for good. He had sent his brother Frederick Bruce home in the summer with the Treaty of Tientsin, and it had since been announced that Frederick was to be the first British Minister accredited to the Chinese Empire. The two brothers met briefly in Ceylon at the beginning of April, Elgin on his way home, Bruce travelling eastward to carry out his first task, the agreed exchange of ratifications of the Treaty at Peking.

[1] This is an interesting judgment in the light of the argument now often advanced that the Taipings were a genuine popular force. Elgin formed his negative opinion long before there was any question of the West helping the Emperor against the Taipings.

15

BEFORE THE STORY of Frederick Bruce's misfortunes is told it may be useful to give a fuller account of the Treaty which he was to carry to Peking. The Treaties of Tientsin between China and the British, French and Americans remained in force with little change for almost half a century, and provided the framework within which China's relations with the West developed, finding their most striking expression in those extraordinary and exciting excrescences, the Treaty Ports. The most important provision of the British Treaty was that which allowed diplomatic representation in Peking; of this enough has been said. The other provisions can be quickly summarised. As a result of the three treaties ten new ports were opened to trade, and an eleventh (Tientsin) was added in 1860. Of those new ports only three (Tientsin, Hankow and Nanking) were to develop into big partly Europeanised cities on the scale of Shanghai and Canton, and Hankow and Nanking were not opened until the Yangtze was clear of Taiping rebels. It was also provided that foreigners might travel for their pleasure or for purposes of trade to all parts of the interior, i.e. outside the treaty ports to which they had previously been confined. This was almost as revolutionary a step as the admission of diplomats to Peking.

The British merchants tried to interpret another section of the Treaty[1] as meaning that they could not only travel but also reside wherever they wished outside the treaty ports. This interpretation was clearly against the purpose

[1] Article XLI.

of the Treaty and was firmly resisted by the British Government. There was a simple but effective clause for the missionaries:[1] 'The Christian religion as professed by Protestants or Roman Catholics, inculcates the practice of virtue, and teaches man to do as he would be done by. Persons teaching it or professing it therefore shall alike be entitled to the protection of the Chinese authorities; nor shall any such, peaceably pursuing their calling, and not offending against the laws, be persecuted or interfered with.' An indemnity of 4 million taels was to be paid by the Chinese to the British for the losses which the British community had suffered as a result of Yeh's activities in Canton and for the expenses of the British military expedition, and another indemnity half the size was payable to the French. The principle of extraterritoriality was extended; that is to say the British Consul in a treaty port was given jurisdiction over disputes between British subjects, and over British subjects who were defendants in civil and criminal cases brought by Chinese. The Chinese authorities in practice kept jurisdiction where the defendant was a Chinese.

In the commercial negotiations at Shanghai a Chinese tariff of 5 per cent was agreed on both imports and exports of most goods, though because of special French interest the export tariff on silk was to be lower. After the 1842-4 treaties merchants had complained that in addition to the tariff levied at the port, the goods which they sold or bought in China had to pay all kinds of mysterious inland revenu duties as they crossed from one province or city to another. It was now agreed that a merchant could now pay an extra $2\frac{1}{2}$ per cent on top of the normal tariff, in return for which he would get a certificate exempting his consignment from any further inland payments to the Chinese revenue authorities.

Little or nothing has been said so far in this book about opium. This may seem strange, as the events related are known to the modern Chinese as the Second Opium War,

[1] Article VIII.

171

and many Western commentators have assumed in ignorance of the facts that this is a fair description. The true facts can be summed up in three propositions. First, the opium trade was of great importance. Second, in spite of this it was not among the causes of the war of 1856-8. Third, the legalisation of the opium trade in 1858 was a much less revolutionary step than it appears. In order to explain these propositions, the opium trade must be described in some detail.

The people of China were <u>forbidden to buy or consume opium on pain of death</u>. From time to time there was debate in Peking about the wisdom of this law, but it remained on the books. From time to time attempts were made to enforce it, and one of these attempts in 1839 in Canton led to the First Anglo-Chinese War of 1839-42. There is therefore some justification for calling that war the First Opium War. It is however a title which most historians would probably wish to qualify, if only because when at the end of that war the victorious British suggested that the opium trade should be legalised, the Chinese refused and the British did not insist. The opium trade thus continued to be illegal from 1842 to 1858, and flourished exceedingly. Imports into China from India were estimated in 1842 at just over 28,500 chests and in 1857 at 60,385 chests. Lesser supplies came from Turkey and the Malay States. The opium was shipped mainly in British ships, and the two firms most heavily engaged were Dents and Jardines, both of Hong Kong. The brilliant organisation of the trade has often been described. At the time of which we are writing <u>fast armed steamers carried the opium from Bombay and Calcutta via Hong Kong to the ports of China</u>. Because of their speed and reliability the opium steamers were often given mail to deliver in the Far East, and developed the amiable habit of holding up delivery for a day or two of the mail for their firm's competitors so that their own firm could profit from prior knowledge of commercial prices in India and Europe. The opium was not delivered to the

Chinese ports themselves but to receiving stations organised a few miles off. Thus the opium for Shanghai was unloaded at Woosung, a few miles down the river. By this system everyone was saved embarrassment. The opium firms found no difficulty in selling the drug or in bribing the local authorities to let it in. The profit was sure and quick and the trade in every way easier than that in textiles. There was no pressure for legalisation of the trade from the opium firms themselves, who were doing very nicely. Legalisation would probably bring new firms in to compete for the business; it would mean a Chinese tariff on imported opium which might well be more expensive than the bribes paid so long as the drug was contraband; and it would almost certainly mean that opium would be grown in large quantities in China to compete with the imports.

The British Government was uncomfortably placed. It was under eloquent pressure from a section of British radical opinion, led by Lord Shaftesbury, to abolish the opium trade. There was no doubt that its standing abroad would be improved if it did so, as many foreigners took it for granted that opium was Britain's only real interest in China. On the other hand a ban on the opium trade would run contrary to the philosophy of free trade. It would be difficult to enforce even against British ships, and impossible to enforce against foreign ships, particularly the Americans who already had a significant share of the opium trade and would no doubt move in to replace the British if the British Government prevented its nationals from taking part. The export of opium to China was of economic benefit to the China trade as a whole. During the period 1842-58 the balance of trade turned in favour of China. The tea served at mid-Victorian tables was China tea, the silk of the ladies' gowns was China silk. India had not yet emerged as a main exporter of tea nor Japan of silk. The demand for China tea and China silk rose rapidly with growing prosperity in Europe and America; but as we have seen the Chinese demand for Western goods remained stagnant. The gap was filled by sales of bullion—and sales of opium. Bullion was hard to find and difficult to negotiate, as the Chinese trusted only certain types of minted coin, notably the Spanish Carolus silver dollar, and rates of exchange fluctuated widely. Opium was easy to find and easy to sell. In 1857 it was estimated that $\frac{1}{3}$ of the imports into the Shanghai district was bullion, $\frac{1}{3}$ opium and $\frac{1}{3}$ other goods. The abolitionists argued that if the Chinese were not able to spend money on opium they would have more with which to buy Western manufactures; in fact as shown earlier the Chinese were not deterred from this by lack of purchasing power but because Western goods were so rarely competitive with the home-made article. But the main reason which persuaded successive British Governments not to act against the opium trade was that the revenue of the British East India Company and later of the Government of India depended so largely on the tax levied on the drug before it left that country. About a sixth of the Indian revenues came from this source, and this was not a sum which could easily be waved aside.[1]

The British Government would not act to suppress the opium trade but it was not happy at the way it was run. The idea that British traders were engaged in two separate types of operation in China, one legal conducted with the help of the Consul and backed by a formal treaty, the other illegal and carried on just beyond the Consul's horizon, was distasteful even to those whom the opium trade itself did not shock. After some uncertainties at first, the British Government instructed the Consuls at the treaty ports that it was not part of their job either to help the opium traders or to help the Chinese carry out Chinese laws against the drug. The Consul was in fact to ignore as best he could the business on which many of his British and Chinese acquaintances thrived with little concealment. In practice this was often impossible. Traders were tempted to use for smuggling

[1] Compare the modern dependence of the British and other exchequers on the taxation of tobacco.

174

other goods the smooth quick mechanism of bribes and receiving stations which had been designed for opium. From time to time local rebellions or piracy made the receiving stations unsafe, lying as they did beyond the protection of the big towns; when this happened opium smuggling was transferred to the towns themselves, and it was even harder for the Consul to keep his eye blind.

In short, the trade, though profitable for the Chinese official and the British opium merchant, added notably to the confusion and burdens of a British consul's life. It became steadily clearer that Anglo-Chinese affairs could never develop in a rational and orderly pattern so long as an illegal trade thrived alongside the legal. Since they regarded suppression as out of the question the British Government favoured legalisation. But they were in no great hurry, and in any case looked on legalisation as a suggestion to be put to the Chinese Government, not as a demand. Lord Clarendon's instructions to Elgin in April 1857 made the British attitude clear: 'It will be for your Excellency when discussing commercial arrangements with any Chinese plenipotentiaries, to ascertain whether the Government of China would revoke its prohibition of the opium trade, which the high officers of the Chinese Government never practically enforce. Whether the legalisation of the trade would tend to augment that trade may be doubtful, as it seems now to be carried on to the full extent of the demand in China, with the sanction and connivance of the local authorities. But there would be obvious advantages in placing the trade upon a legal footing by the imposition of a duty, instead of its being carried on in the present irregular manner.' Elgin agreed so strongly with this tentative approach that the British never mentioned opium to the Chinese during the negotiations in Tientsin in June 1858. Elgin was painfully conscious that at Tientsin he was negotiating with armed force close at his back, and that the concessions asked of the Chinese there, however reasonable, were not freely given. He was not prepared to force through the legalisation of opium in this way. He waited until he met the Commissioners in Shanghai in the autumn to discuss commercial arrangements; there the discussions were calm and on more equal terms. Meanwhile he had been encouraged to raise the matter by the American plenipotentiary Mr. Reed. The policy of the American Government favoured the suppression of the opium trade despite the part taken in it by American shippers, and Reed brought instructions from Washington in this sense. But he quickly became so sceptical of the possibilities of suppression and so horrified at the evils of the existing illegal trade that he abandoned his instructions and urged Elgin to suggest legalisation to the Chinese. At the same time he wrote to the State Department: 'Most honest men concur that nominal prohibition is in point of fact encouragement, and that the only remaining chance of restraint is making the drug dutiable and placing it under direct custom house control.' When the suggestion was made the Chinese did not object. It was quickly agreed that opium should pay a tariff of about 8 per cent (compared to the 5 per cent for most goods) and that merchants should not be allowed to commute the inland revenue charges on opium as they were on other goods. Elgin, like Clarendon, thought the change would do little to increase the trade. In fact though the figure for opium imports remained high, they represented by the end of the century a far lower proportion of China's total imports than they had in 1850. The main change was that, the Chinese laws against opium consumption having fallen into further disuse, China's own production of the drug grew fast. The American scholar Fairbank ended his essay on the legalisation of the opium trade as follows: 'It is no more than a half truth to say therefore as has generally been the fashion that in 1858 England forced the Emperor of China to legalise the opium trade. In the 1850s opium in China needed no advocate and recognition came as the result of domestic problems.'[1]

[1] *Chinese Social and Political Science Review* 1941, vol. 17.

Such was the Treaty of Tientsin. In Hong Kong it was accepted as a reasonable settlement. The critics complained not of its content but of the way it was achieved. Men such as Parkes considered that Elgin should have gone to see the Emperor in Peking, and that he should not have agreed to recommend that the right of residence in Peking should be waived. In England the chorus of approval was almost unanimous, and the verdict of *The Times* which welcomed Elgin's 'manly and consistent policy' was typical. One of the few critics was Karl Marx whose flair for scenting improbable conspiracies enabled him to inform Engels in a letter of October 10th 1858 that the whole thing was a Russian plot. 'The present Anglo-Chinese Treaty which in my opinion was worked out by Palmerston in conjunction with the Petersburg Cabinet and given to Lord Elgin to take with him on his journey is a mockery from beginning to end.' In fact, as we have seen the Russian negotiator thought that Elgin had asked for dangerously much, and Elgin himself thought that one of the Treaty's main advantages was that it had put a spoke in Russia's wheel. But there was some logic in Marx's analysis. He had no evidence whatever for connivance between Britain and Russia except his belief that obviously Russia with a frontier less than 1,000 miles from Peking would benefit more than anyone else from the terms of the Treaty and in particular the right of residence in the capital. This is certainly a defensible point, and indeed fifteen years ago one could argue that history had proved Marx right, and that of all the great powers only Russia had secured a lasting position in China. Now the wheel has turned again. It now looks as if each of the major powers, Britain, the United States and Russia has in turn enjoyed its years of predominance in China, but that in the end after much tribulation the main beneficiaries from the forced opening-up of the country were the Chinese people themselves.

In their own comments on the Treaty Elgin and his brother Frederick made repeatedly a point which would have astonished Marx. In private and public letters they rubbed in the fact that however reasonable its terms the Treaty of Tientsin had been exacted from the Chinese by force, and that in return the British owed it to the Chinese to behave with moderation and forbearance. Only if they did so would the settlement last. Elgin wrote as follows to the Prime Minister, Lord Derby, on October 23rd: 'Though I can hardly expect to bring them [the Chinese Commissioners] to regard the Treaty which we have extorted from them otherwise than as a great calamity to the Empire I hope that I may be able to induce them to acquiesce in it as an accomplished fact, and to accept the necessity of carrying out its provisions loyally. This done we shall have to convince them that if we are rigorous in requiring that good faith should characterise their conduct towards us we are no less scrupulous in adopting it as the rule of ours to them. I confess that for my own part if I were obliged to choose between the two I would much rather have it written on my tombstone that I had moralised the trade of China than that I had battered down the Great Wall.'

16

ELGIN RETURNED thankfully to his family and his life as a Scottish dignitary. At first he took little part in politics, though his views were so clearly in the centre of the party spectrum that both sides thought to make use of him. In a letter to the Prime Minister on May 8th 1859 Disraeli suggested strengthening the Government by bringing in Elgin as Foreign Secretary in place of Malmesbury. But within a week or so the Tories were out, and Palmerston and the Whigs back again. Elgin accepted the job of Postmaster General with a seat in the Cabinet; but he was not to escape so easily the burden of China. In mid-September he was attending the Queen at Balmoral, and on the 13th wrote to his wife: 'Dearest, you see the dreadful news from China. I am quite overcome by it: I never closed my eyes last night.' Indeed the news was so bad as to be hardly credible; Frederick Bruce, carrying the Treaty of Tientsin to Peking for ratification, had been repulsed at the Taku forts, with three gunboats sunk and heavy loss of life.

It had always seemed prudent to assume that there might be trouble over the ratification of the Treaty, which was to take place at Peking within a year of signature. Before he left China Elgin, by now wise in the deliberate speed with which his Admiral acted, had asked Seymour to collect a force of gunboats to escort his brother to the north. The instructions which Malmesbury sent Bruce on March 1st warned him to watch for trickery. As it was later argued that Bruce had gone beyond his instructions it is worth quoting an extract from them: 'The Admiral in charge of Her Majesty's naval forces in China has been directed to send up with you to the mouth of the Peiho a sufficient naval force and unless any unforeseen circumstances should appear to make another arrangement more advisable, it would seem desirable that you should reach Tientsin in a British ship of war. It is impossible for Her Majesty's Government, and indeed it would not be wise, to lay down any definite rules to be rigidly adhered to in regard to your approach to and your communication with the Chinese Court. The acquaintance which you possess with the Chinese character will enable you to judge when you may give way and when you must stand firm, bearing in mind that your treatment in your first visit to Peking will always be appealed to on the occasion of future visits as establishing a precedent not to be departed from.'

Bruce spent five weeks in Hong Kong and reached Shanghai on June 6th. He had heard stories in Hong Kong that those who favoured a tough line with the West had gained the upper hand in Peking and that the forts at Taku were being strengthened. At Shanghai he and his French colleague de Bourboulon were told that Kuei Liang and Hua Sha-na, the two Commissioners who had negotiated the Treaty of Tientsin, had arrived and wished to discuss a number of points with the British and French. Bruce and de Bourboulon replied that before there could be any discussion of substance the Treaty would have to be ratified at Peking. The Commissioners continued to prevaricate and Bruce and de Bourboulon left Shanghai for the north without seeing them. By June 18th they were anchored in the familiar waters of the Gulf of Pechihli beyond the bar of the river at Taku, where a little more than a year before Elgin and Bruce had fretted impatiently for Seymour's gunboats. This time there was no delay. Sir James Hope, who had succeeded Seymour in the spring, had mustered sixteen warships of which thirteen were the indispensable gunboats. Most of the French naval force was busy in Indo-China but de Bourboulon was supported by two warships. Admiral Hope had already established that the Taku forts had been greatly strengthened since they had been taken with such ease in May 1858, and that formidable booms of bamboo trunks lashed together had been laid across the approach. His landing party had been told that these works had been undertaken by the local militia on their own initiative as a precaution against attack by the Taiping rebels. He asked that the obstacles be removed so that the plenipotentiaries could continue their peaceful journey to Tientsin and Peking. Nothing happened, and on June 21st Bruce and de Bour-boulon formally authorised their naval commanders to clear the obstacles.

Meanwhile a new American representative named Ward had arrived off Taku, intending like the British and French to take his Treaty to Peking for ratification. He quickly made contact with the Chinese authorities on shore and was invited to move to Peking by way of Pehtang, a small town on the coast about ten miles from Taku. On the morning of June 25th Bruce received a letter two days old from the local Viceroy Heng Fu making the same proposal. The letter reached him at 9 o'clock in the morning on board the *Magicienne*, which lay about eight miles out to sea. He be-lieved that in an hour's time Admiral Hope would begin his attack on the forts. He had no means of communicating with the Admiral within that time even had he wished to do so. In any case he did not believe that the Chinese proposal would justify him in calling off the attack. Lord Malmes-bury had advised him to go as far as Tientsin in a British man-of-war. This was not just to strike an attitude. If the city of Tientsin were once again under the guns of the Royal Navy, the chances of a British envoy being safely and decently received in Peking would be good. Now it was suggested that Bruce should land at Pehtang and journey overland to Peking, leaving his gunboats before the forts at Taku. From there they could put no useful pressure on the Chinese Government, and Bruce's chances in Peking would be correspondingly less bright. There seemed everything to be said for a quick blow at the recalcitrant forts and a dignified journey up the river to Tientsin. So no reply was sent to the Viceroy's letter and all aboard the *Magicienne* crowded on deck to watch for the first puffs of smoke from the Taku forts, just visible on the horizon.

Admiral Hope had planned to advance through the first boom at 10 o'clock, but in fact spent the morning manœuvring his ships into position. It was not until 2 in the afternoon that the *Opossum* began to cut a passage through the first barrier. The forts remained strangely silent until the *Opossum*, closely followed by three other gunboats, one of them carrying the Admiral, reached the second barrier. Then they opened simultaneous fire with between thirty and forty guns. Resistance in itself came as no surprise to the Admiral, but his plan was entirely without guile. He expected that after an hour or two's pummelling from his gunboats the forts would be ripe for storming by a landing party. In his bluff confidence in the superiority of his forces he had contented himself with a sketchy reconnaissance and had no idea of the number or calibre of the guns waiting for him behind the Chinese embrasures. He quickly learned the truth. Within a few minutes the leading gunboats were forced to retreat heavily damaged behind the first boom. The admiral himself on the *Plover* was hit in the leg and severely bruised in falling. The artillery duel continued for three hours until both sides were exhausted. The fire from the forts slackened towards evening, by which time six of the eleven British gunboats were out of action, most of them aground with heavy casualties.

It was by now six o'clock. If the forts were to be taken that day the landing party must go ashore without more delay. But several of the big guns on the forts were still in action and it was clear that they were heavily garrisoned by men with small arms. On the other hand the British were unable to withdraw in good order and return another day. Four gunboats were aground within easy range of the forts, and even though the crews could be taken off no admiral would leave these ships to their fate if there was a chance to save them. It was a desperate choice, and Admiral Hope, fainting from his wound, was in no state to make it. Finally Shadwell, his second in command, decided to press the attack. It was the wrong decision. The tide was by now out and the landing launches had to leave the marines to struggle across hundreds of yards of mud before they reached land. Weapons and ammunition were by then soaked and unusable. The Chinese opened a heavy and effective fire. Although it soon became obvious that the forts could resist successfully 150 men were put ashore. Wells Williams, the secretary of the American mission, watched them preparing themselves. They talked in low voices without shrinking or bravado, quietly carrying out their orders, as they watched their comrades shot down in the mud. The American Commodore Tatnall could not bear merely to watch in the attitude of neutrality which his instructions laid down. He ordered a small steamer under his command to tow away from the action several of the launches filled with British wounded, and justified himself with the famous remark: 'Blood is thicker than water.'

The landing party pressed ahead as far as they could, and 50 arrived close under the walls of the southern forts. There they were pinned down, and reported to Shadwell that they could not storm the forts without reinforcements. Reinforcements did not exist, and the landing party was ordered to retire with their wounded to the boats. They struggled back in the darkness, and the evacuation was complete at 1.30 a.m. The cost could now be counted. During the day the British lost 89 killed and 345 wounded. It was a shattering reverse, the more so because everyone had been confident of success. The veterans of the Crimea murmured that they would rather fight Balaclava over three times than face again the forts of Taku. As the missing were counted and the wounded given some care Bruce and his party on the *Magicienne* went cheerful to bed. They had remained out of touch with the battle from their position eight miles away, and when the firing stopped they assumed that all had gone well.

In the next few days Hope, quickly recovering from his wound, gathered his force together. Three of the crippled gunboats, the *Plover*, *Lee* and *Cormorant*, could not be saved; the rest were patched up. On July 1st Hope formally reported to Bruce that no further attempt could be made against the forts.

Faced with so complete and unexpected a defeat those immediately concerned quickly assumed that they had been the victims of a conspiracy. The Chinese, it was said, had never intended to ratify the Treaty of Tientsin. They had prepared a deliberate ambush designed to humiliate the British and bring the Treaty to nothing. They had probably been helped by the Russians. The sailors soon told how men with cropped hair wearing fur hats and European trousers had been seen manning the guns in the forts.[1] Palmerston was firmly convinced that Russians had stood behind those murderous batteries. However that might be most people in England assumed that there had been a Chinese plot to attack and maul the British as they went about their peaceful occasions.

The evidence does not support this explanation. The Chinese certainly wanted to reopen discussion of part of the Treaty of Tientsin, but they expected to be able to do this without more fighting, as they had with Elgin in October 1858. They would almost certainly have agreed to exchange ratifications with Bruce in Peking as the Treaty provided. But they were anxious to handle his visit in as nearly as possible the traditional way. They genuinely believed that the presence of a European envoy in Peking

---

[1] The Chinese of the north commonly wear fur hats in winter; but the man who wears a fur hat at Taku in June is indeed a hero, whatever his nationality. There was no report of snow left by the Russian boots.

treating on equal terms with the Imperial Government would give a severe, perhaps fatal, jolt to the Emperor's authority. They had persuaded Elgin not to insist that an envoy live permanently in Peking; now it remained to receive his brother courteously but in something as near the old style of tributary as he would stomach. But for this tactic to succeed it was essential that Bruce should leave his gunboats at Taku. It would not be politic to patronise him and treat him as a subordinate if British warships again dominated the city of Tientsin. That was why they suggested that he should travel overland to Peking instead of up the river as far as Tientsin. That was why the Taku forts had been strengthened and encouraged to resist.

This explanation is borne out by the way the Chinese treated the American envoy Ward. Ward agreed to land at Pehtang. He was kept hanging about off that unsavoury little town for three weeks after the engagement at Taku, holding desultory talks with Heng Fu the Viceroy of Chihli. Heng Fu pressed Ward hard to persuade the British to follow his example, an odd move if in fact the Chinese had planned and been satisfied with the repulse of the British on June 25th. Finally the American party was allotted a number of unsprung carts in which, apart from one day in a river boat, they accomplished the journey to Peking. The final stretch of road was so bumpy that the Americans dismounted and walked beside the by now intolerable carts. They entered Peking on July 27th, the seventh day of their journey, and were received by a great crowd. They were given a house, servants and food, for none of which they were allowed to pay. They were prevented from moving freely about the city or from making contact with the Russians who lived there. Ward's two aims were to exchange ratifications of the American Treaty and to hand over a letter from President Buchanan to the Emperor. The Chinese said that this last must be done in person, but immediately plunged into the great question of the kowtow. Here Ward was at a disadvantage even compared to the British. Elgin and Bruce, being accustomed to kneel on one knee before Queen Victoria, would have been willing to offer the same courtesy to the Emperor. Kneeling of any kind before a fellow-human was however a rank offence to the republican principles of the Americans. Patiently the Chinese explained the custom. Lesser breeds like the Siamese and Burmese were required to kneel three times and knock their heads on the ground before the Emperor nine times. As a concession to the principles of the Americans, Ward need only kneel once and knock his head three times. The argument went to and fro, the Americans becoming increasingly uncomfortable in their allotted quarters. The heat increased, and they had brought no light clothes; strangely enough they also complained of a surfeit of iced water. Ward made a written proposal: 'I would enter the presence of His Majesty with head uncovered and bowing low; I would stand and not sit; I would not speak unless addressed, and retire by walking backwards, never turning my back until out of his presence.' It was not enough. The Chinese asked if he would bow so low as to touch the ground with his fingers; Ward refused and the discussion broke down. Buchanan's letter was handed to Kuei Liang for transmission to the Emperor, and the Americans returned to Pehtang. Their Treaty, unlike the British and French, did not lay down specifically that ratifications should be exchanged in Peking, and they carried out this formality at Pehtang on August 16th before embarking for home.

The news of Ward's visit to Peking was received with scorn by the British. Bruce wrote to the Foreign Secretary on September 3rd that the treatment given him showed that 'the Chinese Government are still far from recognising the rights of foreign Envoys; that whatever they may have conceded on paper, they practically refuse to admit diplomatic intercourse on a footing of national equality, and that a visit to the capital is only acceptable if it can be converted into a means of flattering the pride, and acknowledging the superiority of the Emperor of China.' It was a fair comment. The Chinese had skilfully managed to fit Ward's visit to Peking into the tradition of visits by tributary princes without actually driving him to take offence. True, he had refused the kowtow, but equally he had not seen the Emperor without performing it. No doubt they would have tried almost identical tactics with Bruce. He would certainly have felt bound to urge more forcefully than Ward that he must be treated as the representative of an equal ruler. Whether he could with greater firmness have obtained better treatment than Ward no one can say. He would have had the bargaining asset of his fleet. Gunboats left off the bar at Taku would not have been as valuable a bargaining asset as gunboats up the river dominating Tientsin; but they would have been better than nothing, and a great deal better than gunboats helplessly aground and gunboats limping sadly back to Hong Kong.

The real criticism of Bruce as a diplomat in 1859 is thus that he never gave diplomacy a chance. His later career shows that he was naturally a man of peace, and he shared his brother's critical views about the part of the British in China. But in this his first independent mission he was so frightened of being tricked that he was too quick to use force. He hurried north from Shanghai without even seeing the Commissioners. He made no real effort himself to find out why the river was barred at Taku or to persuade the Chinese to let him pass. He handed the problem to his Admiral to solve by force and then stationed himself so far from the resulting action that even if he had wished he could not have intervened to stop it on the morning of the 25th when he received the Viceroy's proposal that he should land at Pehtang. It may be that he would in any case have had to resort to force if he was to carry out his instructions, but he was in such a hurry that the point was not proved.

As for Admiral Hope he had shown himself a gallant ass. Everyone liked him for the cheerfulness with which he bore defeat and a painful wound. But he had attacked a strong position without full reconnaissance, using a plan innocent of any guile or ingenuity, and then by wasting the morning hours of the 25th further reduced the chances of success. He was careless because it never occurred to him that precautions or ingenuity were necessary against a Chinese adversary.

17

———— ⚬ ————

THE BAD NEWS from China took the usual eleven weeks to
reach England, and arrived in the middle of September
when Ministers were scattered on holiday across the kingdom. Because of this chance of the calendar dozens of
letters survive, written by Ministers to canvass one another's
views, exchanges which at other times of the year would
have taken place at the Reform Club or in the smoking
room of the House of Commons without leaving a trace
for the historian. The tireless Permanent Secretary at the
Foreign Office, Hammond, was at his post and strongly
placed to influence Ministers' thoughts. His own thoughts
were clear. By and large the Foreign Office did not favour
a strong forward policy in China during the nineteenth
century. It usually set itself to moderate the ambitions of the
merchants and the men on the spot. But this time, as over
the *Arrow* two and a half years earlier, Hammond was certain that the man on the spot must be supported and the
adverse tide turned in favour of Britain by sending an expedition. He saw that it would be much more difficult than
in 1857 to persuade his masters to agree. For the two most
powerful Ministers under Palmerston in the Government of
1859 had passionately opposed and voted against Palmerston's support for Bowring over the *Arrow* in 1857. Could
Gladstone, now Chancellor of the Exchequer, and Lord
John Russell, now Foreign Secretary and Hammond's immediate master, support an expedition to salvage Bruce
when they had denounced the expedition to salvage Bow-

ring? Even Palmerston, now seventy-five, seemed at last to have lost some of his zest for an energetic China policy, and his first reaction to the news was definitely subdued. He wrote to Hammond from Broadlands on September 12th: 'This is very unpleasant news from China, and I fear that our people must have allowed themselves to be much over-reached by the Chinese and not to have taken proper precautions for reconnoitring the ground before they advanced up the river. But there is no use in criticising the past. The question is what is to be done now. . . . We must I think resent this outrage in some way or other. To make an attack on Peking would be an operation of great magnitude, but we might blockade the Grand Canal at its mouth in the Yangtze Kiang, or we might take possession of Chusan; but the objection to that latter operation would be that we would be obliged to occupy it jointly with the French.'

With the Prime Minister thus writing despondently of half-measures and the Foreign Secretary far off in Scotland and also likely on past form to hesitate, Hammond may well have felt that his chances of getting the Cabinet to stand up to Gladstone and the Chinese were not good. *The Times* was in an extravagant rage against the Chinese and against Admiral Hope, exclaiming on September 12th that the Chinese had brought the Treaty of Tientsin to an end 'by an act faithless, barbarous and treacherous' and urging that 'England and France, or England without France if necessary, shall teach such a lesson to these perfidious hordes that the name of European will hereafter be a passport of fear, if it cannot be of love, throughout their land.' The *Daily Telegraph* insisted two days later: 'There must be no faltering while the blood of our murdered soldiers remains unavenged.' But when the Cabinet met on September 17th, Lord John Russell still being absent, Gladstone prevailed. He had written a paper for the meeting in which he agreed that a sufficient force should be sent to China in co-operation with the French; but Bruce's action should not be approved, and the object of the new expedition would simply be to secure ratification of the Treaty of Tientsin. For this purpose the British representative should agree to travel to Peking by any honourable means and should not insist on sailing up the river to Tientsin. The Cabinet on September 17th took no decisions, but Gladstone was pleased with the tone of the discussion and wrote to the Duke of Argyll the next day: 'There was not the slightest indication anywhere to treat the present question, which is entirely new, according to the traditions of the last [i.e. Bowring]. . . . There was a unanimous disposition to send a powerful force and on the other hand a great degree of doubt about Bruce's proceedings. I wish I could feel sure that he was up to his very difficult work. It was determined to get an opinion as to the principles of law on which he acted and it remains in reserve to what extent and in what form satisfactions, as well as obtaining ratifications, are to be made the object of the force.'

Gladstone and his friends thus favoured sending a force but wanted it to behave as if Bruce had never been repulsed at Taku. To Hammond it seemed essential that Bruce's action be approved and the Chinese forced to pay for theirs. He wrote almost every day to the Foreign Secretary in Scotland, arguing Bruce's case again and again. The Chinese offer that he should go to Peking by way of Pehtang had not been serious and in any case, 'It would be absurd to to say we do not prevent you going to Edinburgh, but you must go round by Glasgow . . . and instead of going at your ease in a carriage you must either walk or ride.' Lord John Russell was at first perplexed and wrote for advice to Clarendon. Clarendon was in close touch with Hammond: 'I had a long letter yesterday from Lord John,' he wrote to Hammond on September 19th, 'asking my opinion about the best or least bad mode of dealing with China. Three courses he said were open to us: 1, reaching Peking by force; 2, blockade of the Yangtze Kiang; 3, occupation of Chusan. I pointed out the reasons why the two latter would settle nothing and be only attributed to fear by the Chinese and that if we abated our original and notorious intention of getting to Peking our position in China would be untenable and our trade greatly damaged. This is inconvenient, costly and hazardous advice, but I am convinced that any temporising course or attempt to evade the real difficulty of avenging our honour would only make matters worse.'

By now Lord John was convinced. 'It seems strange,' he wrote to Palmerston on the same day, 'that I who objected so much to Bowring's proceedings about the Lorcha should be so ready to support Bruce. But so it is, and I do not think we can do otherwise than to agree to act with the French and only make peace at Tientsin.'[1] Hammond was urging him to come south to deal with his reluctant colleagues, but the Queen, with whom he talked about China at Balmoral on September 20th, asked him to stay in Scotland a little longer. So he wrote a series of strong letters to those Ministers who according to Hammond were wavering. To the Lord Chancellor: 'I hope you do not think that the Law Officers ought to be consulted about this China affair. It seems to me a high question of policy. If Bruce could have been sure that the Chinese would have ratified the Treaty had he gone alone to Peking, and without any degrading ceremony, he might be wrong to insist on going by the river. But this reliance he could not have had. Indeed the certainty was the other way.' To Sir George Lewis: 'A gentleman has made an agreement with me which is to be confirmed on a certain day at his house. At the time named I go along the direct road to his house. Finding stakes stuck up in the road I try to remove them, upon which he fires upon me from behind the hedge and kills several of my servants. Query, was this murder or justifiable homicide? I should say murder, and as such to be punished. Mine appears to be the general opinion.' To Sir Charles Wood (Secretary of State for India): If Bruce

[1] PRO 30/22/30 The last word is surely a slip for 'Peking.'

had accepted the last Chinese proposal 'I dare say that after some weeks' delay a messenger or a great officer would have appeared to conduct Bruce to Peking. He would have been insulted on the road and led a captive to the capital. There he would have been required to perform the kowtow. He would have said no, and some time in August would have got back to the Peiho. What then? An attempt to force the river? That would have failed after two months' sickness on the part of our fleet and two months' more preparation on the part of the Chinese. But what would have been the language held in England? That Bruce ought to have gone to Tientsin when it would have appeared he could have done so.'

Lord John put up a stout argument, but he and Palmerston had other thoughts which they kept more closely to themselves. The two old gentlemen were at this time passionately interested, not in China, but in Italy. In the summer of 1859 Napoleon III had picked a quarrel with Austria and the entry of his army into the Austrian provinces of Northern Italy set in motion a tide which quickly escaped his control. Napoleon beat the Austrians but was content to take from them Lombardy for his ally the King of Piedmont and Sardinia, leaving Venetia under their rule. British opinion, apart from the Court and some Tories, was heartily in favour of the freeing of Italy, but almost equally suspicious of Napoleon's motives in appointing himself the liberator. During 1859 there flared up one of those scares of French invasion which recurred so oddly at intervals during the first half of Victoria's reign. The ally who had fought alongside the British in the Crimea four years before was again feared and distrusted. Russell and Palmerston had no illusions about Napoleon, but they knew that with his shifts and his selfishness the Emperor combined a misty liberalism which made him more of a friend than an enemy to England in the confusion of European politics. A joint Anglo-French expedition to China would help to calm public opinion and give it something to worry about other than the Emperor's alarming installations at Cherbourg. There was moreover the simpler point that the Emperor would certainly go it alone if need be. The French had been only thinly represented in the clash at Taku and lost 4 men killed and 10 wounded, a tiny proportion of the British casualties; but the reports coming in from Paris in September made it clear that the Emperor was determined to react fiercely. Who could tell what dangerous annexations or concessions might be achieved by a French expedition sailing alone to China? Common prudence as well as European policy argued for a British expedition of at least equal size; and as it happened that after the Mutiny India was, as *The Times* put it, 'gorged with soldiers,' the practical difficulties were for once not too great.

Fresh news came in to strengthen the hand of Hammond and Lord John Russell. The Emperor of China formally approved what his subjects had done at Taku. The news of Ward's treatment at Peking was received by the Foreign Office with delight, and lost nothing in the telling. It had a powerful effect on the Duke of Argyll, one of those Whig magnates who formed the backbone of all Liberal Cabinets until the time of Home Rule: 'In respect to the Chinese,' he wrote to Granville, 'I am all against submitting to any nonsense such as they seem to have practised on the Yankee Minister who was sent to Peking, caged in a van like one of Wombwell's wild beasts. Better to have none at all than submit to this. It is supreme nonsense to talk as if we were bound to the Chinese by the same rules which regulate international relations in Europe.'

Not all the news supported Bruce's defenders. The British Ambassador in St. Petersburg passed on a report that the Chinese had prepared a house for Bruce in Peking, which, as Sidney Herbert, the Secretary of State for War, pointed out to Granville, showed that they had not intended to prevent him getting there.

While other Ministers corresponded copiously, one of them found himself greatly embarrassed. Elgin as Postmaster General had a seat in the Cabinet. He had himself returned from China so lately that his colleagues were inevitably anxious to have his opinions. But what could he say? His brother Frederick, of whom he was very fond, had taken a fearful beating. Frederick's defenders were now saying that the idea that he could go peacefully to Peking to exchange ratifications of the Treaty had always been wholly unrealistic, in fact that the arrangements which Elgin had negotiated the year before were unsound. Some of his colleagues waited maliciously to see how he would escape from the dilemma that either Frederick had been wrong in 1859, or he himself in 1858. One of his friends, Sir Charles Wood, urged him to attend all Cabinets on China 'as it is obvious that the executability of your treaty except by force will be questioned.' 'I don't know whether Elgin will have much to say,' wrote Granville to Canning on September 16th. 'Some of the caution which he deplored so much in Sir Michael Seymour would have been of use in this occasion.' Lord Stanley of Alderley, who was to take Elgin's place as Postmaster General in the following year, harked back to Elgin's trip up the Yangtze: 'If the Chinese had only done then what they had done now, palisaded the river and attacked him on his return that great addition to your Government would have been now exhibited in a cage at Peking instead of as a mandarin at the Post Office.'

With greater logic Hammond argued that Elgin had erred in giving up the demand for permanent residence in Peking, and told him so bluntly in a conversation on September 27th which he described to the Foreign Secretary as 'warm.' 'I gave him a thrust, a deadly one, which he was not prepared for . . . I said that although at the time I thought he Lord Elgin had done perfectly right in yielding on the point of permanent residence, the result had proved that he had done perfectly wrong, for by making that concession he had encouraged the Chinese to suspect they could obtain more, and was therefore responsible for all that had now happened. He was not pleased.' Hammond clearly disliked Elgin and took an unkind interest in his embarrassment. He heard a story that Elgin had criticised Frederick's action in Cabinet and asked Clarendon if it was true. Clarendon told him it was not, but ten days later wrote again: 'I have since seen Rumbold to whom he [Elgin] opened himself freely and who was disgusted at the manner in which he threw over Bruce and thought only of how he could extract some credit for himself out of the disaster.'

This was probably unfair. Elgin believed his brother had made a bad mistake, but he is unlikely to have criticised him to anyone except his wife. He was not ready however to go so far in defending his brother as to admit that the whole settlement of 1858 was defective. He explained himself in a letter to his wife in Scotland on September 22: 'The truth is that John Russell and Pam go the whole hog with him (Frederick), throw all the blame on the Chinese, assume that they meditated treachery, and are rather delighted with the prospect of another war in China to be undertaken in concert with the French. There are others in the Cabinet who take a different view, who think it by no means proved that the Chinese intended treachery, and who consider that our attempt to force the barrier of the Peiho was unjustifiable. . . . My own view is that the admiral acted like a madman, and that Frederick was misled by him. However there is no chance of any blame being cast on an admiral.'

In this last Elgin was quite right. *The Times*, which had sharply criticised Admiral Hope at first, relented within a month: 'If we would keep up the old tone in our Navy we must hold it through good and through evil fortune as a maxim that it is not want of success but want of audacity that can alone ever be imputed as a disgrace to an English admiral.'

At its second meeting on China the Cabinet agreed what should be said to Bruce. It was already almost three months since his defeat, and it would be two more before he learnt what his masters thought of it. Lord John Russell's official letter was a good example of the gobbledegook of compromise. Gladstone, Wood, Lewis, Herbert and others would not agree that Bruce's action should be approved, nor Lord John and Palmerston that it should be disowned. So 'I can only say therefore,' wrote the Foreign Secretary on September 26th, 'that Her Majesty's Government without being able in the present state of their information to judge precisely what measures it might have been most advisable for you to adopt at the moment, see nothing in the decision which you took to diminish the confidence which they repose in you.' Lord John followed this up with a friendly private letter saying that the Queen was looking forward to the day when Bruce would obtain the ratification and execution of the Treaty of Tientsin.

While British Ministers were weighing these rights and wrongs the Emperor Napoleon was collecting his troops. Different stories reached England; some said the French would send 12,000 infantry, with two squadrons of cavalry, six batteries of artillery and 20 small gunboats. He was warned by his Ambassador in London that under Elgin's influence the British Cabinet was reluctant to press the Chinese hard, and he blandly suggested that if the British did not want to match the size of the French expedition they might help by providing transport for it. This had the effect which the Emperor presumably intended: 'Now I decidedly object,' wrote Lord John, 'to being again beasts of burden for the French. I think it absolutely essential we should send of Europeans an equal number with that of the French infantry, and as many cavalry if not more.' The peace party in the Cabinet were despondent. 'Palmerston insists that we should send as much or more [than the French],' wrote Wood to Elgin, 'and a pretty penny we shall have to pay for our preparations however it ends. . . . I am almost *aghast* at the thought of what I am convinced we should have to send if we really do send a large joint expedition with our ally.' Elgin was dismayed for another reason. He remembered the eloquence with which the

Chinese Commissioners had pleaded with him at Shanghai a year before against sending a British Ambassador to live permanently in Peking. They had said that this would weaken the prestige of the Emperor so seriously that the dynasty might collapse and the country decline into chaos. If the arrival of a British Ambassador was to have this effect, what would be the result of thousands of allied infantry and cavalry knocking at the gates of Peking? He explained his doubts to Wood: 'If you humiliate the Emperor beyond measure, if you seriously impair his influence over his own subjects, you kill the goose that lays the golden eggs, throw the country into confusion and imperil the most lucrative trade you have in the world. . . . I know that these opinions are not popular. The general notion is that if we use the bludgeon freely enough we can do anything in China. I hold the opposite view so strongly that I must give expression to it at whatever cost to myself.' The cost, as the poor Postmaster General knew by now, included the sneers of Hammond, Granville and Lord Stanley of Alderley.

Elgin had been long enough in government to know that if he was to carry conviction he must put forward a plan of his own. The problem was to find an effective means of pressure on Peking short of an armed attack on the city. In May of the year before Elgin had sat helpless on the *Furious* in the Gulf of Pechihli waiting for Sir Michael Seymour's lagging gunboats, and watching the sails of hundreds of junks carrying the annual tribute of rice into the Peiho river on its way to Peking. If the junks could be stopped, surely the capital would starve; the Imperial Government would come to heel without an allied soldier having to land. Elgin wrote a memorandum for the Cabinet, having earlier put the notion to his friends. First of all he made the old false point about the short campaigning season in North China. The allies would hardly be able to put a force into the field before July 1860, but July and August were almost unbearably hot. By November on the other hand it was almost unbearably cold. The Chinese would spin things out until the winter, and the Emperor might retreat into his Manchurian homeland until shortage of supplies forced the allies to abandon Peking. There was also the great danger that the dynasty would collapse, leaving anarchy from which no one would profit. Instead of marching on Peking the Allies should concentrate on sealing up the Gulf of Pechihli, occupying one of the Meatou Islands in the Gulf as a temporary base. Deprived of the rice junks, the Chinese Government would probably come to terms. Even if a military expedition was thought necessary, it should try to come to terms short of Peking, either at Tientsin, or at T'ungchow (at the head of the canal a few miles short of the capital).

Elgin's paper was plausibly argued, and there was no one available to point out that Peking did not depend on the tribute junks for its food. Rice is the staple food of the south of China, not the north. The court, the army and the gentry ate the tribute rice in Peking, but if it was stopped they could fall back on the corn and bean products which the ordinary people ate. The Emperor was not likely to capitulate merely because he had to return to the diet of his ancestors. But the British were not yet experts on Chinese cooking, and the Cabinet approved Elgin's plan while insisting that an expedition must be prepared to match the French and act with them if the blockade failed in its purpose. On October 29th Lord John Russell instructed Bruce to send the Chinese a 30-day ultimatum asking for an apology for the repulse at Taku, for an indemnity for the damage then done, and for early ratification of the Treaty of Tientsin. At the same time Bruce was told of his brother's plan and authorised to put it into effect if the Chinese did not accept the ultimatum.

The autumn and winter of 1859-60 passed peacefully in China, but it would be difficult to say whether the Chinese or British there were more worried about the future. The Chinese, so far from exulting in their success at Taku, were notably nervous about its probable results, which is in itself an indication that they had not meant to give the British such a conclusive slap in the face. The Mongol general who led the war party, Sang Ko Lin Chin,[1] thought it wise to explain to the Emperor in July that it had been necessary to use force against the British and French because they had come to make new demands, not simply to ratify the Treaty of Tientsin. Some unofficial hints were given to Bruce that if he wished he could still ratify the Treaty at Peking by travelling as Ward had done by way of Pehtang. The Chinese heard with alarm the news of allied military preparations. One high official near the Russian frontier reported to Peking that a Russian had suggested to him that the Chinese should stir up trouble in India. The official thought that this combined with a refusal to trade would stop the British. 'We need only start a boycott and stop the supplies of tea and rhubarb to increase the enemy's difficulties.' But the Chinese Government did not trust advice from the Russians whom they believed to be in league with the British and French: 'Let the Brigadier General reply,' ran his instructions, 'that the Heavenly Dynasty, in dealing with the outer barbarians, has always emphasised truthfulness. It never resorts to plots leading to war.'[2] The Heavenly Dynasty waited helpless for the next assault, knowing enough about the barbarians to be sure that the blow would come, but not enough to be able to ward it off. An attempt was made to draw Bruce into informal discussions in Shanghai through a Chinese merchant, but Bruce would not agree, having nothing to say.

Bruce indeed was not to be envied as he sat in Shanghai, brooding over those incredible few hours of June 25th and wondering how his masters would judge him. Inevitably he slipped more and more into the theory that there had been a treacherous conspiracy against him which no diplomacy on

[1] Known to the British soldiers as 'Sam Collinson.'
[2] Tsiang, 'China, England and Russia in 1860,' *Cambridge Historical Review*, vol. 3, p. 115.

his part could have prevented. This was believed by almost all his advisers, who were convinced that the war party must be crushed before the Treaty of Tientsin was safe. Parkes wrote to him on February 11th: 'Those princes and other notables who compose the war party, backed as they are by Sang Ko Lin Chin and other ignorant Mongol blusterers, did not I fear see enough of us at Tientsin in 1858 to feel assured that we had strength sufficient to compel the strict execution of the Treaty.'

When at last Bruce received his instructions he did not find them helpful. There was a muddle with the French; de Bourboulon's instructions required him to ask for a further indemnity, while Bruce's did not. Worse than this, Elgin's plan for stopping the rice junks seemed less of a brainwave in Shanghai than it had in Whitehall. Wade was quick to point out that only the court and army ate rice. In any case the timing was wrong. Bruce was told to send an ultimatum at once, that is in January, and if it was rejected to start the blockade. But no rice junks sailed till March, and in any case the Admiral could not promise enough gunboats until April. So Bruce asked and received permission to delay putting in his ultimatum and it was not until March 8th, almost nine months after their defeat, that Bruce and de Bourboulon gave the Chinese their Governments' reaction to it. The ultimatum asked for an apology for the attack on the gunboats at Taku, for the return of the captured ships and guns, for ratification of the Treaty at Peking by Ambassadors who were to travel via Taku and Tientsin, and for prompt payment of the 1858 indemnity. A further indemnity might be insisted on if the reply was unsatisfactory. The British Government was no longer bound by Elgin's undertaking of October 1858 that they would not exercise the right to station a representative in Peking. Bruce thought there was a chance that the Chinese would accept these terms, but the reply on April 5th was firm and negative. The Chinese rejected Bruce's version of the events of June 1859 and suggested for the rest that he proceed to Pehtang, exchange ratifications there, and discuss matters with an Imperial Commissioner. Finally he was rebuked for extravagant and insubordinate language and told that in future he must not be so wanting in decorum. The Chinese, encouraged out of their nervousness by nine months of allied inactivity, wrote as if they were ready for another round.

18

As we have seen Lord John Russell had told Bruce that the Queen looked forward to the day when he would bring home the ratified Treaty of Tientsin. This was a veiled way of telling him that despite his defeat he was not to be replaced. Great therefore must have been Bruce's disappointment to learn in April that his brother was coming out to take command. Lord John wrote lamely that the Government's confidence in Bruce was undiminished, but perhaps the Chinese might find it difficult to make concessions to the men they had repelled the year before. The truth was that the Government wanted a man of greater political standing than Bruce who could keep an eye on the French and give the whole expedition a grander air. Elgin was unwilling, but accepted after he had made a speech in the House of Lords defending his settlement of 1858. Hammond thought that Bruce would resign when he heard the news. Certainly some of his advisers were dismayed: 'If it be true that Lord Elgin be returning,' writes Parkes, 'I doubt not he will again attempt negotiation. There will then be no end to the Chinese troubles.' But Bruce was not a proud man nor a firebrand. His instincts were peaceable and liberal, but unlike his brother he distrusted his own judgment, and was thus normally to be found in a state of conscientious worry, wide open to the advice of those around him. In later years he seems to have developed self-confidence, but in 1860 he was still very much a younger brother and it probably never occurred to him to resign when he heard that he was again to work under James.

Elgin visited Paris after his appointment to see the Emperor, who to his relief said nothing of any French plans for territorial gains in China, and to revive his friendship with Gros, whom he found feeling sorry for himself at the prospect of having to brave again the discomforts of China. Just before he left London Elgin received his formal despatch of instructions. He was to go to Peking with his French colleague and insist on being received there with honour. He was further to insist on an apology for the events of 1859, on an indemnity for the losses suffered, and on ratification of the Treaty of Tientsin. He had discretion as to whether a British Minister should be left permanently in Peking. He was authorised to annex the peninsula of Kowloon, opposite Hong Kong, if this could be done without causing trouble with the French. He was warned of the risk which he himself had pointed out in Cabinet, that if the Emperor retired into Manchuria rather than wait in Peking for the allied expedition, the Empire might dissolve into chaos. The Foreign Office gave no hint as to how it would expect Elgin to deal with such a situation, but performed a graceful sidestep for which the ironical Hammond was surely responsible: 'In these circumstances Your Lordship and your enlightened colleague Baron Gros will be required to exercise those personal qualities of firmness and discretion which have induced Her Majesty and her ally to place their confidence in you.'

So Elgin sailed east again, hoping each day while he was still in range of the telegraph to hear that Frederick had settled the business without him, and that he could return to the Post Office and to Fife. He travelled in the congenial company of *The Times* correspondent Bowlby. In Egypt they were much struck by the expression of the moonlit Sphinx. 'There was a singular gentleness and hopefulness in the lines of the mouth which appeared to be in contrast with the anxious eye.' Mr. Bowlby agreed that the upper part of the face denoted intellectual striving and the lower part moral confidence. Elgin sent his wife a camomile plant with a little blue flower. In the Indian Ocean he tore up old letters and threw them overboard, read Thiers and Tennyson, and bitterly regretted having agreed to come. His gloom was increased by reading about the Indian Mutiny and as usual took the form of violent invective in his diary against his fellow countrymen: 'Can I do anything to prevent England from calling down on herself God's curse for brutalities committed on another feeble Oriental race? Or are all my exertions to result only in the extension of the area over which Englishmen are to exhibit how hollow and superficial are both their civilisation and their Christianity?' He was by now in company again with Baron Gros, and just as they were leaving Ceylon they suffered a dramatic accident. Their P. and O. steamer *Malabar* struck a rock in a thunderstorm. 'Going to sea?' said the captain. 'Why, we are going to the bottom.' Luckily the ship was beached and everyone taken off, but most of the luggage was under water, and Elgin and Gros had to wait a fortnight while the divers fished it up. The two elderly gentlemen recorded with mild relish each other's discomfiture. Gros fussed about his set of plate and Elgin was surprised to learn that it was not insured. Elgin worried about his secret instructions which were also submerged. Gros found this concern sinister, and connected it with a remark of Elgin's that a new war in China would be so unpopular in England that rather than drag it on into 1861 it might be better to help the pseudo-Protestant Taiping rebels and set them up as rulers of the Empire. Could this be the plan authorised in the secret instructions for which the divers were fishing assiduously in the wreck of the *Malabar*? Gros thought so, and over the next months the thought slowly grew into a bad dream in his mind. In fact Elgin's secret instructions dealt with the possible annexation of Kowloon.

While the two plenipotentiaries were sailing east the allied expedition had been assembling in Hong Kong. The massive figures for the French force which had so impressed Ministers in London were never turned into reality and the

British, having begun by worrying that there would be so many French that they would swamp the expedition, ended by worrying that the proportion of British was so high that the French would take mortal offence. In fact there converged on Hong Kong about 11,000 British and Indians, and about 7,000 French. There was no room for so large a force on the island, but Parkes had solved the problem by renting from the local authorities for £160 a year the peninsula of Kowloon opposite Hong Kong. The Viceroy at Canton was happy to turn an honest penny by renting to the allies a training ground on which they could prepare the force which was to attack his Emperor, and the British thus entered peaceably into possession, before Elgin's arrival, of the territory which his secret instructions authorised him to annex. There, on the strip beside the harbour where the Peninsula Hotel stands today, the two armies camped, trained and recruited their coolies. The British paid their coolies £1 17s. 6d. a month, with rations and two suits of clothes; the terms were so attractive that the Chinese assumed that they would be required to fight in the front line, and recruits were slow to come in. The British commander, Sir Hope Grant, was a general favourite. No one claimed that he was a military genius, indeed it was said that he owed the decisive promotion of his career to the need of his commanding officer for an adjutant who could play the violoncello to accompany his violin. Sir Hope was spare, weatherbeaten and very much a Scot. He read the Bible, rode to hounds, and was particularly popular with the Sikhs with whom he had served at Lucknow three years before. Elgin wrote of him: 'There is a great simplicity and kindliness about his manner which in a man so highly placed must be most winning.' His French counterpart, de Montauban, though perhaps the abler soldier, was a flamboyant and prickly colleague, always on the point of quarrel. There were plenty of minor squabbles in Hong Kong. As the forces were gathering, news came of the French proposal to annex Nice and Savoy and of the resulting coldness between

London and Paris. The alliance with the French was unpopular with the officers and the community in Hong Kong, and they were quick to believe rumours that it was about to break down. There were local causes of friction too, in particular a tense rivalry about the height of the flagpoles over the two headquarters. But on the whole the spring of 1860 passed pleasantly enough. Social life in Hong Kong was more serene now that at last poor Sir John Bowring had gone. His place as Governor had been taken by Sir Hercules Robinson, who was, to Elgin's relief, 'a gentlemanlike person, and the tone of the community has undergone a great change for the better.' Lady Robinson gave cheerful routs for the officers, and on fine days the local residents crossed the harbour to catch the evening breezes on the Kowloon side, to admire the new Armstrong guns and the Indian cavalry at their manœuvres, and to hear Sir Hope Grant at his violoncello.

The first military move was to occupy Chusan, the island off the mouth of the Yangtze which had had a big part in the first China war twenty years before. It had no strategic importance in an operation against Peking, but could be used as a pledge in future negotiations. Meanwhile the commanders and the bulk of their forces moved north from Hong Kong to Shanghai in May. There the social round resumed; the French Minister's wife Madame de Bourboulon smoked cigars, and Sir Hope Grant was again assiduous on his 'cello. But young Colonel Wolseley recorded that Shanghai for a stranger 'is one of the dullest places under heaven . . . nothing but a desire to grow rich could induce men to reside there.' The style of living was already expensive, luxurious and dull; the rent of a small house was as much as £400 a year, and merchant princes like John Dent had acquired French cooks. There were now more serious troubles with the French. The Chinese Viceroy at Shanghai was hard-pressed by the Taiping rebels, and appealed to the allied commanders for help. De Montauban was in favour of sending an expedition against the

Taipings, who offended him by being not only Chinese but also a sort of Protestant. Bruce agreed that Shanghai should be defended against any rebel attack but otherwise refused to be drawn from the official policy of neutrality in internal Chinese matters and Gros when he arrived agreed with Bruce rather than de Montauban. Elgin's feelings as he returned to Shanghai after nearly two years' absence were gloomy even for him. 'If I had been anything but the greatest fool that the world ever saw I should never have been where I now am. I deserve to suffer for it, and no doubt I shall do so.' His reunion with Frederick must have been awkward, but the two brothers were genuinely fond of each other and Frederick seems to have returned almost with relief to the role of adviser and lieutenant. Elgin's main worry was the expense of the large forces of which he disposed. His last remark to Palmerston had been that he would rather march on Peking with 5,000 men than with 25,000. The sight of the forces on the ground did nothing to reassure him. To Wolseley, the soldier, it was a matter of pride that 'England has never before opened a campaign with such a well organised or a more efficient force.' Elgin the administrator, judged dourly that three times as much as necessary had been spent. 'What will the House of Commons say when the bill which has to be paid for this war has to be presented . . . the Admiral is doing things excellently well if money be no object.' Elgin's recent experience of admirals had not been cheerful, and he held Hope largely responsible for his brother's discomfiture the year before. He himself soon had a brush with Hope when the Admiral denied his right to fly a flag on the ship in which he travelled. Elgin won and the flag flew, but it was not a happy beginning to their co-operation.

The military commanders and the two Ambassadors held a meeting at Shanghai on June 16th to work out a plan of action. The Chinese having already in April rejected the allied terms, it was agreed that there was no point in starting negotiations at least until the allies had reached Tientsin.

Attack on the Taku forts by the British and French fleets, May 1858

The storming of the Taku forts by the French, August 1860

The shipwreck of the *Malabar*, Ceylon, May 1860; Lord Elgin and Baron Gros on board. 'An amiable altercation takes place between their Excellencies as to whether France or England shall leave the sinking vessel first.' Below, identification of the murdered prisoners, Peking; 1860. From sketches by Colonel Crealock

It was also agreed that Admiral Hope should not again be asked to mount a frontal attack on the terrible guns at Taku, even though his own and the French forces were now much stronger than they had been a year before. There was to be a pincer attack, the French to land south of the forts, the British east of them at Pehtang, both to advance by land to take the guns on the flank and in the rear. But the troops were not yet ready for action, the French in particular being short of baggage animals. Separate camps were therefore to be established from which the attacks could be launched. The French were to set up at Chefoo on the coast of Shantung, and the British across the Gulf of Pechihli at Talienwan, near what was to become Port Arthur. It was a sign of the uneasiness of the alliance that the plan of operations provided for the British and French forces to be kept apart until the last possible moment. All worked reasonably well. The French made themselves comfortable at Chefoo and had no difficulty in buying meat and vegetables in the nearby villages. The young officers played whist and read aloud to each other the fashionable socialist novels of Eugene Sue. They fretted over the shortage of ponies and mules. The French had no India or Hong Kong near at hand to supply them, and their agents trying to buy ponies in Japan for £5 each complained that the British had been there first and were spoiling their prospects. Elgin visited the French camp in mid-July and was entertained by the staging of a play whose lack of merit was attributed by one Frenchman to the fact that its author was only a sergeant. There was no British sergeant to write plays, good or bad, for de Montauban when he visited Talienwan. Instead the Sikh cavalry carried out the manœuvre which had so charmed the ladies of Hong Kong in the spring, the lancing at the gallop of tent pegs fixed into the ground. The landing at Talienwan had not been without incident, for the sailors in unloading the stores had happened upon the officers' champagne. The countryside around was barren, and the cavalry found foraging difficult. There were plenty of oysters by the shore, and the coolies smoked a great deal of opium, but neither was exactly the right diet for a fighting force. The troops slept fourteen in a bell tent, twelve foot in diameter and eleven foot high. It was in fact far from ideal, and the British waited impatiently for the French to find their transport. Neither the French nor the British were pleased to discover the arrival in the Gulf of Ward the American, and a new Russian called Ignatieff, both instructed to hover in their customary neutral role on the fringes of the expedition. On July 19th when all seemed almost ready, the agreed plan collapsed. The French found that the coast to the south of the Taku forts where they were supposed to land sloped so gently out to sea that they would have to wade through up to two miles of mud to get ashore. There was a hasty conference and it was agreed that the French should join the British in the landing at Pehtang. Some of the British thought that the French were scared not of the mud but of the glaring deficiencies in their own equipment which a separate landing would reveal, but Elgin dismissed this as unfair.

Finally on July 26th the British embarked from Talienwan, in more than 150 ships and boats, and made their way slowly along the coast. On August 1st they and the French landed at Pehtang. The British troops were in theory heavy-laden. According to their orders: 'Every man will land with three days' cooked provisions, 56 rounds ammunition, greatcoats, canteens, water-bottles full, and haversacks. They will wear cloth trousers, summer frocks, worsted socks, and wicker helmets.' Faced with wading through half a mile of mud the orders were sensibly forgotten and one brigadier led his men clad only in a short shirt and jacket. The landing would have been difficult if the Chinese cavalry had opposed it, but they did not appear. The forts of Pehtang (far less formidable than those of Taku) were left empty but mined for the invaders. The small town of 20,000 inhabitants was quickly occupied. The next move was to march south-west for seven miles from Pehtang to the town of Sinho and the Peiho river. Once the river had been reached behind the fearsome forts of Taku which guarded its entrance they could be attacked from their weaker land ward side. But the march to the river would not be easy. The ground was mostly swampy, and the one causeway which led across it was easily defensible. On August 3rd a reconnaissance in strength out of Pehtang by 2,000 British and French was pinned down on the causeway by Chinese fire and could make no progress. De Montauban refused to do any more until his stores were unloaded. This took ten days as there was a shortage of boats and no proper jetty. It began to rain and the stinking streets of Pehtang were turned to mud. Hundreds of its citizens, turned out of their homes by the soldiery, camped helpless in the open. The dangers of fire and disease in the squalid overcrowded little town grew with each day. The French soldiers became skilled at chasing and capturing stray pigs in the narrow slippery streets, but their officers claimed that for more serious plunder the British and Indians were the worst offenders: 'Quant aux anglais,' wrote one of them, Armand Lucy, 'leur réputation est faite de longtemps, ce sont nos maîtres: on ne trouve pas un clou où ils ont passé.' Elgin had no doubt that the opposite was true: 'This dreadful alliance, what will it not have cost us before we are done with it. The French by their exactions and misconduct have already stirred to resistance the peaceful population of China. They are cautious enough when armed enemies even Chinese are in question—but indisputably valorous against defenceless villagers and little-footed women.' The argument about plundering was to splutter on for months and reach an angry climax when the Summer Palace was burned. The judgments of the eye-witnesses vary so widely that it is not possible to do more than pity the Chinese householder whose possessions lay in the path of the advancing army.

The Chinese were encouraged by the result of the action on August 3rd and a few days later Heng Fu, the Governor of the local province of Chihli, wrote to Elgin suggesting discussions. The allies having already agreed not to enter into negotiations until they had reached Tientsin, Elgin sent a politely negative reply. Finally on August 12th the army was ready. Hope Grant and de Montauban had decided to follow the sometimes disastrous precedent of the Roman consuls and take it in turns to command the joint force on alternate days. Hope Grant forced de Montauban's hand by saying that he intended to order an advance on the 12th whether or not the French came with him. In fact the action was successful. Sir R. Napier and the Second Division of cavalry were sent on a northward movement across the swampy plain to outflank the Chinese position on the causeway while the French and First British Division advanced slowly along the causeway itself. Several thousand Manchu cavalry harassed these movements and attempted to charge, but were disorganised by steady artillery fire in which the new Armstrong guns first showed their paces. By the end of the day the town of Sinho at the south-west end of the causeway was captured. De Montauban wanted to push on down the river the same day and take the neighbouring town of Tangku, but it proved to be defended and he had to pause.

It was during the engagement on August 12th that one of the most celebrated casualties of the war occurred. An Irish sergeant and a private of the Buffs were in charge of a party of Chinese coolies carrying in carts the rum ration of Napier's 2nd Division. They drank too much, lost their way, mistook for Sikhs a troop of Manchu cavalry and after a scuffle were captured. A week later the Irish sergeant made his way back to the allied camp with a stirring tale to tell. The prisoners had been brought before a mandarin and ordered on pain of death to kowtow. All obeyed except for Private Moyse of the Buffs, who was at once beheaded. The sergeant's story appeared in *The Times*, and was read by Sir Francis Doyle. Sir Francis had been Gladstone's best man, and was for many years receiver-general of customs. He was also a poet, and he rose to this patriotic occasion:

Last night among his fellow roughs
He jested, quaffed and swore
A drunken private of the Buffs
Who never looked before.
Today beneath the foeman's frown
He stands in Elgin's place,
Ambassador from Britain's crown,
And type of all her race. . . .

Far Kentish hopfields round him seemed
Like dreams to come and go
Bright leagues of cherryblossom gleam'd
One sheet of living snow.
The smoke above his father's door
In grey soft eddies hung,
Must he then watch it rise no more,
Doomed by himself so young?

Yes, honour calls! with strength like steel
He puts the vision by;
Let dusky Indians whine and kneel,
An English lad must die.
And thus with eye that would not shrink,
With knee to man unbent,
Unfaltering on its dreadful brink,
To his red grave he went . . .

So let his name through Europe ring
A man of mean estate,
Who died, as firm as Sparta's king,
Because his soul was great.

Unfortunately Sir Francis had jumped to several wrong con-
clusions. The 'dusky Indians' were in fact Cantonese coolies.
Despite his regiment, Moyse was no Kentish lad but a hard-
boiled Scot of 32 with an army record of insubordination.[1]
All the more likely perhaps to have refused to kowtow; on
the face of it there seems no reason why the sergeant, though

[1] J.P. Entract, Journal Society for Army Historical Research.

Irish and intoxicated, should have invented a story which put a dead man's courage at so notably different a level to his own. But most witnesses of the war thought the sergeant was deranged, and a doubt must continue to hang over Private Moyse's act of heroism.

On August 14th the allies took without difficulty the small town of Tangku, and the way was clear for an attack on the rear of the Taku forts. There were four main forts, two on either side of the Peiho river, and the allied commanders differed as to how they should be tackled. De Montauban wanted to push the allied army across the river and attack the forts which stood on its farther or southern bank. There were sound military arguments for this. If the southern forts were attacked it would be easier for the naval force gathered on the sea side of the forts to give supporting fire. More important, the Chinese forces would be able to retreat from the forts towards Tientsin if the allies controlled only one bank of the river. If, as de Montauban proposed, the allies were established on both banks before they attacked the forts then the Chinese garrisons would be cut off and their destruction made certain. It was not easy for Hope Grant to contest de Montauban's professional opinion, for the reputation of the French army and its generals still stood high; but he managed to do so successfully without causing a breach. Hope Grant wanted to capture the forts, not necessarily to destroy the garrisons. He was told that the fort nearest to the allied position at Tangku, i.e. the inner northern fort, was the least strongly defended but that by virtue of its location it controlled the other three. An attack down the northern bank would not involve the allies in crossing the river and so lengthening and exposing their line of communication with the port of Pehtang. Hope Grant was a cautious man, always ready to worry about his supplies, and the thought of his mule convoys being attacked by clouds of Mongol cavalry as they struggled through the mud flats was not to be endured. He had his way, and on August 21st the allies attacked the inner northern fort, with careful artillery support. Despite the bombardment which they had suffered the defenders kept up a punishing fire on the parties of attackers as they made their way over the canals and ditches which surrounded the fort. The attackers were handicapped by having to carry large and clumsy pontoons which proved useless for the narrow waterways to be crossed. After some hours enough men were gathered under the walls of the fort to make an assault possible. The French and British vanguards planted their flags on the walls of the fort at almost the same time, and the fighting was then soon over. The Chinese had resisted with great determination. It was not true as was later reported that they had been tied to their guns by their officers, but it was true that the elaborate system of obstacles which they had built all round the fort made it difficult for them to retreat. Their bodies lay strewn inside the fort; the gruesome scene was recorded by Signor Beato, the Italian photographer who had somehow managed to attach himself to the expedition. He flitted enthusiastically among the corpses, insisting that they should not be moved until he had finished. The British casualties were about 200 killed and wounded, the French roughly the same. Six Victoria Crosses were awarded for the storming of this single fort. In the evening there was a torrential downpour which quickly swamped the allied camp at Sinho and the surrounding country; if it had happened in the morning the Chinese would have been safe for the day.

Hope Grant was proved right in thinking that the fort which had been taken was the key to the whole position. A few hours of confusion followed its fall, during which Parkes was sent to persuade the Chinese commander to surrender. White flags soon appeared on all three remaining forts and without more fighting the allies took possession. Two days later Admiral Hope and his gunboats sailed up the river to Tientsin which they found undefended. Elgin wrote on August 26th: 'The martial crust under which China conceals her military weakness and disorganisation has been more tough and difficult to break through, but that object once accomplished the power of resistance seems to have been paralysed on this as on the former occasion.'

The parallel with 1858 seemed complete when a letter arrived from Kuei Liang, one of the negotiators of the 1858 Treaty, saying that he had authority to negotiate all matters in dispute. Elgin and Gros installed themselves comfortably in Tientsin, and Parkes was sent to present the allied demands. They required an apology for the events of 1859, an indemnity for the losses suffered, ratification of the Treaty of Tientsin, the advance of the army as far as T'ungchow, a town only a few miles from Peking, and an audience for the Ambassadors with the Emperor. As Kuei Liang dickered over these terms the allied army moved up to Tientsin. The bell tents were stiflingly hot in the August sun and good trade was done by the hawkers who slipped among them selling ice. Elgin noted that the army thrived: 'beef and mutton at about 3d. a pound; peaches, grapes and all sorts of vegetables in plenty . . . a man scorns his grog if it is not well iced.' He and Gros and Parkes all believed that the war was over, and de Montauban began to issue fancy scarves to the units which were to escort the Ambassadors into Peking. There was news of trouble in Shanghai where allied troops had helped to beat off a Taiping rebel attack, but in spite of this the army was beginning to hope for Christmas at home. Great was the disappointment when on September 6th it was learned that negotiations had broken down. Kuei Liang had accepted the allied terms but it turned out that he did not after all have sufficient powers to sign a binding document. The soldiers bitterly criticised the diplomats for having been deceived by an obvious Chinese delaying tactic, and it does seem out of character that Parkes should not have insisted on seeing Kuei Liang's powers before he began negotiations. Elgin himself did not think the Chinese had gained anything by the delay: 'the blockheads,' he wrote on September 8th, 'have gone on negotiating with me just long enough to enable Grant to bring all his army up to this point. Here we are with our base established in the heart of the country, in a capital climate, with abundance around us, our army in excellent health, and these stupid people give me a snub which obliges me to break with them.'

On September 9th the army began to advance northwards from Tientsin up the Peiho river towards Peking. With them went the two Ambassadors; Gros would have preferred to stay in Tientsin, but Elgin decided that he had to keep an eye on the allied commanders and Gros felt that even at the sacrifice of his comforts he must keep an eye on Elgin. As they moved north the Ambassadors were peppered with Chinese letters urging them to turn the army back. Ts'ai Prince of Yi and Mu Yi, President of the Board of War, wrote on September 11th that Kuei Liang had confused matters, that all the allied demands were agreed, and that they were about to leave for Tientsin to conclude the necessary agreement. Elgin replied that after what had passed he would sign no agreement until the army was at T'ungchow, almost at the gates of the capital. The next day another letter suggested a compromise; could not the army stop at Ho-se-wu, about halfway between Tientsin and Peking? It so happened that this was what Hope Grant wanted to do anyway—the army had met no resistance on its slow march north, but he was in a fluster about supplies. The Chinese mule drivers had bolted the first day out of Tientsin, and the Peiho river, which was to be the main supply line, was running dangerously low. Hope Grant told Elgin that he needed a week's pause to bring up his heavy guns and form a depot at Ho-se-wu. Elgin was not pleased; he knew that he and Gros had been criticised for the delay in Tientsin by the same officers who were now proposing a further delay at Ho-se-wu. 'Entre nous,' he wrote in his diary, 'the difficulty of getting our army along is incredible; our men are so pampered that they do nothing for themselves and their necessities so great that we are almost immovable.' But he decided in the interval to try again for an agreement with the Chinese, and Wade and Parkes were sent to see Ts'ai and Mu at T'ungchow on September 14th. Wade described Ts'ai as 'a tall dignified man with an intelligent countenance, though a somewhat unpleasant eye'; Mu was 'softer and more wily in his manner, but also intelligent.' They worked for eight hours and seemed near agreement. Once again Parkes dominated the proceedings; as Elgin wrote at this time: 'Parkes is one of the most remarkable men I ever met; for energy, courage and ability combined I do not know where I could find his match; and this joined to a facility for speaking Chinese which he shares only with Lay makes him at present the man of the situation.' It was a far cry from the discords of 1858 when Elgin had dismissed Parkes as a bigoted creature of Bowring's. Unfortunately for Parkes the Chinese also thought he was 'the man of the situation,' and were tempted into a foolish act of treachery against him.

There remained among the captured documents of this campaign a number of memorials to the Emperor which show that in late August and early September there was a strong clash of opinion among his advisers. Behind the traditional courtliness of phrase in these papers can be found a mounting anxiety for the future of China. The main point at issue was whether the Emperor should stay in Peking. Sang Ko Lin Chin advised him to take a hunting trip to the north. His arguments were those natural to any military commander who finds his plans complicated by the presence of royalty near the front line, and it is not necessary to assume as some have done that Sang wanted to seat himself on the imperial throne. Other voices urged that for the Emperor to leave Peking would damage public morale, that the barbarians were only interested in trade and could be fobbed off. The Emperor himself suggested a compromise: he would announce that he intended to take personal command of his armies, and would then leave Peking ostensibly for the battlefield, but in fact for the north. This produced a masterpiece of respectful protest from his ministers: 'At a period of public distress the man of heroic character is prepared to die at his post, and at such a time the most perfect sincerity and truthfulness befit the conduct of both high and low. Your Ministers have today respectfully read the Vermilion Decree stating that the arrangements for Your Majesty's hunting expedition are to be presented as preparations for taking the field in person, and that if the enemy is met in the vicinity of Matow or Tungchow Your Majesty will proceed with a strong force as originally intended to a place north of Peking and there take up a position. They admire the awe-inspiring demeanour and the well-devised strategy thus displayed. But the common people are extremely slow of apprehension; they easily suspect and with difficulty appreciate, and they will say that as the barbarians are to the south-east of the capital the change of plan from a hunting tour to taking the field in person should induce Your Majesty to remain at Tungchow for the support of Sang Ko Lin Chin; that the taking up a post to the north of the capital would be a deviation from the seat of war; and accordingly that what in name was campaigning was in reality a hunting tour.' Another minister was less circumspect: 'In what light does Your Majesty regard your people? In what light the shrines of your ancestors or the altars of the tutelary gods? Will you cast away the inheritance of your ancestors like a damaged shoe? What would history say of Your Majesty for a thousand generations to come?'

At the back of the minds of those who wrote must have been the memory of the last Ming Emperor, who two hundred years earlier at the news of the approach of the barbarians had hanged himself on a tree on Coal Hill in the middle of Peking, overlooking the gardens and palaces of his ancestors.

19

As we have seen recorded, Parkes and Wade had reached a broad agreement with the Chinese negotiators on September 14th. The allied army was to halt short of T'ungchow, and Elgin and Gros were then to enter Peking with an escort of 1,000 men each to ratify the Treaty of Tientsin. A few points remained to be settled, for example the exact site for the army's camp and whether Elgin was to deliver in person to the Emperor the letter which he carried from Queen Victoria. On September 17th Parkes went again to T'ungchow to settle these points, accompanied by Henry Loch (Elgin's private secretary), Bowlby (*The Times* correspondent), de Normann (an attaché belonging to Frederick Bruce, whom Elgin had brought north with him), Colonel Walker (Quartermaster General of cavalry), Thompson of the Commissariat and an escort of six dragoons and twenty Sikhs under the command of Lieutenant Anderson. It was a bright morning with a touch of autumn coolness and the party rode cheerfully through the high-standing corn. They reached T'ungchow without incident and in the early afternoon Parkes and Loch called on the Chinese Commissioners, led by the Emperor's cousin, Ts'ai, Prince of Yi. The Commissioners, who had been so conciliatory three days earlier, were fretful and nervous. They fastened on one of the outstanding points and declared that it was out of the question for Elgin to deliver the Queen's letter personally to the Emperor. Parkes replied soothingly that this was not a point of the first importance and that it could be peacefully settled later on. The argument went fitfully to and fro and it was not until evening that Parkes managed to agree exactly where the allied army was to camp the following day. The whole British party spent the night of the 17th in a house at T'ungchow. The next day Parkes, Loch, Colonel Walker and Thompson rose early to ride back to the army with the news of what had been agreed. The rest of the group stayed in T'ungchow to wait for Parkes and Loch, who were to return to the town that night as an advance party to prepare for Elgin's arrival. As Parkes and his companions neared the allied army they noticed that several units of Chinese infantry and cavalry were on the move. The high corn and the watercourses which intersected the countryside made it difficult to be sure what was happening, but it was clear that a large-scale surreptitious military movement was under way. Parkes and his companions hastily consulted; the plan on which they decided showed courage and a startling self-confidence. One would have thought that in those threatening circumstances the first instinct of the party would have been to stay together; instead they decided to split into three. Loch was to ride with two Sikhs to warn the allied army that instead of advancing peacefully to an agreed encampment it was about to move into an elaborate trap; Walker, Thompson and the five dragoons were to stay where they were, in the middle of the Chinese position, to watch developments; Parkes, with one dragoon and one Sikh, was to ride back to T'ungchow to demand an explanation from the Commissioners. Loch found Sir Hope Grant, who had already halted the army after noticing Chinese cavalry on his flank. He persuaded the General to wait two hours before advancing again, to give Parkes time either to persuade the Chinese to desist or to bring back Bowlby, de Normann and the rest of the escort from T'ungchow. Then, almost incredibly, Loch asked and was given permission to return through the Chinese lines to T'ungchow, and a Captain Brabazon of the Royal Artillery was allowed to go with him. There was little he could tell Parkes which Parkes did not already know or guess, and it was foolish courage to add in this way more lives to those already in the power of the Chinese.

Colonel Walker and his tiny party in their red coats were clearly visible from the allied lines as they moved among the grey uniforms of the Chinese. Colonel Walker came upon a French officer who was in the hands of the Chinese. He tried unsuccessfully to rescue the Frenchman; after this scuffle he clearly could not stay where he was and he and his men galloped through Chinese fire to their own lines. The two hours' respite promised by Hope Grant to Loch soon came to an end, and there was no further sign from the direction of T'ungchow. The French had for some time been pressing Hope Grant to attack, and the order was given in the middle of the morning. In the engagement which followed the Anglo-French army of about 4,000 had no serious trouble in breaking a Chinese force about five times the size and capturing the town of Chang-chia-wan on which the Chinese front rested. As usual there was no lack of courage on the Chinese side; but the skilful use of the allied artillery prevented them bringing their numbers to bear, and the fiery disciplined Indian and Spahi cavalry struck decisively at their weak points. After the fighting the town of Chang-chia-wan was given over to plunder, and the following day Gros wrote to the French Foreign Minister what was probably a just verdict in advance on the controversy which was to break out about looting: 'J'ai le coeur serré par les actes de vandalisme que j'ai vu commettre par nos soldats, comme par nos alliés, charmés de pouvoir rejeter mutuellement les uns sur les autres les actes abominables dont ils se rendaient coupables.'

The allied army pushed slowly forward, vainly seeking news of Parkes and his missing party. They outflanked T'ungchow, and on September 21st fought a second battle to force a crossing of the canal which links that town with Peking. This sharp engagement round the bridge at Pa-li-ch'iao brought particular glory to the French infantry who carried the Chinese batteries at the point of the bayonet, and consequently to de Montauban, who chose the place for the title of nobility which Napoleon III later bestowed upon him.

No further obstacle lay between the allies and Peking, and the Emperor now left the capital for his hunting trip to the north. He did not put his trust in the last massive weapon of defence which earlier dynasties had bequeathed him, the walls of the city itself. Yet Hope Grant was sure after reconnaissance that the small force and light guns with which he had won at Chang-chia-wan and Pa-li-ch'iao would be quite unable to storm the walls of Peking if they were defended with anything of the determination which the Chinese had shown behind the humbler fort at Taku. He and de Montauban were clear that nothing could be done until the siege guns had been brought up by river from Tientsin. Elgin and Gros fretted at the delay, Gros in particular fearing that by the time the allies broke into Peking the missing prisoners would be dead and the Chinese authorities vanished. The Ambassadors were now in touch with the last and most exalted of the Chinese statesmen with whom they had to deal, Prince Kung, younger brother of the Emperor; but no progress was being made because the Ambassadors insisted that all those who had been captured should be returned before negotiations could start. No violent language was used, and it was left open to Kung to disclaim the violation of the flag of truce as a mistake of subordinates. His failure to do this or to produce the prisoners increased the fears which were felt for their lives. It was an odious dilemma for Elgin, particularly when Kung promised to release the prisoners if the allied army withdrew and hinted that they would be killed if Peking was attacked. It was unthinkable to give up the purpose of the expedition to save the lives of 37 men, who indeed might already be dead, but the burden of continuing operations as though the Chinese held no hostages must have been great.

The allied army had last seen Loch riding with Brabazon back to T'ungchow on the morning of September 18th.

When they reached the town they found that Parkes had already gone to remonstrate with the chief Commissioner, Prince Ts'ai, about the military movements, and that de Normann and Bowlby were out shopping, not knowing that anything was amiss. Parkes soon returned, having had a fruitless argument with Prince Ts'ai and as soon as the whole party was assembled they left in the direction of the allied army. They had ten miles to ride through a hostile army, and little prospect of doing it before the end of the two hours' respite which Hope Grant had promised, particularly as de Normann and Bowlby were poorly mounted. As they had feared the allied artillery began to fire just as they reached the centre of the Chinese position. They were stopped by a mandarin who, noticing their flag of truce, offered them a safe conduct if two of them would come to discuss the matter with his general. Parkes and Loch followed him and found themselves in the presence of the commander-in-chief Sang Ko Lin Chin. Sang questioned them angrily and ordered Parkes to arrange for the allied army to retreat. When Parkes said that this was not in his power, Sang lost his temper and ordered that they be taken to Prince Ts'ai in a cart. Prince Ts'ai was not to be found, but they were questioned again by another general at Pa-li-ch'iao, and at one time thought they were about to be beheaded. Eventually they were bound, pushed again into a cart, and carried on the paved road to Peking. The same journey over deep ruts in a springless cart had been suffered by the American, Ward, the year before; but Loch and Parkes were bound and unable to protect themselves against the agonising jolts which hurled their bodies against the hard sides of the cart. In Peking they were thrown into separate prisons, each chained and confined with a batch of criminals. Loch wrote a detailed account of the week which he spent in this prison. The food was poor but adequate, and his fellow prisoners kindly; his fear was that the gall-marks of the chains on his neck and wrists would become infected by the maggots which abounded. It was to be seen that

Prince Kung, from a lithograph published 1862 by J. Hogarth

Clock Tower of the Summer Palace by the lake. The photograph, taken by Signor Beato in 1860, bears the inscription: 'Fired by Hon. Stuart Wortley'

this was not an idle fear. He tried to attract Parkes' attention by singing 'God Save the Queen' but found he could only manage a few bars. Meanwhile the Chinese were at work on Parkes in his separate prison. One of the Commissioners, Heng Chi, who had known Parkes in Canton, was sent to persuade him to write to ask Elgin to abate his demands. Parkes eventually agreed to write to Elgin provided that he was moved out of prison and allowed to join Loch. On September 29th the two men were moved to a temple in the north of the city and served an excellent dinner, brought in boxes from a nearby restaurant, of sixteen main and thirty-two minor dishes, which unfortunately they were too weak to eat. The luxury of a bath was more completely welcome. Parkes wrote in Chinese to Elgin, praising Prince Kung's qualifications and suggesting that the allied army should not advance farther until there had been a conference. Loch managed to scribble in Hindustani at the foot of the letter that it was written at the order of the Chinese Government. This letter was the first news which the allies had that any of the missing men were alive. The Chinese allowed clothes to be sent from the army to Parkes and Loch, and on an embroidered handkerchief of Loch's an ingenious craftsman wove the message (again in Hindustani) that the allied bombardment was to start in three days' time. It was a message of doubtful cheer, for Loch and Parkes had been assured by the mandarins who came to see them in their temple that the first shot of the bombardment would be the signal for their execution. While they waited the two men played backgammon on a board of their own design. They were sent by Prince Kung a small quantity of tea specially grown for the imperial court, of a flavour so exquisite that officials who had no particular business with the prisoners formed the habit of dropping in to take tea.

The siege guns had by now arrived and on October 5th and 6th the allied army moved slowly from Pa-li-ch'iao towards Peking. Its purpose was to engage once more Sang Ko Lin Chin's army which was said to be encamped immediately outside the north wall of the city. Cavalry were seen from time to time but there was no serious fighting. On the 6th Hope Grant sent a message to the French suggesting a rendezvous that night at the Imperial Summer Palace at Yuan Ming Yuan which lay some six miles to the north-west of the northern city wall. Later in the day contact was lost with the French; the main British force was held up by skirmishing Manchu cavalry in difficult country and spent the night in camp some miles short of the Summer Palace. Meanwhile within the city there was confusion and disagree-ment. The Emperor was gone, Sang's army was melting away to the north, and Prince Kung was left in the capital with orders to resist and a quantity of advisers who were divided as to whether this was possible. On the 5th Heng Chi announced to Parkes and Loch that it had been decided to reject the allied demands and that they themselves would be executed in the evening. He returned to Parkes a mini-ature of his wife and gave both men paper to write their last letters. The evening passed, and the next day, without any definite news. On the morning of the 7th Loch was awakened by the sound of artillery. He assumed that the long awaited bombardment of Peking had begun and that he and Parkes would be immediately executed. In fact the guns were fired from the British camp to tell the French army and the British cavalry of its position.

Hope Grant soon regained contact with his allies, and found they had business on hand which ruled out any further military operations for some days. The Summer Palace at Yuan Ming Yuan, which the French occupied on the evening of October 6th, was not a single palace, but a huge park crowded with pavilions, lakes and gardens, into the adorn-ment of which had been poured the wealth and ingenuity of successive Emperors. The park extended over eighty square miles and contained two hundred main buildings. Here were baroque halls designed by Jesuits two centuries earlier to suit the fantasy of their imperial clients; pavilions roofed with gold; the Hall of Audience with the rosewood throne; toy warships for naval warfare on the miniature lakes; marble bridges, gardens of twisted rock and carefully stunted trees; everywhere decoration and prettiness rather than grandeur; and here above all, scattered about for the taking, was an accumulation of bronzes, enamels, clocks, silks, furs, jade and ornaments such as none of the victors had seen before. Across the lake from the Hall of Audience were found the Emperor's private rooms, his cap on his bed, his pipe beside, the satin cushions with dragons and flowers worked in the imperial yellow, the chests and cupboards crammed with jade. The French army fell upon its prey. When Hope Grant's messengers arrived the next morning they found what one of them described as a temporary insanity. In vain de Montauban ordered that looting should be suspended until the British arrived; in vain did the French officers try to get their men on parade. They wandered from pavilion to pavilion, ripping and destroying, trailing treasures of whose value they had little idea, trying to find horses or peasants to carry their loot back to their quarters. The ground was soon littered with silks and furs. As the day wore on British officers began to appear on the scene to take their share; by the evening Hope Grant realised that he was faced with a grave problem of discipline. There was no question of trying to preserve the contents of the palace. By the rules of war as then understood they were lost, particularly as they belonged not to ordinary Chinese citizens but to the Emperor, who in allied eyes had brought his loss upon himself. What was intolerable to discipline was not the looting but the fact that it was confined to the French and to such British officers as had managed to visit the Palace on the 7th. The next day Hope Grant negotiated with de Montauban a share of a roomful of gold ingots which had been found in the Palace. He ordered all under his command to hand over at once all the objects which they had seized, and these were auctioned publicly over two days. The sum realised was £8,000; the objects sold must even then have been worth many times that amount. The splendid fruits of that auction are to be seen today on the walls and in the chests and cabinets of many an English and Scottish country house. The proceeds of the auction together with the ingots gave Hope Grant enough money to make a cash distribution to the whole army according to rank, each private soldier receiving £4; he and his immediate subordinates renounced their share. Nothing he could do could alter the fact that the smaller French force had much the richer share. The French army reached the Summer Palace almost without transport; it left with three hundred loaded wagons. It was widely believed by the British that de Montauban had deliberately lost contact with the British on October 6th in order to reach the Summer Palace first and alone. But Hope Grant himself had suggested the Summer Palace for a rendezvous that evening and the French cannot be blamed for his own delay in reaching it. They were indeed amazed at their own fortune; one young officer wrote home: 'Je prends la plume, mon bon père, mais sais-je que je vais te dire? Je suis ébahi, ahuri, abasourdi de ce que j'ai vu. Les mille et une nuits sont pour moi une chose parfaitement véridique maintenant. J'ai marché pendant presque deux jours sur plus de 30 millions de francs de soieries, de bijous, de porcelaines, bronzes, sculptures, de trésors enfin! Je ne crois pas qu'on ait vu chose pareille depuis le sac de Rome par les barbares.'

While the new barbarians were at work on the Summer Palace the long anxieties of Parkes and Loch were coming to an end. They passed the days, comfortable and well fed, in their temple in the north of Peking waiting for the turns of Chinese policy to bring them either release or sudden death. On the 8th Heng Chi came again to visit them. He had spent the day before in negotiation with Wade, having been lowered over the city walls in a basket because the Chinese soldiers, suspicious of his loyalty, refused to open the city gate to let him pass. He mentioned none of this to Parkes and Loch but sat for three hours drinking the imperial tea and discussing among other topics whether the earth revolved round the sun or vice versa. Parkes and Loch, determined not to show anxiety for their own safety, kept up the charade, until about noon when Heng Chi received a message and told the prisoners that Prince Kung had ordered their release that afternoon. At two o'clock they were placed in a cart and escorted out of one of the northern gates. Their escort left them, and on emerging from the cart they found that with them in other carts were a French officer and four soldiers, and a Sikh, all of whom had also been captured on September 18th. They reached the allied camp without difficulty, after twenty days of captivity. Heng Chi later told Parkes that he, but not Prince Kung, knew from a private message that the Emperor had been persuaded to sign an order for the immediate execution of the prisoners, with which an imperial courier was riding to Peking while Heng Chi was discussing the sun and the earth. Heng Chi had not dared to anticipate the hour fixed by Prince Kung for their release, although he feared that at any minute the courier might reach the Prince with the overriding order of execution. Heng Chi claimed no sympathy from Parkes and Loch, explaining that he had argued on their behalf with Prince Kung not because of any sympathy with them but simply because he judged that their death would bring a great weight of vengeance on the city and the imperial throne.

The released prisoners soon learned how lucky had been their lot. Four days later three Frenchmen and eight more Sikhs were sent to the allied camp, and two days after that another two Sikhs. Within the next few days there were brought to the British camp coffins containing the bodies of de Normann, Bowlby, Anderson, Private Phipps and the remaining Sikhs; the French also received the bodies of most of their missing men. The Sikhs who remained alive were able to tell some of the story. The prisoners had been escorted to the Summer Palace and then split up into four groups and taken to different prisons outside Peking. They had been chained or tied and in some cases left day and night in the open. Those who died died in great agony, through the infection spreading from their bound and swollen hands. The gaolers had in some instances increased the agony by wetting and so tightening the cords. Captain Brabazon and a French abbé were fortunate in that they were almost certainly beheaded at Pa-li-ch'iao on the day of the battle for the bridge over the canal. The coffins of the British and the Sikhs were buried in the Russian cemetery north of the city on October 17th; on the following day the French held a more elaborate ceremony for their compatriots at which the British generals were asked with others to sprinkle water over the graves. The Scottish spirit of General Hope Grant was dismayed, but 'as I perceived Sir Robert Napier, an excellent man, occupied with the same business I no longer hesitated.' During the funeral it was noticed that the far ranges of the Western Hills were white with snow.

20

THOSE SNOWY RIDGES of the Western Hills weighed on the minds of the allied leaders. The formal record of the next few weeks reads outwardly as a story of almost uninterrupted and inevitable success. In fact they were for Elgin a time of great stress and difficulty. Now that the fighting was over he and Gros moved back to the centre of events, but they were by no means free to make their own decisions. The generals who had up to now moved with great prudence, accepting delays rather than risks, were now led by the same prudence to argue that everything must be concluded in a great hurry. Hope Grant told Elgin that the British army must be back in Tientsin by the beginning of November if it was to avoid the risks of the severe Peking winter. He and de Montauban brushed aside the suggestion that if necessary the army might winter in Peking itself; the danger to their supplies would be too great. This time-table left the Ambassadors no room for subtleties or setbacks; they had to hammer Prince Kung into submission as hard and as fast as they could.

The first need was to dominate the city of Peking. An ultimatum was sent to Prince Kung requiring him to surrender the Anting gate of the city by noon on October 13th. The more light-hearted civilians assumed that there would be no further trouble from the Chinese, but those in the know waited anxiously for Prince Kung's reply. The military position of the Chinese was by no means desperate. The army of Sang Ko Lin Chin was defeated but not destroyed. The walls of Peking were forty foot high, sixty foot thick

231

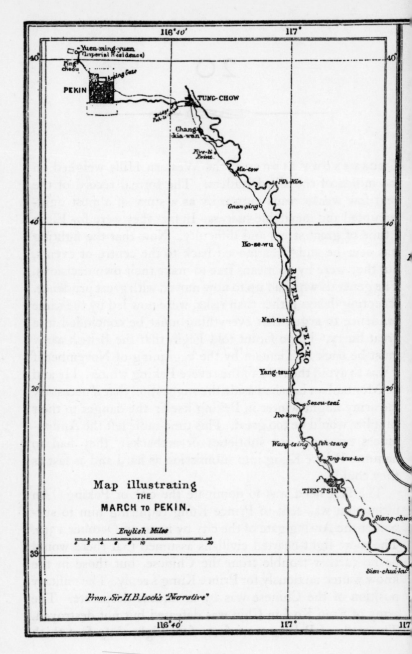

Map illustrating
THE
MARCH TO PEKIN.

English Miles

From Sir H.B.Loch's "Narrative"

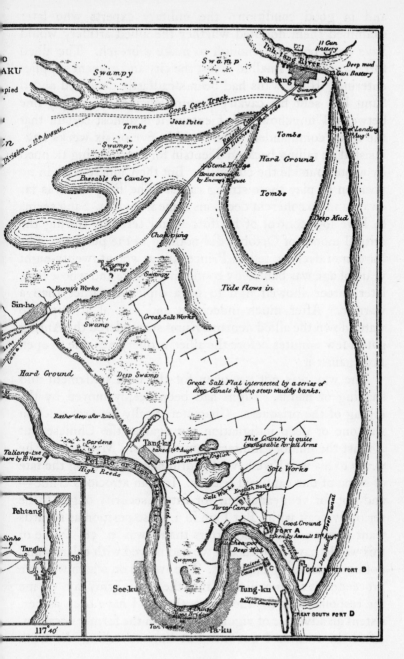

Swampy

Swamp

Pei-tang River

11 Gun Battery

Peh-tang

Gun Battery

Deep mud

Swamp Canal

Good Cart Track

River of Landing 1st Aug.

Tombs

Joss Poles

Swampy

Tombs

Hard Ground

Stone Bridge
House occupied
by Enemy's Picquet

Tombs

Deep Mud

Raised Causeway
with Ditches on each side

Passable for Cavalry

Division 12th August

Cha- pung

Enemy's Works

Swampy

Tide flows in

Enemy's Works

Sin-ho

Swamp

Great Salt Works

Ho Junk?

Ho Canal?

Hard Ground

Deep Swamp

Raised Causeway

Great Salt Flat intersected by a series of
deep Canals having steep muddy banks.

Rather deep after Rain

Gardens

This Country is quite
impassable for all Arms

Tang-ku
taken 14th Aug.

Taliang-tze
here by R'. Navy

Salt Works

Pei Ho or Peiho

High Reeds

Road made by English

Raised Causeway

Salt Works

English Batts.

Tartar Camp

Good Ground

FORT A
Taken by Assault 21st August

Cha-pou
Deep Mud

C

GREAT NORTH FORT B

Swamp

See-ku

Tung-ku

GREAT SOUTH FORT D

Ta-ku

Raised Causeway

Pehtang

Sinho

Tanglar

39

117° 40'

233

and in good condition; the military experts who later examined them doubted whether the allied artillery would have been powerful enough to make a breach. The allied force was far too small to invest the city and prevent supplies entering. If the walls had been steadfastly defended and if Sang had sent his cavalry ranging against the supply line between T'ungchow and Tientsin, it is almost certain that the allied commanders would within five or six weeks hav insisted on falling back on Tientsin for fear of being trapped by winter outside the city walls. But the Chinese were in no position to play these strong cards. The Emperor was far away, and no coherent decisions came from him. Sang seems to have lost control of his forces and certainly during the critical month of October did nothing to the purpose. The burden of decision fell on Prince Kung, who at twenty-eight years of age was baffled by conflicting advice and whose long later career showed him to be a diplomat rather than a warrior. After much indecision and several attempts to water down the allied demand Kung surrendered the Anting gate a few minutes before the allied artillery was due to open fire against it.

The way was not yet open for the final settlement and shaking of hands. Elgin had been deeply moved by the killing of the prisoners. Characteristically his first reaction was one of deep indignation not against the Chinese but against the dilatory military commanders. 'My dearest,' he wrote to his wife, 'we have dreadful news respecting the fate of some of our captured friends. It is an atrocious crime— and not for vengeance but for future security ought to be seriously dealt with. But I am in a worse position as regards want of energy at headquarters than I was in '58. None of this would have happened if we had moved with celerity and not been scared by bugbears. The system on which we have proceeded is so inexplicable that the whole army lays on me the responsibility for the delays though I have been as persistent an advocate of vigour as I was on the former occasion. After the trouble I got into last time by telling the truth [i.e. about Admiral Seymour] I shall keep silence now, but when we meet I shall say a good deal to you which I do not care to write even to you. God bless you.' The criticism is unfair since it is by no means certain that the lives of the prisoners would have been saved if the allies had attacked Peking immediately after the battle of Pa-li-ch'iao on September 21st; they might well have been executed at once.

Elgin was determined on some spectacular act of redress for the atrocity, but was not at first sure what this should be. Further military action was impracticable: 'I should have preferred crushing the Chinese army which is still in this neighbourhood, but as we go to work we might have followed them round the walls of Peking till Doomsday without catching them.' If he asked for the officials responsible for the maltreatment of the prisoners he would probably have been sent some innocent wretches of low grade. He felt bound by his negotiations with Kung over the Anting gate not to harm Peking itself. The Emperor was out of his power. But within his power was the Emperor's Summer Palace, already stripped of its glory by allied looting. There was evidence that de Normann and his party had for a time been held there. The destruction of the Summer Palace would not be a blow at the people of China but at the prestige of their ruler. It was something which could be done at once without complicating the further negotiations with Prince Kung.

Elgin's proposal to destroy the Summer Palace was popular among the British, but was opposed by Gros and most of the French. 'C'est détruire pour le plaisir de détruire,' wrote one French officer, who had been enthusiastic about the looting a few days earlier. Gros and de Montauban were genuinely shocked at the thought that a place of such delicate beauty should be destroyed and worried that Prince Kung might be driven to break off negotiations. But Gros was careful not to push his opposition too far. 'Soyez persuadé,' he wrote to de Montauban, 'qu'aux yeux de l'Europe, comme parmi les populations

235

de la Chine, le beau rôle sera pour nous dans cette affaire.'
Gros's counter-proposal to Elgin is hard to reconcile with
this 'beau rôle'; he suggested that if Prince Kung refused
their demands the Imperial Palace in Peking itself should be
destroyed, which would have been an act of vandalism much
greater than the one performed.

The French did not press their objection though they
refused to join in the work. On October 18th and 19th the
First Division under Sir John Michel moved slowly through
the vast park of the Summer Palace, setting fire methodi-
cally to the buildings which it contained. Being mostly of
wood, they burned easily. A heavy pall of smoke rose from
the Palace, obscuring the light of the sun; it drifted over
Peking and deposited an ominous layer of ashes in the
streets of the city. 'The world around looked dark with
shadow,' wrote Colonel Wolseley. 'When we entered the
gardens they reminded one of those magic grounds described in fairy tales; we marched from them upon the
19th October, leaving them a dreary waste of ruined
nothings.' In the outlying buildings, hitherto neglected by
the British, French and Chinese plunderers, the soldiers
happened on unexpected treasures, such as a heap of gold
which the Punjabis found, and two carriages presented by
Lord Macartney to the Emperor sixty-five years before.

The ruins of the Summer Palace remain, though they are
not easy to find; the Communist Government has not so far
tried to exploit the propaganda value of the place. For the
most part the site looks prehistoric, showing only mounds,
ditches and lakes as if they were traces of some long-
vanished civilisation. But the outer walls of the stone
buildings designed by the Jesuits survived the fire, and have
only slowly crumbled in the intervening century; broken
baroque arches and intricate fallen capitals overgrown with
flowers suggest a folly contrived by some romantic lord to
close a vista. A few miles away at the foot of the Western
Hills are the bright-painted halls and temples of the new
Summer Palace of Wan-Shou-Shan, enlarged by the Em-

press Dowager in the eighteen-eighties out of funds raised for the navy. It is now a cheerful People's Park and thronged on holidays with thousands of blue-clad citizens who row on the magnificent lake and munch their meals happily beneath the scarlet rafters of the imperial pavilions.[1]

The arguments brought by Elgin and many others to support the burning of the Summer Palace were cogent, and in Britain were generally approved. According to Clarendon, Lord Palmerston in particular was 'quite enchanted.' Modern historians are unanimous in condemning it, sometimes without giving a fair account of the reasons for Elgin's decision.[2] There is no doubt that the act is looked on by modern Chinese as a prime example of imperialist methods. It is ironical that this should be for many the best-remembered act of a man whose years in China were spent in a search for a settlement resting on something more than force and destruction. Elgin always tried to deal justly, and was always conscious of the sufferings of the people of China. Unfortunately he had no corresponding sense of the beauty of their civilisation or of the pride which regardless of class they took in its creations. It was this gap in his education or his imagination which brought about the burning of the Summer Palace.

There was a final week of negotiation with Prince Kung, during which the tension between the British and French grew uncomfortably. Elgin and Gros had never resumed on this expedition the easy co-operation which had grown up naturally in 1858, and each suspected the other of hidden motives. Gros feared that Elgin's demands on Kung were

[1] The park is a victim of the Cultural Revolution. Because of its imperial past it has been closed, and the rafters stuck over with posters, but not destroyed, the Red Guards being in this respect more civilised, or more farseeing, than Cromwell or Elgin.

[2] For example the late Dr. Victor Purcell wrote in his *History of China* that the palace was burned in retaliation for the violation of a flag of truce. This is like saying that Charlotte Corday was guillotined for breaking and entering a bathroom.

so severe that the dynasty would collapse. Was not this probably the secret intention of the British? Gros recalled the secret instructions which Elgin had lost that spring in the shipwreck off Ceylon. Was it not likely that Elgin was authorised by those instructions to replace the Manchus by the Taiping rebels, who already dominated the Yangtze Valley? It would suit England to have a semi-Protestant junta ruling China, with the capital at Nanking within range of the English fleet. Gros felt helpless before these imagined intrigues and implored the Russian Ambassador Ignatieff to persuade Kung to give way to Elgin's demands and so avoid the provocation which he thought the English were seeking. Elgin on his side found Gros over-sentimental about the dynasty. He suspected the influence of Jesuits and a design to convert Prince Kung to Catholicism. He allowed himself to be persuaded out of some of his demands, but held to the rest. These were finally accepted by Prince Kung, and on October 24th Elgin was carried in state through the streets of Peking in a large red sedan chair with streaming tassels of many colours, escorted by 100 cavalry and 400 infantry. He was received by Prince Kung in the Hall of Audience, the new Convention of Peking was signed and the old Treaty of Tientsin ratified. The proceedings were dignified on both sides, apart from the surprise shown by the Chinese at the antics of Signor Beato, who with the persistence of his race and profession managed to photograph Prince Kung at close range. The next day was the turn of the French; Baron Gros was careful to put a little special cordiality into his meeting with Prince Kung, and Signor Beato was not present.

The generals were now more than ever anxious to get away. The plan was to leave a garrison for the winter in Tientsin, but to ship home the greater part of the expedition. Ice was beginning to form in the Peiho river between Tientsin and the sea, and it would soon be impassable for the gunboats which were to carry the troops out. Elgin insisted on remaining in Peking a further fortnight. This enabled him to introduce his brother Frederick to Prince Kung as the first British Minister to be accredited to the Chinese Government, and to choose a princely town palace as the site for the Legation. Finally he left Peking on November 10th, leaving an interpreter named Adkins behind to represent the Legation until Bruce should return in the spring. He was in no hurry to leave China and spent a restful month in Shanghai, during which he read Dr. Thorne, John Halifax Gentleman ('stupid') Aurora Leigh ('I admire greatly') and the Origin of Species ('audacious'). He defended this choice characteristically in his diary: 'It takes a great deal of time to read through *The Times* and is a considerable expenditure of eyesight. When one knows from one's own case how worthless their information is one begins to think that it is just as well to spend one's leisure in reading better print and more amusing fiction.' By January he was back in Hong Kong and on the 19th formally annexed the peninsula of Kowloon. Two days later he left China for the last time.

The news of the final settlement at Peking was received with great relief in England. Ministers had realised that the 1860 war, though more easy to justify than the war started by Bowring over the *Arrow*, was less popular with public opinion. This was particularly galling for the old Peelites who had to their cost opposed the popular war and were now in office saddled with running the unpopular one. Gladstone had warned Elgin at great length in a letter of September 5th: 'Unless happily you shall have been enabled to get that most miserable business composed before next session I think it very likely to be made the subject of some vote which will overthrow the Government . . . It is undoubtedly a most singular contrast which is offered to view between the way in which the Chinese war of 1857 was hugged and glorified by the British people, and the mixture of indifference and disgust which now marks the public sentiment. The comparative moral character of the two wars, however little the present one may be satisfactory, would have told at least in its favour as compared with that flagrant business. I suppose then that the causes of the difference are two; first some glimmerings of perception that these wars do not produce the benefits that are desired and expected, secondly the enormous charge which the people are now for the first time, most happily, called upon to meet in ready money'[1] [as opposed to credit from the East India Company]. Lord John Russell, also writing to Elgin, and Sidney Herbert, writing privately to Hope Grant, continually harped on the unpopularity of the war and the anxiety with which they heard of the delays in ending it. The news of success arrived in mid-December and Sidney Herbert wrote from Wilton on Christmas Day to congratulate Hope Grant. The Prime Minister too was pleased: 'This China success ushers well in the New Year, but we must not wish many returns of such an event as the capture of Peking. I wish Elgin had doubled the indemnity, but I suppose he had good grounds for sticking to the sum before demanded.' Gladstone was more sententious: 'It is with joy that I snatch a moment to tell you Lord John has just brought in to us after the Cabinet had ceased to sit a telegram come this day from St. Petersberg. . . . This really seems to be sure; let us thank God for his goodness. We had just before determined to take another million in consequence of the winter occupation. This is gone; and never did I get a million with greater pleasure than I surrender the chance of this one.' The telegram was followed by Loch who arrived on December 27th with the Convention and the ratified Treaty. His imprisonment by the Chinese had made him a national hero, and he was amazed to be welcomed ceremonially at Dover. He was received at Windsor, where Prince Albert cross-examined him about the stability of the Manchu dynasty, and the Queen about

[1] Gladstone to Elgin 5-9-60. British Museum, Gladstone. The later part of the letter is a strong attack upon the whole idea of overseas empire, written several years before Disraeli moved this idea into the centre of party controversy.

the looting of the Summer Palace.[1] Lord Palmerston told him that no one could have done as well as Elgin, and the railway porters were equally enthusiastic.

When Elgin finally reached England the formalities of triumph were repeated. He had at long last finished with China, having imposed a settlement which lasted forty years and having acted, he believed, 'as China's friend in all this.' Within a few months he was to set his hand to an even greater task as Viceroy of India, and within three years was to die prematurely in the middle of this new work.

Elgin had carried to China in 1857, and again in 1860, letters written by Queen Victoria in her own hand to the Emperor of China. It is a symbol of the story that these two letters of friendship are preserved at Broomhall, undelivered and unopened.

---

[1] The Queen was presented with a Pekingese Lion Dog which had been found in the Summer Palace by Captain Hart Dunne of the Wiltshire Regiment. Aptly named 'Lootie,' the dog had its portrait painted by Keyl and lived happily till 1872.

Principal Works
Consulted

Index

Principal Works Consulted

A. PAPERS

Archives Diplomatiques, Paris.
Elgin mss at Broomhall, Fife.
Foreign Office Papers at the Public Record Office, London.
Gladstone Papers, British Museum.
Jardine, Matheson and Co. archive, University Library, Cambridge.

B. BOOKS

Argyll, 8th Duke of, *Autobiography and Memoirs* (1906).
Bonner-Smith, D., and Lumby, E. W. R., *The Second China War 1856-60* (Navy Records Society 1954).
Bowring, Sir John, *Autobiographical Recollections* (1877).
Cordier, *Expedition de Chine 1857-8. Expedition de Chine de 1860.*
Fairbank, J. K., *Trade and Diplomacy on the China Coast* (1953).
Fortescue, *History of British Army*, vol. XIII.
Garnett, Robert, *English Historical Review*, October 1901, pp. 739-42; article on diversion of China regiments to India 1857.
Hsieh, Fu-Ch'eng, *Harvard Journal of Asiatic Studies* (1941), Vol. 6., p. 37: article on Yeh at Canton.
Knollys, edited *Diary* of General Sir Hope Grant.
Lane-Poole, Stanley, *Life of Sir Harry Parkes* (1894).
Loch, Lord, *Personal Narrative of Occurences during Lord Elgin's Second Embassy to China in 1860* (1869).
Lucy, Armand, *Lettres intimes sur la Campagne de Chine en 1860* (1861).
McGhee, *How we got to Peking* (1862).
Michie, Alexander, *The Englishman in China* (1900).
Morison, G. L., *The Eighth Earl of Elgin* (1928).
Morley, John, *Recollections*.
Morse, H. B., *The International Relations of the Chinese Empire* (1910-17).
Oliphant, Laurence, *Narrative of the Earl of Elgin's Mission to China and Japan* (1860).

Osborn, Captain Sherard, *The Past and Future of British relations in China* (1860).

Panmure, Earl of, *Collected Papers*.

Pelcovits, Nathan A., *Old China Hands and the Foreign Office* (1948).

Rennie, D. F., *The British Army in N. China and Japan* (1864).

Southgate, Donald, *The Passing of the Whigs, 1832-1880*.

Swinhoe, Robert, *Narrative of the North China Campaign of 1860* (1861).

Tsiang, T. F., 'China after the Victory of Taku' (*American History Review*, vol, 35, p. 79). 'China, England and Russia in 1860' (*Cambridge Historical Journal*, vol. 3, p. 115).

Varin, Paul, *Expédition de Chine* (1862).

Walrond, *Letters and Journals of James, 8th Earl of Elgin* (1872).

Williams, S. Wells, *Journal of N. China Branch of Royal Asiatic Society*, vol. XLII (1911).

Wolseley, Lt. Col. G. J., *Narrative of the War with China in 1860* (1862).

Blue Books, *The Times, Punch, Economist, Edinburgh Review, Hansard* and the standard lives of nineteenth-century statesmen.

Index

Ht · Thick

walls 40 x 60